THE POWER OF ROME

IN THE
TWENTIETH CENTURY

THE
POWER
OF
ROME

IN THE
TWENTIETH CENTURY

The Vatican in the
Age of Liberal Democracies, 1870-1922

ANTHONY RHODES

SIDGWICK & JACKSON

LONDON

First published in Great Britain in 1983
by Sidgwick & Jackson Limited

Copyright © 1983 by Anthony Rhodes

ISBN 0-283-99003-1

Printed in Great Britain by
Biddles Ltd, Guildford, Surrey
for Sidgwick & Jackson Limited,
1 Tavistock Chambers, Bloomsbury Way,
London WC1A 2SG

Contents

Acknowledgements

The longest part of this volume deals with the reign of Leo XIII (1878-1903). Three years ago the present Pope, John Paul II, shortened the 'Hundred Year Rule' for the consultation of the Vatican Secret Archives to seventy-five years, thereby opening up the Leonine Pontificate. Much of the new material made available has been incorporated here. The research for, and writing of, the book has been made possible by generous grants from the Arts Council and the Society of Authors, and by the help of the English College in Rome; to all of whom I wish to express my thanks.

This volume is written largely from the following national archival sources:

1 The Vatican *Archivi Segreti* ('Secret Archives'), at the Secretary of State's Department; here referred to as 'Vat. Sec. Arch.'

2 The Italian State Archives at the Ministero degli Affari Esteri (the Italian Foreign Office); this office is commonly known as the 'Farnesina' from the building in which it is located, and that name is used here for the source.

3 The *Correspondance Politique* ('Political Correspondence') of the French Ministry of Foreign Affairs, at the Quai d'Orsay, from which it takes its common name; here referred to as 'Quai d'Orsay'.

4 The British Foreign Office documents in the Public Records Office, Kew; here referred to as 'F.O.'

Details of other sources quoted are given in the Bibliography, p. 271.

Preface

The twentieth century began for the Papacy in 1870, when Rome was occupied by the new Italian State, and Papal fortunes fell to their lowest ebb since the Reformation. In the decade leading up to that year, the Papacy had gradually been dispossessed by the Italian State of territory over which it had exercised sovereignty for a thousand years, since Pepin, King of the Franks, had bestowed on it the broad lands of central Italy, from Terracina on the Tyrrhenian to Fano on the Adriatic. This territory, about twice the size of Wales, with a population of some three million souls, was known as the Papal States.[1] Sovereignty over it had enabled the Popes to defend the Church for a millennium against the incursions of lay rulers, the Kings of France and Spain, the Emperors of the Holy Roman Empire, the Italian provincial despots. In the words of Bossuet, 'The temporal sovereignty ensures that the Pope cannot be at the mercy of any one state.' Two centuries later, the English statesman Lord Palmerston endorsed this: 'It is clearly desirable that a personality who in his spiritual quality possesses such influence over most European countries should be in an independent position so that he cannot be used by any one European power as a political tool, to the disadvantage of other powers. From this point of view alone, it is desirable that the Pope should remain sovereign in his own state.'

These are two representative modern views supporting the temporal claims of the Papacy. There were of course equally representative contrary views, maintaining that an essentially spiritual power such as the Papacy should divorce itself entirely from things material; in Dante's phrase, 'The crosier should not be joined with the sword.' In his treatise on government *De Monarchia*, Dante denounces the temporal claims of the Papacy as 'unscriptural, unhistorical and illogical'; he laments that Constantine the

9

Great (who everyone then believed had made the 'Donation' of these States to the Papacy in A.D. 322) had ever been born. Dante contended that there should be two distinct, independent powers in the Christian world – the 'Caesar' or Emperor, the temporal ruler; and the Pope, the spiritual ruler – working together in harmony, but confining themselves strictly to their respective spheres. With his grotesque mediaeval imagery, Dante depicts the Papacy, as he saw it in his own time under the worldly and gubernatorial Boniface VIII, as a 'sewer of blood and Stench'.[2] Dante would have approved the events of 1870, believing that they must benefit the Papacy by confining it to its proper, exclusively spiritual role. Nevertheless, in 1870 when these views prevailed, and the Papal States were forcibly sequestered by the new 'Caesar', Victor Emmanuel II of Italy, many people thought that the power of Rome, spiritual as well as material, was over for ever.

Nor was its humiliation confined to Italy. In the two preceding decades, liberal and anti-clerical governments had come to power all over Europe, and they turned vengefully on a Church which had, in their opinion, exercised power in their lands for too long. France became a Republic in 1870, and revived the anti-clericalism of the French Revolution. In Germany in 1870 Bismarck, fresh from his triumphs of Sadowa and Sedan, began his *Kulturkampf* ('Battle of culture') to eliminate entirely Papal influence in the much enlarged Catholic territories which Prussia now ruled over. In Spain in 1868, Queen Isabella was expelled and Sorrano's liberal government began suppressing the convents and monasteries. In Mexico, Napoleon's Catholic and Latin bulwark against the Anglo–Saxon Protestants had been overthrown by Juarez and the firing squad of Queretaro. Even His Apostolic Majesty in Vienna, the Emperor Franz Josef, was obliged to sign anti-clerical decrees legalizing civil marriage and lay education. While in Geneva, a Congress of Anarchist Revolutionaries was acclaiming Bakunin, who had just announced the end of Christianity. In Dante's imagery, the barque of St Peter was indeed in 'dire tempest'.

It was a tempest such as the Church had not known since the French Revolution or the sack of Rome in 1527, when the Constable of Bourbon's *Landsknechte* (mercenaries) danced with prostitutes on the high altar of St Peter's, and then paraded a donkey caparisoned with Pontifical vestments through the streets. If now in 1870 such acts of physical violence were less in evidence, those of blasphemy were not. On 8 December 1870, three months after the Italian seizure of Rome, a man walked into St Peter's with his hat on, ostentatiously lit a cigar from the high altar, and blew out all the candles. In earlier times, no Roman citizen would have dared to commit such sacrilege, for fear of the eternal fires. Now in 1870, the liberals and socialists taught that the eternal fires were so much superstitious rubbish.

Eighteen hundred and seventy was the beginning of the twentieth century for the rest of Europe too. Everywhere in that year, the nation states were introducing parliamentary government: France, Germany, Austria, Belgium. Even Spain had, in theory at least, handed power over to its assembly, the Cortes. And with this new type of government went a new type of ruler. Hitherto, the Popes had been accustomed for centuries to dealing with European monarchies and aristocracies which, however refractory they might on occasion be, generally accepted a traditional code of behaviour, and paid at least lip-service to religion. But the new type of ruler, the democratically elected liberal or socialist politician, often repudiated religion altogether. Nor were these men much concerned with the niceties of language. Signor Farini, the Liberal President of the Italian Parliament in 1888, said when speaking in a debate on the Guarantee Laws for the Papacy, 'Let us stop all this fornicating with the Pope!' while the French Deputy Zavaès declared in 1875 in the Palais Bourbon, 'Let us make a bonfire of that heap of old rubbish piled up for centuries on the right bank of the Tiber!'

These men, or their prototypes, were not unfamiliar to the Church. For a short time – between 1793 and 1803 in France – the followers of Voltaire and the Encyclopaedists had repudiated religion and spoken equally offensively about the Pope; in Voltaire's celebrated couplet:

Les prêtres ne sont pas ce qu'un vain peuple pense;
Notre crédulité fait toute leur science.

('Priests are not what foolish folk suppose;
our credulity is all there is to their science.')

But the Voltairean scoffers were a restricted intellectual élite; whereas after 1870, their descendants proliferated all over Europe,

11

flaunting their contempt for the Catholic Church in a variety of ways. Sainte-Beuve, the French literary critic, ostentatiously offered a meat dinner on Good Friday 1868 to his friends Flaubert, Renan and Taine. Renan's book *La Vie de Jésus*, discrediting the supernatural and miraculous element in Christianity, was acclaimed by George Sand with the words, 'And here Jesus is demolished for good!' The greatest Italian poet of the time, Giosuè Carducci, wrote a poem in praise and defence of Judas Iscariot, and an adulatory *Hymn to Satan*. Books with patently irreligious titles such as *Les Fleurs du Mal* ('The Flowers of Evil'), whose poetry, though beautiful, is ostentatiously pagan, and *À Rebours* ('Against the Grain'), were standard reading for all self-respecting European liberals.

Together with this iconoclasm went a fervent belief in the perfectibility of man, thanks to his wonderful scientific discoveries. Auguste Comte wrote, 'Humanity has passed through three stages – the religious, the metaphysical, and now it has reached the positive stage, in which the reign of science will replace belief in the supernatural.' In the last decades of the nineteenth century, a great new era seemed to be dawning, the product of man's inventive genius and his domination over matter. In future, these men believed, the self-enlightened human intellect would solve all problems, social and economic. Marcellin Berthelot, the savant and French Minister of Education, announced, 'The world today is no longer mysterious. The conception of miracles has vanished like an empty mirage. Reason and science have ruined the basis of Catholicism. There are no more religious problems, only scientific constatations. . . . By the year A.D. 2000, man will have gained in sweetness and morality, because he will have ceased to live by carnage and the destruction of his fellow creatures. . . .' An English Liberal Member of Parliament at the opening of the twentieth century, G. P. Gooch, was even more utopian: 'We can now look forward with something like confidence to the time when war between civilized nations will be considered as antiquated as a duel.'

The English Cardinal Henry Manning, who played such a part in the Vatican Council of 1870, summed this up: 'The special character of our age is the tendency for a party of educated men to overturn the ancient Christian institutions which are based on the supernatural – by which man is elevated to a higher knowledge and destiny – and to erect upon these ruins a new order founded upon natural reason alone. . . .'[3] Another Catholic apologist, Dr Murri, in his *Battaglia d'Oggi*, writes, 'The rise of the middle classes has culminated in a movement of intense hostility to the Church and the Faith. . . . This spirit is to be found as much in a university professor as in some peasant in a village of the central Appenines, who has become literate enough to read the *Tribuna*. . . .'

Now if man could so easily resolve the enigma of his own destiny, what place remained for God? In the Vatican Secret Archives is a despatch from the Papal Nuncio in Munich, Mgr Melli, in 1871, reporting a public speech by the unfrocked priest Hyacinthe Loison: 'If twelve ignorant heads could regenerate the world [Loison is referring to the Apostles], what shall we not be able to do – *we* who have the power of science on our side?'[4] Nor was this attitude any longer confined to the educated classes. The father of Benito Mussolini, a village blacksmith, published a tract in 1891 under the title, 'Science is illuminating the world! Reason is mastering Faith! Free Thought is overthrowing Religion!'

The enemies of the Church in 1870 bore little resemblance to her traditional enemy in the preceding millennium, the militant Mohammedans, who reached Poitiers and besieged Vienna. In 1870, her enemies were atheists, radicals, anarchists, communists, socialists of all kinds, using weapons which were more effective than the swords and scimitars of the Turk – speeches and writings propagated all over Europe by printing press and pamphlet. They can be compared with Julian the Apostate, whose persecution of the Christians in the mid fourth century was a model for the French and Italian liberals of the late nineteenth century. Julian's persecution was quite different from that of his predecessors – the savage cruelty of Nero and the early Roman Emperors – for the measures Julian took against Christianity were non-violent, but more insidious. Christians were forbidden to teach or take part in any educational programme; public employment was reserved for pagans; the pagan priesthood was recognized as the official Church of Rome. Julian's persecution was to be repeated *mutatis mutandis* all over Europe between 1870 and 1914.

Yet today, when over a century has passed since 1870, the history of the Papacy has not followed the course the liberals and atheists anticipated: gradual erosion of the Church under their unceasing attacks, finally lapsing into total disintegration. In the period from

1870 to 1922, the Church lived through one of the bitterest, and yet most subtle, attacks on the realm of the Spirit which has ever been known. How did the Papacy defeat this and retrieve its fortunes, which had sunk so low in 1870 – so that today under Pope John Paul II, its prestige in the world is as high as, if not higher than, that of any lay state? And with prestige goes power. Napoleon understood this well when he said at the end of his career to the Marquis de Fontanes, 'There are only two powers in the world – the sword and the spirit. In the long run, the sword is always defeated by the spirit.'

Some Catholic apologists have seen a parallel between the Goths, Huns and Vandals who destroyed the Roman Empire in the Dark Ages, and the liberals, socialists and freethinkers of the nineteenth and twentieth centuries. But this is inexact. There is far greater recuperative power in the Church of Rome today than there was in the effete Empire of Honorius. To quote Cardinal Manning again:

> In the course of history, some forty Popes have at one time or another been expelled from Rome – nine times by Roman factions, seven times by foreign invaders. Six times the city of Rome has been held to ransom by usurpers. Twice it has been nearly destroyed. Once, it was so utterly desolate that for fifty days nothing human breathed in it, and no cry was heard but that of the foxes on the Aventine. Warfare, suffering, exile – that has been the lot of many Popes. Yet with imperishable vitality and invincible power they persist, they remain. . . .'[5]

In the pages of this book, an attempt will be made to describe the vicissitudes through which the Papacy passed under the four Popes of the 'Liberal' era, from 1870 to 1922: Pius IX, Leo XIII, Pius X and Benedict XV.

1

The Italian Seizure of Rome

Pius IX had inaugurated his Pontificate in 1846 with none of the intransigence for which he was later to become famous. Although he came of a family which had been ennobled in the seventeenth century, the Counts of Mastai in the Romagna, he had supported the new liberalism then abroad in Europe. A month after his accession, he proclaimed an amnesty for political prisoners in the Papal States, and recalled those who had been exiled under his predecessor, Gregory XVI. He relaxed the censorship laws. He granted Rome a constitution with a lay Prime Minister. He sympathized with the cause of Italian unity, and proposed a customs union between the various States and Principalities. He founded an Accademia Biblica for the diffusion of Hebrew learning, very much on the lines of the Protestant Bible Societies.

In those days when Austria was all powerful in the Italian peninsula, these measures shocked Prince Metternich, who exclaimed, 'We had foreseen everything in Italy – except a liberal Pope!' The Austrian Foreign Minister need not have feared. The liberal policy of Pius IX lasted exactly two years, until the upheavals of 1848 which undermined the old order everywhere in Europe, including the Papal States. The Pope's concessions were regarded as weakness by his subjects, and the amnesty he had granted attracted a host of revolutionary elements to Rome. In that year, they murdered his new lay Prime Minister Rossi in the Cancelleria; and besieged the Pope himself in the Quirinale. His private secretary was shot dead before his eyes, and he was forced to flee for his life down the back stairs, disguised as a servant. For two years, he found asylum with the King of Naples in Gaeta.

From here he contemplated the Triumvirate ruling Rome, which

15

declared a Republic and the 'Religion of the People'. 'The People' sacked churches and palaces, made bonfires of confessionals in the Piazza del Popolo, and murdered a score of priests in the Trastevere slums. They also instituted a body of anodyne name but sinister precedent, the 'Committee of Public Safety'. This lasted two years, until the French Army expelled the Triumvirate, and Pius IX returned to his city. However, the mob rule in Rome during that period had turned the erstwhile liberal Pope into an arch-conservative.

Twenty-eight years were to pass between this episode and his death in 1878, during which time he became more and more intransigent. The most important of the measures he introduced in the last years of his reign was the Dogma of Papal Infallibility. He believed that had he proclaimed it at the beginning of his Pontificate, instead of introducing the liberal reforms of 1846, the Triumvirate revolution of 1848 would not have taken place. The Dogma of Infallibility was based on Christ's famous words in St Matthew's Gospel: 'Thou art Peter, and upon this rock will I build my Church.... And I will give unto thee the keys of the Kingdom of Heaven', and in St John's Gospel: 'There shall be one fold, and one shepherd'. This had been the doctrine of the Primitive Church when the infallibility of '*one* shepherd' had been universally recognized. To this, Pius IX now intended to return.

The Dogma states that decisions of the Pope speaking *ex cathedra* are infallible in all matters concerning faith and morals. In 1870 this presumption was hotly contested by the nationalistic lay rulers of Europe, who feared that their subjects would thus be directly subordinated, or a part of their loyalties would be, to a foreign potentate. These fears were expressed by William Gladstone in his famous pamphlet, *The Vatican Decrees and their Bearing on Civil Allegiance*. They would, he said, deflect a man from his allegiance to his country, making him a Catholic first, an Englishman second. 'With this decree,' wrote Gladstone, 'the claims of Innocent III over mankind have been resurrected in the nineteenth century – like some mummy picked out of its dusty sarcophagus.'

It is perhaps hard for us today to understand the passions aroused in 1870 by the Papal claim to infallibility. In its fierce day it shook the hearts of men, ruffled the smooth surface of diplomacy, and agitated all the chancelleries of Europe. Most Europeans assumed that 'infallibility' entailed that the Pope could exercise absolute power in all domains, secular as well as religious. This was in fact not the case, as was explained by Cardinal Merry del Val (later Secretary of State): 'Our Church does not contend,' he wrote, 'that in matters political, scientific and historical, the Pope's authority is in any degree superior to that of other men. Nor does it mean that in dealing with contemporary events, men and affairs, the Pope cannot make errors of judgement.'[1] Yet few people appear to have been aware of this considerable limitation.

If Gladstone expressed the doubts and fears of most Europeans, it was another Englishman, the convert, Mgr Henry Manning, who repudiated them. To Gladstone's contention that the Dogma would weaken a man's allegiance to his native land, Manning replied, 'On the contrary, our civil allegiance exists not *in spite of* the teaching of the Roman Church, but because of it. The Church expressly enjoins, "Give unto Caesar what is Caesar's." This predicates a man's loyalty to his native land.'

The role played by Manning during the Vatican Council of 1870, which prescribed the declaration of Infallibility, cannot be overestimated. During it, he became Pius IX's closest adviser and confidant. It was said he had a latchkey to the Pope's private apartments, as Manning later confirmed: 'I had access by a private passage to the Pope's rooms. Once, when the Cardinals and Ambassadors had come into the antechamber and were waiting for the Pope, I saw their marked surprise when I entered it from the other side.'[2] Many in the Curia objected to this Englishman, an ex-Protestant clergyman who had been married; they distrusted his late and sudden conversion, and his habit of continually going into print (Manning published some twenty books and numerous articles). During the deliberations on Infallibility he was dubbed by some of them '*il diavolo del Concilio*' ('the devil of the Council'). Nevertheless, it was this very articulacy which enabled him to state clearly the disasters which would befall the Catholic Church if the Dogma was not accepted. Although he was a deeply religious man, his reasoning was notably pragmatic.

While many eminent politicians and scientists towards the end of the nineteenth century believed that the world was moving into a utopian age created by science, in which there would be no more war, Manning totally rejected this sanguine view. Europe as he saw it, far from entering an era of peace and tranquillity, was about to destroy itself. Rumours of wars, and assassination of public men, were on every side. Anarchy was rife, and the Church was threatened by a new enemy, more dangerous than Luther: atheistic communism. He showed that the assembling of Catholic bishops to take decision for the benefit of the Church might have sufficed at the Council of Trent in the sixteenth century; but today, in an age requiring quick thought and quicker action against the modern enemies of religion, it would be useless, a clumsy method of defence in face of a determined, fast-moving enemy, 'as clumsy in its working as the wooden ships of Nelson's day against the new Ironclads'. The most effective remedy, he advocated, was to concentrate the supreme authority of the Church in one man, who could take swift decisions and forestall the assault. Such a lurid picture did Manning draw of the dangers ahead, of the bloodletting to come in an atheist twentieth century, that the Bishop of Mainz exclaimed, 'He made all our hair stand on end.' With his apocalyptical vision, Manning seems to have foreseen 1914 and 1939.

Some 530 bishops congregated in Rome for the Council in January 1870. They came from all over the world so that – in the words of Lytton Strachey – 'As if she knew her doom was upon her, the Eternal City arrayed herself in all her glory to meet it. Her streets were filled with crowned heads and princes of the Church, ambassadors, great ladies and great theologians. The rival parties, for and against the Dogma of the Infallibility, were entertained in a series of lavish receptions given by the Roman ladies, who entered into the controversy with equal zest – *Les Commères du Concile* ["the godmothers of the Council"] they were known as.'

When the Dogma was mooted before the Grand Council, almost half of the bishops opposed it. They represented some ninety million souls all over the world, as imposing an array of moral force as had ever confronted the Papacy. Yet in spite of this, the Curia – that is the Roman cardinals, who were of like mind with Manning, and under the inspired leadership of Pius IX – had in less than six months defeated the opposition, and reduced the two hundred dissenting bishops to silence and acquiescence.

Pius IX's methods of dealing with refractory bishops were drastic and effective. The Roman Cardinal Guidi had argued eloquently at the Council against Infallibility, on the ground that it would injure relations with the European powers. Pius IX summoned him and reprimanded him severely. When Cardinal

Guidi protested, 'But Your Holiness, European tradition is unfavourable to the Dogma', Pius IX silenced him with a curt '*I* am Tradition!' He then condemned Guidi to a course of religious exercises in the Convent of the Minerva, where he was forbidden to receive visitors, except those likely to persuade him to retract his heterodoxy. The result was a complete recantation. When the vote was taken on 18 July 1870, Cardinal Guidi cast his in favour of Infallibility.

The Pope treated his own staff in much the same manner. Mgr Mérade, his personal almoner, who had voiced certain objections to Infallibility, was confined to his cell with a copy of the Dogma, which he had to learn by heart. Another Vatican dignitary, the Vicar of St Peter's Chapter, Mgr Passorelli, was removed from his post for failing to attend the fourth session of the Grand Council.[3]

The majority in favour was 532 votes to 2. What could have been responsible for this episcopal volte-face? Odo Russell, the British Minister to the Holy See, explained it as due to 'Pius IX's imperative way with his subordinates. They receive their orders and obey without daring to discuss them. Notwithstanding his proverbial goodness of heart and benevolence, he seems to inspire them with unreasoning apprehension and inexplicable fear.'

There was much celebration that night in Rome and, as was the custom, windows were decorated with symbolic 'transparencies' lit from inside. The Papacy seemed in its strongest position since the days of Innocent III. But was it not ominous that on this very day, 18 July 1870, the Franco–Prussian War was declared? Or that amid all the jubilation that night, the Ambassadors of France and Austria alone did not illuminate their windows?[4]

In the months before Sedan and Metz, Pius IX showed complete confidence that the Italians would not invade his city, a belief which seems to have been sustained by the notion of his infallibility. A further, more pragmatic, reason was that the French Second Empire was his friend. France was then regarded as the greatest military power in Europe, and Napoleon III had installed a powerful French garrison in Rome, with which the new and largely untried Italian Army would hardly dare to cross swords. At Mentana three years before, Napoleon had given practical proof of this by decisively defeating the forces of Garibaldi marching on Rome.

Why did France, the very land of atheist revolution since 1789, support the Popes' temporal power throughout the nineteenth century – to the extent that the Geneva-educated Guizot could exclaim: 'The temporal power of the Pope is a necessity for France'? The reason appears to be that the Papacy had been for centuries a most effective element in keeping the Italian peninsula disunited, a position which was of the greatest importance for countering France's traditional enemy there, the Habsburg Empire. After the battle of Novara (1848), Austria had obtained such predominance in the peninsula that France became alarmed. The French expedition to Rome in 1849, which restored Pius IX to his throne, as well as the earlier one to Ancona in 1832, which supported Gregory XVI against the revolutionary Camorra, were undertaken less on behalf of the Papacy than to thwart Austria. Faced by the threatened Austrian hegemony of Italy, Napoleon III had to maintain a strong military force there, and the most convenient way of doing this was through the Pope in Rome. For the French, the question of who occupied the Legations or the Patrimony of St Peter was a matter of relative unimportance; but Napoleon III was far from indifferent about being able, at Papal invitation, to support the Pope's temporal claims. The division of Italy depended upon the existence of the Papal States.

It would not be the place here to analyse the character of that ambivalent ruler, the Emperor Napoleon III. Sufficient to say that he was aware he owed his position to the Catholic groups of France, whose power had greatly increased during the nineteenth century in reaction to the anti-clerical excesses of the French Revolution. Although he had as a young man flirted with Italian liberalism, and had even supported the cause of Italian unity, he had now, with the acquisition of power, become a conservative French nationalist. He regarded the Papacy as a stabilizing force in a Europe which since 1848 was becoming increasingly revolutionary. He now disapproved of revolutionaries – chiefly no doubt because one of them had tried to blow him up. Moreover, he was under the spell of the Empress Eugenie a devout Spanish Catholic. In 1868, he invited Pius IX to stand as godfather to his son, the Prince Imperial. This explains why the British representative at the Vatican, Odo Russell, could report in July 1870, 'All the elements of Italian opposition to the Pope can be easily overcome, so long as the French garrison remains ... the Church of Rome is shielded by France ... the embarrassment which a renewed invasion of Rome would cause throughout Europe [he is referring to Pius IX's expulsion from Rome in 1848], together with the religious feeling in France, render the withdrawal of the French garrison impossible.'[5]

In 1861, Napoleon III expressed this support for the Papacy in a letter to King Victor Emmanuel II: 'I declare frankly to Your Majesty that, while recognizing your new Kingdom of Italy, I shall leave my troops in Rome until Your Majesty is reconciled with His Holiness, the Pope.' Three years later, he prevailed upon the Italian government in Florence to subscribe to the September Convention of 1864, by which the two Powers guaranteed the Pope's possession of Rome. Of this document the British Ambassador to the Italian state, Sir Augustus Paget, reported, 'Nothing can be clearer than this declaration by the Italian government that it will not invade Rome.'[6] According to R. de Cesare in *Gli Ultimi Giorni di Roma Papale* ('The Last Days of Papal Rome'), the exact words to which Italy subscribed in the September Convention were: 'Italy will prevent, by force if necessary, any attempt made from the interior against the territories of the Pope.' Such were the solemn promises of the Italian Government.

Pius IX, although somewhat piqued that two great European powers should have made arrangements for his future behind his back, was at least reassured. Then came the defeat of Garibaldi at Mentana, which reassured him further. But what none of the parties involved had foreseen was that fatal day at Sedan three years later, 2 September 1870. In a campaign of under two months, the legend of French military might was shattered; and the Emperor, in need of every available soldier, withdrew his entire garrison from Rome overnight. The Eternal City lay defenceless, protected by only a handful of Papal Zouaves.[7] It was at this conjuncture, which might never occur again, that the Italian Government decided to seize its chance and crown the unification of Italy with occupation of its first city.

It seems incredible that all the great powers still thought that Italy would not take this step. In the Vatican Archives is a despatch from the Nuncio in Vienna, Mgr Falcinelli, reporting that Graf Beust, the Austrian Foreign Minister, had told him, 'The Italians will go no further than occupying Viterbo on one side and Frosinone on the other – and only for the purpose of maintaining order.'[8] The British Ambassador in Florence, Sir Augustus Paget, was of the same opinion. 'I do not believe,' he wrote, 'that the Italian Government will take advantage of France's present distress to march on Rome, as advocated by the Italian Socialists and Radicals.'[9] He added however that the Socialists were now exerting pressure on the government, 'crying Patriotism at every turn'. 'This word, which is not normally the Socialists' strong card,' he wrote, 'is now their watchword. Their exhortations to the government are full of such phrases as, "We need Rome for the sake of our country!" "We are citizens and lovers of Italy!"; "We will not fail in our patriotic duty!"; etc.'

It seems that even as late as September, the Italian Foreign Minister, Visconti-Venosta, counselled against occupying Rome. Mr Jervoise, the British representative at the Vatican (he had replaced Odo Russell), reported, 'Visconti-Venosta considers Rome's strategical position poor as a capital; its climate unhealthy; and with insufficient accommodation for government offices. Nor does he wish to alienate Catholic opinion throughout the world by occupying Rome. He thinks that Rome should be left completely Papal, including territory within a radius of 15 miles.'[10]

Events now proceeded rapidly. On 10 September 1870 the Italian Ambassador in Paris, Count Nigra, informed the French Government that in view of the changed circumstances (the French capitulation at Metz), Italy considered that the September Convention of 1864 guaranteeing Papal sovereignty had lapsed.[11] The day before this, Italy had sent a special envoy, Count Ponza di San Martino, to the Pope with a personal letter from King Victor Emmanuel II. In this, the King explained that, in view of the dangerous socialist and revolutionary movements now afoot in the peninsula, his forces would have to occupy certain parts of Roman territory, even a part of Rome itself – to maintain order, to protect His Holiness and to prevent the establishment of revolutionary rule in the Eternal City. He added, however, that the occupation would be undertaken only after consultation with the great powers. Rome would be treated as an international, not an Italian, issue. A violent occupation, as advocated by the Garibaldians, would not be permitted.[12]

Pius IX was now in the thirty-fourth year of his reign, and the seventy-first of his life. The tribulations he had undergone during and since the Roman Republic of 1848 had in no way diminished his native courage. Rome, he considered, was his by imprescriptible right, handed down to him from 263 predecessors. He fully believed that martyrdom at the end of his stormy Pontificate would be the reward from Heaven he had prayed for all his life. Having read the King's letter, he replied to Count Ponza that not only would he not cede one square inch of his territory, but that he was perfectly capable of maintaining order in it; he required no assistance from the King of Italy. According to R. de Cesare in *Gli Ultimi Giorni di Roma Papale*, he threw the King's letter on the table with the exclamation, 'You are all a nest of vipers! Of whited sepulchres! I am no prophet, but I tell you – you will never enter Rome!' Whereupon Count Ponza di San Martino took his leave, adding that as His Holiness refused to negotiate, General Cadorna would march on Rome within the next twenty-four hours.

With the threat of invasion imminent, Pius IX made desperate last-minute attempts to enlist the support of the European powers. France being otherwise occupied, the most important of these was Austria; and he instructed the Nuncio in Vienna, Mgr Falcinelli, to approach His Apostolic Majesty. In the Vatican Archives are Falcinelli's despatches describing his efforts.[13] His communication of 9 September 1870 reads:

> I waited on the Austrian Foreign Minister, Graf Beust, yesterday and informed him that Italy was about to invade Rome. He replied that His Majesty Franz Josef would be most distressed to hear this, but that Austria could do nothing, as she did not want war with Italy . . . Graf Beust then enlarged upon the devotion of his Emperor to Your Holiness. He said that should Your Holiness require asylum, all the cities of the Habsburg Empire would be at Your disposal. Whereupon I cut him short: 'With what courage,' I said, 'do you invite His Holiness into your house! But you do nothing to prevent him from being expelled from his own.'

It was the same with the other Catholic powers. On 15 September 1870 Mr Jervoise reported to London from a 'reliable informant' he knew, who had just had an audience with the Pope. 'His Holiness told my informant that, in response to his application to foreign governments for support, he had received none. Austria does not want to get involved. Bavaria intends to await an international conference on the Roman question. France can do nothing, being fully occupied in a war with Prussia. Spain is in no position to do anything militarily.'[14] Only Britain, a Protestant power, showed any sympathy. A man-of-war, the *Defence*, was despatched to Civitavecchia, ostensibly to transport the Pope to Malta should he so desire. The Pope expressed the deepest gratitude for this – although, as Mr Jervoise pointed out, the British ship was probably there less to give moral support to the Pope than to evacuate British subjects if this proved necessary.[15]

Otherwise forsaken, with only a small band of Zouaves to defend him, the Pope still would not surrender. He decided that if the Italians attacked Rome, he would make a show of resistance – against overwhelming odds, as it could only be – which would awaken the sympathy of the world, and throw upon the Italian Government the odium of yet another act of spoliation of Papal territory.[16]

The invasion began on 11 September 1870, when the Italian army under General Cadorna crossed the Papal frontiers at Terni, Orte, and Isoletta. There was little opposition, and he quickly occupied Civita Castellana and Viterbo; while another force under General Bixio went south to Civitavecchia. Everywhere, the Italian troops were received with enthusiasm by the population, who hoisted the tricolour in place of the yellow and white Papal flag. General Cadorna had hoped until the last that he would not have to lay siege to Rome itself. On arriving at its gates, he sent an envoy with a white flag to the Pope to request that the Italian troops might enter peaceably. To this the Pope gave a flat refusal.

The attack therefore began at dawn on 20 September 1870. A student at the English College, William Kirkham, entered in his diary for that day,

Awakened shortly after 5 a.m. by a bombardment which seemed to come from the direction of San Giovanni Laterano . . . it continued without interruption, and at breakfast seemed to be nearer, at the Porta San Pancrazio. At 8.30 I was standing at my window on the top floor of the College, when I was startled by a shell bursting on the roof of the house opposite. This seemed too warm for comfort, so I went downstairs. On the way, I met someone with orders from the Rector that we were all to assemble on the ground floor. We had reached the first floor when there was tremendous explosion very near. . . . I was standing by the pulpit in the refectory, and the shell seemed to burst just outside our garden. We heard bricks falling and windows crashing. There was forthwith a general vote to go down to the cellars. The Rector smiled as he led us. *'Silent leges inter arma!'* ['Laws are silent in the presence of arms'], he said.[17]

The student diarist was here referring to the bombardment by General Bixio from the Porta San Pancrazio to the west of the city. (A close friend of Garibaldi, General Bixio had proudly requested that the congenial task of throwing all the cardinals into the Tiber after the occupation should be reserved for him.[18])

As soon as the bombardment was heard in the Vatican, the Pope summoned the heads of the various foreign missions. The scene is described by Mr Jervoise in his despatch of 21 September. The Pope asked them to look out of the window and note the white flag flying over the fortress of Castello Sant' Angelo. The time had come, he said, when he must bow to the will of the Almighty. His principal object had always been to retain for the Church the inheritance he had received from his predecessors, and which he had no power to alienate, even should he wish to do so. But force had now been employed to take it.

This force soon made a breach in the walls near the Porta Pia, through which the Italian troops poured in. They were met with only token resistance from the Zouaves, who surrendered. Official figures for the casualties were: Papal forces – 20 killed and 50 wounded; Italian forces – 27 killed and 140 wounded (most of them during the progress from the frontiers of the Papal States).

Most Romans had stayed indoors during the bombardment, and they did not venture out until it was over. By 10 o'clock in the morning, the solders of King Victor Emmanuel II had advanced to the Campidoglio, where they were greeted by frantic crowds with tricolour flags and cries of *'Evviva'* ('Long live ...'). Mr Jervoise reports that hundreds of sinister characters now appeared on the streets, of whom he had been unaware before. Rome was soon swarming, he says, with people from all parts of Italy. 'In the Corso one heard the many dialects of the Peninsula – but rarely the accent of a native Roman.'[19] The reason for this, he explains, was that the Roman mob had been greatly inflated by hordes of political refugees and turbulent characters from all over Italy, who swarmed in behind the Italian army, hoping for the pickings. Stimulated by these undesirables, the Roman mob insulted and spat upon any priest who dared to show his face on the streets. They broke into the Papal Barracks in the Trastevere, which they sacked to cries of 'Death to the Pope! Death to Cardinal Antonelli! Death to all the Cardinals!' They then proceeded to Bernini's Colonnade before St Peter's, where they pursued with oaths and catcalls all persons entering or leaving through the bronze doors which are the principal entrances of the Vatican buildings. In the first forty-eight hours, says Mr Jervoise, no one dared to enter any church or religious establishment.

Of these two days William Kirkham, the student at the English College, wrote in his diary, 'That first night was something awful. There were no lights on the streets, and a lot of murders were committed. I saw a long procession going down the Via Monserrato with torches and flags – the dregs of Rome, with camp followers of the Italian Army, waving swords and shrieking, "Death to the Pope! Long live Garibaldi!" – any amount of women among them. It all reminded me of what I had read about the French Revolution. Poor Pius IX!'

The Vatican and the Italian authorities took different views about the conduct of the invading Italian troops. Cardinal Antonelli, the Vatican Secretary of State, in a circular to foreign governments, accused the Italian army of having 'taken bloody vengeance on the Papal troops'. He said that for two days they were let loose and sacked the city under the eyes of their own officers.[20] To this the Italian Foreign Minister, Visconti-Venosta, replied indignantly that the Royal troops had been a model of discipline and good behaviour. When the Italian army entered Rome, he said, all the Papal bureaucracy in their offices and establishments had taken to their heels, *leaving the doors open!* It was thanks to the Italian army that these buildings had been protected from sacking, and order maintained.

Within forty-eight hours of the seizure of Rome, the risks taken by the Italian government seemed justified. No European power had lifted a finger to help the Pope. The last step in the unification of Italy, begun by Cavour in 1860, had been accomplished.

2

The Fulminations of
Pius IX

On 10 October 1870, twenty days after the Italian occupation of
Rome, Cardinal Antonelli, the Vatican Secretary of State, wrote
to Mgr Falcinelli, the Papal Nuncio in Vienna, 'The Holy Father
has decided to support all inconveniences and hardships rather
than fail in his duty, and be false to his Coronation Oath. He will
never descend to any kind of dealings with the Italian usurper.
Nor will he enter into any negotiations with the Piedmontese
government, unless they are directly concerned with reintegrat-
ing him into the plenitude of his sovereign rights.'[1]

This was the Pope's answer to the Italian State, when it
informed him immediately after the occupation of Rome that he
was free to move in the city wherever he liked; and that he would
be accorded the full honours due to a sovereign. Instead of
accepting, he made his famous proclamation *Non Possumus*, an
absolute refusal to negotiate. But he had a more practical reason,
based on a precedent, for preferring to remain 'a prisoner in the
Vatican'. He remembered the struggle between one of his
predecessors, Pius VII, and Napoleon I in the opening years of
the nineteenth century. Here, he perceived a close parallel with
his own predicament. On that occasion in 1804, French troops
had broken into the city, and demanded in the name of
Napoleon the Pope's resignation of his temporal power – just as
the Italian usurper was demanding today. On Pius VII refusing,
the Napoleonic troops bundled him into a coach, and abducted
him to the small town of Savona on the Italian Riviera. Here,
apart from occasional sojourns in France, where he was made to
participate in Napoleon's coronation, he remained for six years,
completely isolated from the world. Napoleon had calculated

that the Pope, separated from his counsellors, would finally yield and surrender his temporal power voluntarily. But Pius VII steadfastly refused. Seclusion and separation could not break the will of this ex-Benedictine monk inured to the cloister. Finally, as we know, it was Napoleon who yielded. All this Pius IX regarded as a precedent. Just as a concert of European powers had overthrown the Corsican in 1815, so now a European war would overturn the Savoyard state, and re-establish the Pope in his rightful possessions.

The Pope was also encouraged by a more immediate form of support for his restoration – from France again. There, after the excesses of the Commune in 1871, the Legitimist party had regained power, and had announced, 'The first act of a restored Monarchy in France will be the despatch of an expedition to Rome, because in the words of King Henry V [the Comte de Chambord, the Bourbon Pretender], the triumph of the legitimate Monarchy in France is inseparable from the establishment of the Temporal power in Rome.'[2] Moreover, France gave material testimony to this attitude. While maintaining an Ambassador at the Holy See, France accredited only a Minister to the Quirinale, thereby leaving no doubt as to who, the Pope or the King of Italy, was the more highly regarded.

These were the principal reasons why Pius IX refused the Guarantee Laws which the Italian Government proposed to him.[3] These laws included a large indemnity for the loss of Rome, the guaranteeing as Papal property of a number of buildings including the Cancelleria and the principal Basilicas, the Vatican, St Peter's, St John Lateran and Santa Maria Maggiore. There was even a suggestion of a Papal port on the Tyrrhenian.[4]

But Pius IX announced that he had no confidence in guarantees given by the new democratic governments. In the parliamentary system of the liberal kind which had been operating for the last ten years in Italy, he said, the governments were constantly changing. What was done by one government could be undone by the next a few months later. Within a decade, he pointed out, Italy had had no fewer than nine different administrations. As for the Italian Government's repeated assurance about combating revolutionaries, the Mazzinians, Garibaldians and other atheists, he believed that the Government was secretly in league with these disreputable elements.

The last accusation was fallacious. Although both the Italian Government and the Mazzini-Garibaldi Socialists shared a common goal, a united Italy, the Italian Government was much embarrassed by the republicanism of their leaders both of whom they had exiled on a number of occasions. What *was* true in the Pope's allegations was that a large and vocal element existed in the Italian Parliament, mostly Socialists and Radicals, who were continually pressing the Government to take more vigorous measures against the Pope. These men publicly announced that a commission should be set up to enter the Vatican and its museums, make an inventory of the contents, and sell the works of art for the benefit of the people. They also demanded that all Papal buildings in Rome should be sequestered; that the Jesuits should be expelled from Italy; that the Papal Secretary of State, Cardinal Antonelli, should be arrested and tried for treason; that the Papal guards should be disbanded; and that the position of the Pope should henceforth be simply that of Bishop of Rome elected, not by the Sacred College, but by a city referendum.

The Government thus found itself in a difficult position – in the presence on the one side of a bitter enemy, the Pope; and on the other of a powerful Socialist element, who could seriously impede its legislation. Its policy appears to have been one of hesitation and contradiction, of quibble and subterfuge, the policy – in the old Italian adage – of 'saving both the goat and the cabbages', of appearing to follow the will of the majority, while hoping to conciliate the Pope. Trying to satisfy both sides, finally it satisfied neither.

Under pressure from the Socialists, the Government gave way to one of their demands, that concerning the Jesuits. It suppressed the famous Jesuit Collegio Romano, where Catholic priests from all over the world had been educated since the time of Gregory XIII, who had founded it in 1585.[5] On 20 November 1870, two months after the Italian occupation of Rome, General La Marmora, Rome's new governor, sequestered the Collegio Romano and expelled its teaching staff. This was carried out by needlessly heavy-handed methods, such as in general marked the occupation of Rome in the early days. Over the doors of the College were large armorial shields, on which were engraved the sacred monogram of the Saviour, together with the emblem of the Jesuit Order, dating from the time of Gregory XIII. Scaffolding was erected for masons with hammers and chisels, who effaced these religious symbols. The College was then converted into a repository for storing the manuscripts and historical documents stolen from the monasteries during the campaign against the Papal States between 1860 and 1870. They were stacked on the ground floor under the supervision of a single porter. According to Augustus Hare in his *Walks in Rome*, it was only after a student reported that some butter he had bought in the Piazza Navona was wrapped up in an autograph letter of Christopher Columbus, that it was realized the porter had been selling the manuscripts as waste paper.

The second arbitrary act of the Government which caused great resentment at the Vatican was the seizure of the Quirinale. This palace on the Monte Cavallo had been the summer residence of the Popes since the Papacy of Clement XII in 1730. The Italian Government considered that it would be a suitable residence for King Victor Emmanuel II, after he had made his official entry into the new capital. Accordingly, on 4 October 1870, the Government demanded the keys of the Quirinale, and offered the Pope compensation. When his Holiness refused, Italian troops dispersed the Papal guards on duty outside the palace, and occupied it in the name of the King of Italy.

The King's entry into Rome in December 1870 was attended with all possible pomp and circumstance, with parades, a review of troops in the Piazza del Popolo, finishing with a ceremonial ball on the Campidoglio, which was attended by all the 'White' aristocracy and the diplomatic corps.[6] Concerning these celebrations the British Ambassador, Sir Augustus Paget reported,

> When I recall the language of the Italian Foreign Minister, Visconti–Venosta, to me about the transfer to Rome, I am almost incredulous at the events which have taken place. Visconti–Venosta's tone in speaking of the subject, of not wishing to wound the susceptibilities of the Pope, was almost touching. So the King's grandiose entry into Rome seems to have been a purely gratuitous insult. It was certainly not the King who wanted it. His Majesty, it is well known, has a strong personal regard for the Pope. During the few moments of conversation which I had the honour to have with His Majesty at the Ball, his tone appears to me anything but one of self-satisfaction and contentment. My own feeling is that it is at the complete sacrifice

of his own feelings that His Majesty has consented to follow the advice of his Ministers.[7]

It is confirmed from many sources that King Victor Emmanuel had the highest regard for the Pope, and had never wanted to leave his native Turin for Florence, let alone Rome. Had the decision been left to him alone, it is doubtful if, after his loss of Lombardy under the Treaty of Villafranca, he would have coveted a single square inch of territory beyond Parma and Modena. But he was a constitutional monarch, and he did as his ministers advised him.

On 1 November 1870, Pius IX issued his Encyclical *Respicientes Omnia* ('All those respectful . . .') officially condemning the usurpers of Rome. King Victor Emmanuel II was, it is true, not mentioned by name; but no one could be in any doubt as to who was intended by the Pope's words, '*Eos omnes qualibet dignitate etiam specialissima mentione digna fulgentes*' ('All those of whatever rank, even – specially worthy of mention – the most prominent'). Among the Ultramontane[8] prelates in the Vatican, there had been a call for outright excommunication of the King; and a century or so earlier that might still have been possible. But even Pius IX had to take account of the changed circumstances since the great days of Papal absolutism in Europe.

Throughout the 1870s, Pius IX himself worsened his position by his vehement speeches against the Italian State and its monarch, thus playing into the hands of the Liberals and Socialists, who demanded ever stronger measures against 'this traitor to Italy'. To them, Pius IX was 'the anachronism of the nineteenth century', 'an Old Testament figure out of time and place'. Indeed, there was in him something of the Hebrew prophet pouring forth his vials of wrath, never doubting for a moment that the judgement and punishment of God would descend on the evil men who had committed the great sacrilege. He could quote the Scriptures to good effect: the 79th Psalm – 'O God, the heathen are come into Thine inheritance; Thy holy temple have they defiled, they have laid Jerusalem on heaps.' He would often end a speech notable at its opening for Christian charity and resignation with bitter irony and withering scorn; for he sincerely believed that opposition to the consecrated Pontiff was as unpardonable as rebellion against Heaven. Who should know better in matters of faith and morals than the Infallible? Then he would strike out with whatever verbal weapon came to hand, not infrequently dealing random blows which rebounded against him. There was no crime however heinous, no vice however degrading – murder, theft, blasphemy, adultery – that he did not lay at the door of the House of Savoy which had stolen his inheritance. For him they were 'the sons of darkness', or 'of Belial'; and Victor Emmanuel II was 'the new Sennacherib'. No conciliation could be possible, between Jesus and Belial, between truth and falsehood. He was ready, Pius IX said, to give up his life rather than yield to the devices of iniquity, to be driven down into the catacombs again rather than abandon Rome.

On one occasion, when speaking to a group of foreign pilgrims, he likened King Victor Emannuel to both Holofernes and Goliath, 'those ogres whose heads were severed with their own swords'. Just so, he said, the new Italian State would perish by its own evil devices. On another occasion, he made a direct appeal to Catholics in all countries to persuade their governments to undertake a 'Crusade against Italy for the re-establishment of the temporal power'. On Italian lips other than his, this would have sounded like treason. It caused great uproar in Parliament, where the Socialists demanded his immediate arrest and prosecution.[9] He was equally outspoken in all matters concerning public morals. Odo Russell reported that on one occasion he even expelled from Rome three English spinsters, most respected members of the foreign colony, on the ground that they had too liberally entertained a number of priests in their apartment.[10]

When Pius IX died on 8 February 1878, he left the Church at odds with almost all Europe. Apart from the Italian imbroglio, the Papacy was on bad terms with all the traditionally Catholic states: Spain, Belgium, and Portugal. In Spain, a Liberal government was confiscating ecclesiastical property and suppressing the monasteries and convents. In Belgium, a Radical Prime Minister was laicizing anything Catholic he could lay hands on. The Portuguese, reverting to the practices of Pombal in the previous century, had begun another savage attack on the Jesuits. Even France, the 'Eldest Daughter of the Church', and the Pope's best friend since 1848, was preparing a number of anti-clerical laws. It seemed that Pius IX's reign, during which the entire patrimony of St Peter had been lost, had been a complete failure.

So it seemed; but it is possible for us today to take advantage of hindsight. Ascending the Chair of St Peter when all civilized Europe was mesmerized by the 'Lights of Science', Pius IX alone stood firm for the spiritual against the material values. He was the helmsman who stood fast as the barque of St Peter went into the tempest. When it emerged, he had been swept away; but his example remained. In the words of Cardinal Manning, 'when the history of his Pontificate comes to be written, it will be found to have been one of the most resplendent, and majestic and powerful, to have reached out over the whole extent of the Church with greater effect than that of any other Pope in the Apostolic Succession'.

Pius IX's tribulations during his last years undoubtedly increased the affection in which he was held. In the eyes of all devout Catholics who now flocked to Rome, he had been shamefully dispossessed of his property by wicked men, who had incarcerated him in a Mamertine prison in his own palace.[11] His candid personality and open nature contributed much to this popular affection; for he never harboured personal animosity but always, he said, 'loved the sinner while hating the sin'. To an acquaintance of Garibaldi he said, 'If you see Garibaldi, tell him I know he daily curses me; but that I always bless him.' After Garibaldi's defeat at Mentana, he visited the two hundred or so Garibaldians who had been taken prisoner. 'Behold me, my friends!' he said to them. 'You see before you the man whom your leader has called "The Vampire of Italy"!' The silver hair, twinkling eyes and beaming smile, the round and rubicund face of this 'vampire' seemed to affect the prisoners as he went among them, blessing them: 'You, my friend, want warm clothing . . . you, fresh linen . . . you, shoes. . . .' Overcome with emotion, the men, who only a few days before had loaded his name with every foul term of abuse, grasped at his robe and kissed his hands and feet, weeping.

Metternich had said of Pius IX in the early days of his Pontificate, 'Warm of heart and weak of intellect, he is lacking in practical sense.' In that Pius IX was too impulsive and too great-hearted a man to make a good politician, Metternich was right. Pius was faced with difficulties which would have taxed the ability of the greatest statesmen; yet even in those darkest hours, he displayed a habitual sense of humour which they might have envied. Mr Jervoise relates that he had an audience with the Pope just after the Italian seizure of Rome, and found him 'in a surprisingly good humour'. His Holiness talked about the outcome of the Franco-Prussian War. 'I asked the King of Prussia for help,' he said, 'but he was too busy making peace with France. Now, with which of the French Governments was he making peace? The one in Bordeaux? The one in Paris under M. Favre? Or with the one up there – in the balloon, with Gambetta?'[12] At this the Pope laughed and pointed up as if to Heaven. 'Yes, that's probably the best place for them!'[13]

He found the continuous changes and shuffles of government in the 'constitutional democracies' of Italy and France a source of infinite amusement. 'Here today, gone tomorrow,' he would say. 'How can one make an agreement with a substance which two days later is a shadow?' The new Italy had, he delighted in observing, had nine governments in as many years. Even in the revolutionaries for ever shouting 'Death to the Pope!' he could find something comic. Mr Jervoise relates that he visited him one day when he was recovering from a bout of lumbago and was walking on crutches. When Jervoise enquired sympathetically about this, he laughed at his crutches and put his hand to his hip. 'These pains are like the revolutionaries,' he said. 'They come suddenly, they are hurtful, and they stay a long time.' He rubbed his hip. 'See here – here is a revolutionary! But in the end they always collapse.'[14]

Perhaps the quality by which Pius IX will best be remembered was his pugnacity, his ability to fight back when all seemed lost. Baron de Michelis, the French Ambassador to the Holy See in 1872, said, 'It seems to him that whoever is against him, be it the entire world, is not of the slightest importance. "I have on my side," he once told me, "the great Power which fights for the good cause – and that power is God." '[15] The God, he said, who had wrought great marvels by turning back the waters of the Jordan and the Red Sea, would once again send deliverance to His people; and he expressed his unshakeable faith in a Church 'accustomed to triumph on Golgotha'.

At the end of his life, he made a remarkable prophecy to a group of pilgrims: 'So, they want to make a gardener of me, do they? And leave me only the Vatican and a garden? Instead of the Pope's legitimate possessions? So be it! But in the end, you know, the Pope will be in possession, when the King of Italy will not even have a throne to sit upon. Yes, the Popes are gardeners in a certain sense. But they have been soldiers too.'[16]

Seventy-six years later, in 1946, a Pope of his name was still seated firmly on the Throne of St Peter, while a popular plebiscite evicted the Savoyard Monarchy from the throne of Italy.

Cardinal Antonelli, who was Pius IX's Secretary of State for the unprecedented period of twenty-six years, undoubtedly contributed to his master's intransigence. Born of humble Neapolitan stock (his father appears to have been a bandit), he had shared the Pope's exile in Gaeta, where he remained staunch and loyal when other prelates had forsaken Pius IX. He also remained at his master's side throughout the difficult days after the 1850 restoration in Rome. In those times, a man of his temporizing nature must have been invaluable to Pius IX for dealing with the Garibaldian and Mazzinian revolutionaries. When Perugia revolted against Papal rule in 1859, the crafty Antonelli gave the impression that the Vatican would accept the *fait accompli*; in private, he despatched the Swiss Papal troops secretly to Perugia under Colonel Schmidt, with orders that all rebels captured were to be decapitated instantly (a sentence which the methodical Swiss faithfully carried out). When the Pope was inclined to clemency towards a fanatic who had tried to assassinate him, Antonelli persuaded his master that nothing short of execution would meet the case. He also saw to it that the two Anarchist conspirators, Tognetti and Monti, who had blown up the Seristori Barracks in 1862, killing a score of Papal Zouaves, paid the full penalty.

In the Vatican Archives for 1870 is a curious document, unusual in that here in the archives of the Secretary of State, that is of Cardinal Antonelli, is an arraignment of Antonelli himself.[17] It was drawn up by an Italian State lawyer, Avvocato Achille Genarelli, and it accused Cardinal Antonelli of a number of thefts, including that of having stolen the jewels from the Madonna of Loreto. As legal administrator of the San Loreto sanctuary and its treasure, the author of the document said that he had become aware in 1859 that the most precious gems in that treasure were being removed and sold 'by the clerical administration'. He gave a detailed list of these jewels with their valuation, running into hundreds of thousands of lire, together with the 'Clerical Administration' affidavit stating that they were all handed over to Cardinal Antonelli on 20 December 1859, '*since when they have not been seen again*'. The lawyer recalled that the Renaissance Popes, Nicolas V and Julius II, fulminated their excommunications against 'despoilers of the Virgin of Loreto', and he indicated that this should be the condign punishment for Cardinal Antonelli. He further accused Cardinal Antonelli of stealing Chinese and Japanese vases from the famous Campana Collection.

The only explanation of why this extraordinary document should have found its way into Antonelli's own files must be that it is followed by Antonelli's spirited defence of himself. This was presumably drawn up by a Vatican lawyer under Antonelli's guidance. It quotes receipts to show that these jewels and works of art were indeed sold – for the good reason that the Papal *Casa degli Ornati* (department of Church treasure) was desperately short of funds. 'We have,' said Antonelli's defender, 'a voluminous catalogue listing the whole Campana Collection. We have been through it page by page, article by article, and whereas there are Etruscan and Graeco-Roman vases, there is no mention of Japanese or Chinese ones. . . . If you go to the Church of the Jesù, you will see that the jewels you talk about serve to decorate the high altar.'

Antonelli's defence may well have been valid; but we know that when he died in 1876, his family brought a lawsuit in connection with his will, which revealed that during his long tenure of office, he had amassed a huge fortune, in particular in the form of precious stones, which he liked showing off to Roman ladies. We also know that during Pius IX's reign, he arrogated to himself a number of commanding posts, which made him all-powerful in the Vatican. Avvocato Genarelli listed these in his arraignment. Besides being Secretary of State, Antonelli created for himself the title of Governor of the Holy Palaces, which gave him control over Papal real estate. As we have seen, he became Prefect of the Loreto Congregation and administrator of the Treasure of the Santa Casa. He administered the *Monte di Pietà*, the affluent Papal pawnbroking establishment. He made one of his brothers Governor of the Banco di Roma; for another, he obtained the monopoly of Roman grain imports. The Antonelli brothers fixed the price of corn, so that they and their middlemen amassed large fortunes. All this according to Avvocato Gennarelli; if what he says is true, Antonelli must have been one of the last cases of grand Papal nepotism.

Why did Pius IX choose as his closest adviser such a man, who could hardly be said to be inspired by the zeal for saving souls? In the words of Gregorovius the German historian of Rome, in his

The Roman Journals, 'The upper part of Cardinal Antonelli's face is clear-cut, almost handsome, but the lower part ends in the animal.' Antonelli's value to the Pope appears to have been his understanding of Pius IX's character and weaknesses, so that he never came into collision with the Pope, or provoked his anger: no small achievement in dealing with such an impulsive nature. Equally important was his financial acumen. After the convulsions of 1848, and again after 1870, he restored the Vatican finances. Besides making his own fortune, he made that of the Vatican. In the words of Mr Jervoise, 'Cardinal Antonelli has of late exercised an almost absolute rule over the mind of the Pope. Formerly, the Curia Cardinals were consulted in a body over important decisions; but of late it is only Antonelli. He has become the sole arbiter of Vatican policy.'[18] And yet at the end, Pius IX seems to have become sharply suspicious of this Secretary of State, who combined the astuteness of a Roman prelate with Neapolitan dexterity and cunning. Behind his back, the Pope had been heard to refer to him as 'my Barabbas'; and when Antonelli died in 1875, the Pope remained curiously unmoved.

The last word on Cardinal Antonelli may be left to Dante. He regarded avarice, or the mania for amassing material wealth, as a vice to which high churchmen are particularly susceptible. His fourth Circle in the Inferno is full of Cardinals and prelates, all naked and busily engaged in rolling huge boulders up a hill. No sooner have they reached the top than the boulders topple over and fall to the bottom, so that the damned must start again. It certainly seems odd – and not only to Dante – that some of the very men who by their calling profess to have forsaken the world should be in such bondage to it.

3

The Turbolenti and the Zelanti

It is customary to regard the struggle which was now joined in Rome as between two clearly defined opponents, the Church on the one hand, the State on the other – symbolically 'the Vatican' and 'the Quirinale'. In fact, four groups were engaged in the dispute. To identify them, we may conveniently point to a modern English parallel. We speak today of the Conservative Party as having its right and left wings, just as the Labour Party has two such wings. The views of the left wing of the Conservatives are often not far distant from those expressed by the right wing of the Labour Party; so that the two sometimes find themselves on common ground, more in sympathy than with the wings of their own parties. So it was in Rome after 1870.

The Italian Parliament which now ruled the country through its democratically elected members was composed broadly of two disparate elements; on the one hand the moderate, conservative Monarchists; on the other, socialist Republicans of various brands. The former composed the Government, men like the Foreign Minister, Visconti-Venosta, who wished to antagonize the Pope as little as possible, to go to the limits of concession to conciliate him. In the words of the French Ambassador, the Comte de Bourgoing, 'The moderation of the Italian Minister for Foreign Affairs, and his desire not to exaggerate the differences between the Italian Government and the Papacy, are well known.'[1]

Most of these Moderates were Catholics who, if not devout, at least paid lip-service to religion; some of them even went to Mass. Visconti-Venosta himself stated in a speech in Parliament not long after the occupation of Rome:

We wish to reassure all religious people that we have no intention of exerting pressure on the decisions of the Holy See. On the contrary, we shall grant the Church on our territory total liberty. We believe in liberty. Liberty will prove a corrective to all forms of fanaticism. The only power which we shall exercise in Rome is that of the law. We fervently hope that the day is not far distant when the Holy Father will appreciate the immense advantages accruing to the Church from this liberty. The Holy Father has made the wise decision not to leave Rome. He may rest assured that he will always be accorded in this city the profoundest respect and consideration by the Royal authorities and the Italian nation.[2]

Nothing could be more conciliatory than these lofty sentiments; and these words were on several occasions confirmed by acts. A governmental Order of the Day stated: 'The Royal troops shall render to His Holiness the Pope on all occasions sovereign honours; and to the Cardinals the honours accorded to Royal Princes; and such honours to other members of the Papal hierarchy as have been customary.'[3] On another occasion, at the time of the death of Pius IX in 1878, the Italian Prime Minister, Sig. Depretis, announced, 'The Government wishes to give further proof to Europe of their respect for the spiritual authority of the Pope. It will take every precaution for ensuring complete liberty for the meetings and deliberations of the coming Conclave.'[4]

Had the Government and the Moderates had their way, a *modus vivendi* with the moderate elements in the Vatican might well have been reached. But the Italian Government had to pay attention, if only for voting purposes in the lobbies of the Parliament at Monte Citorio, to the socialist, republican, Garibaldian and atheist elements who were steadily gaining ground, to whom religion was no more than a form of jugglery. Not only were they anti-Papal, they were also anti-Monarchist. They did not refer to the Government as 'The Ministers of the King of Italy', but as 'The Ministers of Italy'; nor to 'King Victor Emmanuel', but to 'Victor Emmanuel'. For them collectively we may use a term coined at the time, and which remained current in Italy for the rest of the century, 'I Turbolenti', to describe a turbulent group of men all imbued with the principles of the French Revolution – socialists, republicans, anarchists, freethinkers, Garibaldians, and communists or 'Red Revolutionaries' (as the latter were then called). All these men were in continuous contention among themselves about the ideal society they wished to introduce into Italy; but one thing they had in common, that the Catholic Church should have no part in it.

The most extreme of these groups was the Alfieri, a secret society which demanded quite simply: 'The abolition of the Papacy; the expulsion of the priests from Italy; the burning of all churches, beginning with the Vatican.' Somewhat less extreme, but equally hostile, was the Central Republican Association, whose meetings took place in the Apollo Theatre. The language they used describes them: '. . . Citizen Carlo Luziano then came to the rostrum and said, "The Rome of the priests is one of idleness and submission to that infirm old idiot called Pius. The Italian people today have had enough of him and his addled Church. The most powerful enemy of Italian liberty is the Vatican." '[5]

In the 'liberal' society of Savoyard Rome, the anti-clerical caricaturists had free run, and the city was placarded with crude portraits of the Pope, Cardinal Antonelli, the Jesuits, and Napoleon III. One of these depicted Pius IX on a donkey, with Antonelli holding a parasol over his head, while a group of Jesuits led them on a rope. Another showed Napoleon III as the crucified Jesus on the Cross, with William II of Prussia as the Roman soldier thrusting the lance into his side.[6]

A representative example of the verbal vituperation directed at the Church is quoted in the Vatican Secret Archives, recording a certain Oscar Lantoni speaking at the inauguration of the Giordano Bruno monument. 'Every page in the history of the Papacy,' he announced, 'reveals an abuse of power, a rape [sic] committed in the name of God. But today humanity is at last rejecting this obscene thing called the Papacy – with all its hierarchy of eminences, sacraments, evangels, breviaries, reliquaries, relics and gallipots ... all this rubbishy junk is on the way out.'[7]

The language of the Turbolenti Deputies in Parliament, if a little more dignified, expressed much the same view. They condemned in particular the Guarantee Laws extending a number of concessions to the Pope which the Government had proposed. These proposals revealed considerable wisdom on the part of the Government. Having deprived the Pope of his temporal power and taken possession of his capital, it should have been the object of all

Italian political parties to conciliate devout and offended Catholic opinion all over the world by large and generous concessions to His Holiness. The Guarantee Laws aimed at providing just this, with the necessary securities for the free and independent exercise of the Pope's spiritual duties.[8] But the provisions of these laws were so violently attacked and amended by the Turbolenti in Parliament that they were finally eroded altogether.

The Turbolenti amendment to Article 7, for instance, completely altered its sense. It had read: 'No officer of the Italian Authority, or agent of its forces, may enter the Papal precincts without the permission of the Supreme Pontiff.' This was clear enough, and would undoubtedly have been accepted by the Pope. But to this recognition of Papal sovereignty, the Turbolenti added the qualifying clause: '. . . or unless the officer is furnished with a decree from the supreme Roman magistrature'. This completely altered the effect, because a simple warrant from the 'supreme Roman magistrature' could authorize the municipal officer to enter the Vatican precincts whenever he wished. In this case, the Pope would be in an even less favourable position than the diplomats of the foreign powers accredited to him, whose embassies and legations were all protected by extra-territorial rights. A host of other amendments of a similar nature were added. The result was that the Pope rejected the Guarantee Laws *in toto*. All hope of an early settlement evaporated.

This surprised the Turbolenti, who had assumed that the Vatican would now be so short of funds that it would gladly accept the Guarantee Laws, and the offer of three million lire that went with it as compensation. It proved a most unwise assumption. The French Ambassador, the Comte de Bourgoing, commented at this time, 'Never has the Papal Treasury been so replete; for the Pope no longer has the bureaucrats of the Papal States on his payroll. Nor has he the Zouave forces to support. And the monetary gifts which now flow into the Vatican from well-wishers all over the world to help him in his predicament substantially surpass the three million lire offered by the Italian Guarantee Laws. His Holiness is confident that the piety of the Faithful will suffice for his financial requirements.'[9]

The spiritual leader of the Turbolenti was Giuseppe Mazzini, who proclaimed 'a new Revelation to supersede effete Christianity'; and its theoretical active leader was the great Garibaldi, 'the hammer of the Church', whom the Government had exiled, after his Mentana escapade, to the island of Caprera. 'Theoretical' is the correct term, for Garibaldi had since then become prematurely senile, and his noisy rodomontades against the Pope were often confused in his mind with those against the Italian Government, whom he kept in a continual state of alarm about what he would do next. In the words of Mr Herries, the British Minister to the Italian Government, 'Garibaldi's language now exceeds in violence, invective and extravagance of metaphor all his previous declarations, if such a thing is possible.'[10] Garibaldi's pretensions had become much inflated after his visit to England, then the first power in the world, by the hospitality of its dukes and the smiles of its duchesses.

Although Garibaldi could not take part personally in the attacks on the Church in Rome, he had plenty of followers: *mangiapreti* (priest-eaters), as they were known, for they delighted in disrupting religious ceremonies and processions. The Jesuit church, the Gesù, was naturally a favourite target. On one occasion while Lenten Mass was in progress there, a *mangiapreti* in a hat, waving a tricolour, rushed in shrieking, 'Down with the Jesuits! Down with the Blacks!' Blows were exchanged and a free fight developed. At one stage before the man was ejected, he seized by the chasuble the Jesuit father officiating at the altar. On another occasion, a number of Turbolenti completely disrupted a service in the Minerva church where a *Te Deum* was being sung in honour of Pius IX's twenty-fifth Pontifical year. The Garibaldian gunpowder conspirators, Tognetti and Monti, had gone even further in blowing up the Papal Seristori Barracks.

Another way of insulting the Church was to select anniversaries of dates important either in its calendar or in the Italian State calendar. One such was 20 September, the anniversary of the entry of Italian troops into Rome, which was annually fêted by the Turbolenti in great style. In 1874, it was the occasion of a celebration on the Campidoglio of 'The New Education for the Young', which had replaced the previous education by priests and Jesuits. In the presence of the Mayor and City Councillors, the Minister of Education delivered a homily to hundreds of university and high school students in which he told them that they were destined to be 'the regenerators of our country'. Referring to the obfuscations of the Vatican, he said that this ceremony signified 'the letting of light into a dark hole, the rescue of youth from the moral degeneration in which it had been kept for centuries by the dark forces of the Church'.

Religious educational establishments appear, in the early days of Italian secular rule, to have excited the greatest wrath of the Turbolenti. Clerical students at the various national religious colleges in Rome were frequently insulted and spat upon in the streets. The Rector of the Belgian College was stoned and seriously injured.

On the other side, in the Vatican, there was a similar division to that in the Italian State, with moderate and extremist elements, the latter known as Ultramontanes or I Zelanti ('Zealots'). The moderators, a body of bishops and clergy inclined to some sort of compromise with the Italian State, argued that sooner or later the Papacy must come to terms with a parliamentary system such as was now general in Europe; but the Zelanti would have no truck with the Italian State, and demanded complete restoration of the Pope's temporal power. They took their inspiration from Gregory XVI's Encyclical *Mirari Vos* of 1832, which teaches that throughout history states have perished as a result of excessive liberty, freedom of speech and the mania for constant reform. That Encyclical condemned the liberty of the press, 'a spreader of errors', and pointed out that the Apostles had burnt bad books; it stated that the Council of Trent was perfectly justified after the Reformation in instituting an Index, on which were placed books containing impure doctrine.

One of the most rabid Zelanti was the Archbishop of Bologna, Cardinal Parocchi, who contributed to the Ultramontane paper *Voce della Verità* ('Voice of Truth'). In an article, he declared they would fight against 'this so-called progress and civilization to the last drop of our blood, to say nothing of our ink'.[11] Another Zelanti journal was *Civiltà Cattolica* ('Catholic Civilization'), the Jesuit monthly. The Pope had become particularly attached to this Order after his return from Gaeta; so that the British Ambassador, Sir Augustus Paget, could report, 'His Holiness is now surrounded by Jesuits, who exert considerable pressure on him'. *Civiltà Cattolica* had been founded during the Gaeta exile (1859), specifically to deal with the most learned questions of the day, philosophical, historical, scientific, economic, as well as theological; its articles were of an exceptionally high literary quality. Once again, as after the Council of Trent three hundred years before, the disciples of Loyola were to be the vanguard of the Papal counter-attack.

In a more practical domain, the Zelanti made no attempt to conceal that the subversion of the Italian State by foreign intervention, if no other means were available, was their aim; and they offered up prayers in church for the success of any political party in a foreign country which declared its hostility to Italy. Mr Herries describes them in his despatch to the Foreign Office:

These prelates at the Vatican neglect no opportunity for fomenting discord and stimulating hate. They leave nothing undone that can be done to inflame passions and provoke conflict. The language of their newspapers such as *Voce della Verità* equals, if it does not exceed, in seditious violence, in outrage to the highest authorities of the State, in audacious defiance of the Laws, that of the worst examples of the Fenian press in Ireland a few years ago. It is clear that these religious fanatics wish to goad the Italian Government into some act of retaliation which the Vatican can denounce as a violation of the Government's solemn pledges to protect the Church.[12]

The opportunity for this 'act of retaliation' arose on the occasion of the transfer of Pius IX's remains to the Basilica of San Lorenzo outside the Walls. In his will, Pius IX had expressed the wish that his body after lying in St Peter's should be transferred to its final resting place in this church. It is one of the most distant basilicas of Rome, and there were fears that, in view of the notorious behaviour of the Turbolenti, there might be incidents on the way there. It was almost as if Pius IX, even from his grave, was determined to keep hostilities alive. The new Pope, Leo XIII, naturally complied with his predecessor's wishes; but he stipulated that the transfer of Pius IX's remains on a bier with its escorting carriages of cardinals and prelates should be of a modest and unassuming kind. As a further precaution, he ordered it to take place at night, when few people were about. He even reduced the number of carriages conveying the cardinals and prelates from twenty to six.

A few days before 12 July 1881, when the transfer was due to take place, the heads of the Zelanti asked permission to take part in the last journey of the Pope they had revered as almost a saint in his lifetime. It appears that Leo XIII was by no means in favour of this, but that on being pressed he finally gave permission.

The Zelanti now advised their faithful of the hour and place where the cortège would form. The result was that a concourse which Leo XIII had hoped would be limited to a few hundred people following the bier numbered three or four thousand. On this the British Ambassador, Sir Augustus Paget, comments, 'The object of the Zelanti was clearly to use the funeral for a political demonstration, which they knew could provoke a violent reaction from the Italian nationalists.'[13]

The clock of St Peter's had sounded the last strokes of midnight, when the hearse hung with red and drawn by four black horses emerged from the cathedral through the archway of the Porta S. Marta, the coffin resting on a bier. The municipal authorities had been informed, and the bier was preceded by a posse of Carabinieri, behind whom walked several thousand persons of both sexes bearing tapers and flares, and reciting the Rosary and other prayers. Behind them moved the cavalcade of carriages conveying the cardinals, prelates and members of the Black aristocracy, in far greater numbers than the six prescribed by the Pope. The Turbolenti had also evidently been apprised, because the Roman pleb had turned out in force. Their bearing was at first respectful, doffing their hats as the bier passed, some even going down on their knees. It was not until the bier had left the Tiber, and was turning into the centre of the city, that it was suddenly confronted in the Piazza Rusticucci by a group of obstreperous persons chanting the Neapolitan *canzone* about a departed loved one, *Addio mia bella, Addio!* ('Farewell, my lovely, farewell!') The sarcastic irreverence of this was soon replaced by something more sinister: cries of 'Long live Garibaldi!', 'Death to the priests!', 'Death to the black vultures!' and finally, 'Let's chuck the Pope's carcase in the Tiber!' They attempted to rush the coffin to do so, but were prevented by the pedestrians behind the bier; they continued to walk beside the cortège uttering obscene and blasphemous cries, spitting on the priests and miming as if to stab them with imaginary daggers. At several places the Carabinieri had to intervene, and near the Termini station bricks were thrown at the cardinals' carriages. As soon as the assailants were driven off at one place, they reappeared in another. By the time the cortège reached San Lorenzo outside the Walls, the obstreperous element had increased to several thousand,

and a real battle seemed imminent. But the Carabinieri now drew their swords and formed a cordon around the basilica where Pius IX's body was to repose. The ceremony of lowering the coffin did not take place until 3 a.m. on the morning of 13 July, four hours after the time planned.

The following day, six men were brought before the magistrates for having 'riotously disturbed a religious ceremony'. Their appearance in court was greeted by a sympathetic public with wild acclamations. Their counsel argued that their behaviour had nothing to do with religion, but was the consequence of the strife stimulated by the clerical party against the liberty and constitution of the nation. They were sentenced to short terms of imprisonment and small fines.[14]

The whole incident reflected badly on the Government, which had been informed that the ceremony would not be on the modest scale originally planned, and who should have provided more forces of law and order than the small posse of Carabinieri. It also reflected on the judgement of the new Pope Leo XIII who had, against his better judgement, allowed the Zelanti to follow the bier.

The episode was unfortunate because the comparative peace which had marked the opening of the new Pontificate was broken, and the extremists on both sides seized the occasion to attack one another again. One sign of the better times had been the order which had been maintained in Rome during the 1878 Conclave which elected Leo XIII, the State authorities stationing troops and police to prevent hostile demonstrations. The world in general was beginning to treat with indifference, or to consider unfounded, the repeated assertions by the Zelanti that the Pope was 'a prisoner in the Vatican'; and there were grounds for hoping ten years after the seizure of Rome that a *modus vivendi* might at last be achieved. But this incident halted the process.

Some idea of the psychology of the Zelanti is given in Émile Zola's fictional but accurate work *Rome*. Here there is a celebrated portrait of Cardinal Boccanera, perhaps the most Ultramontane character in the whole of European literature. To a young priest who suggests to him that because the world is constantly changing, the Church should adapt itself and change too, the Cardinal retorts,

That is not true. The world does not change. It continually tramps the same ground, loses its way, and strays into the most abominable bypaths. Truth is in the past. It is to the past that we must cling, if we are to avoid the snares laid by the present. All your fine novelties, these marvels created by the famous so-called progress, are simply traps and snares laid by the eternal Tempter, the cause of perdition and death. Why seek further, why constantly incur the risk of error, when for 1,800 years *the truth has been known*? Truth is in the Apostolic Succession. What madness to try to change it, when so many lofty minds, so many pious souls have made it the most admirable of monuments, the one instrument of order in this world, and salvation in the next.

The priest he is addressing has written a book setting out the changes he would like to see made for reforming the Catholic Church. On this Cardinal Boccanera comments, 'Why write at all? There is always rebellion in expressing opinions of one's own. It is always the Devil's temptation which puts a pen in an author's hand. I tell you, the only duties you have as a priest are humility and obedience, the complete annihilation of yourself before the sovereign will of the Church.'

As might be expected, often the most extreme of the Zelanti were foreigners, in particular those Catholics from Protestant countries where they were in a minority. Sir Augustus Paget reports that a delegation of English Catholics who presented an address to Pius IX in 1873 were so partisan, and so insulting to the King of Italy, that he was ashamed of his countrymen. It was headed by the Duke of Norfolk and Lord Denbigh 'The words of their address,' Sir Augustus reported, 'seemed to surpass if possible in violence and insult to the King of Italy and his Government anything that has hitherto been uttered. The Pope himself, judging from the opening phrases of his reply, appears to have been most surprised by the vehemence of their declaration. Yet the Italian government makes no objection.' The proper course, Sir Augustus suggested, would have been for the Minister of the Interior to have given the Duke of Norfolk and associates twenty-four hours to leave Italy.[15]

An important element among the Zelanti was the female side of the 'Black' or Papal aristocracy. Many of these ladies, descended from families long enobled in the course of the centuries by the Papacy, regarded the Savoyard Monarch and his Court not only as usurpers but as parvenus. Why should a Colonna or a Massimo bow to people whose ancestors only a century before had been living in a hut on an Alpine mountainside? On the anniversary of Pius IX's return from Gaeta, a number of these ladies presented His Holiness with their own handiwork, a woven carpet; and they asked permission to illuminate their houses that night with transparencies commemorating the event. The more moderate counsellors at the Vatican advised against this. Although their gesture would commemorate an historical event, and was a perfectly legitimate cause for rejoicing, it might be regarded as provocative. Such prudent scruples did not deter two ladies who lived at the top of the Spanish Steps. At 7.30 that night, they lit a number of transparencies and displayed them at the windows on the third floor. These displayed the slogans '*Viva Pio Nono!*'; '*Cuore!*'; '*Lutto!*' '*Fedeltà!*' ('Long live Pius IX!' 'Heart!' 'Mourning!' 'Fidelity!') together with an illuminated Mentana Cross.[16] The Turbolenti immediately assembled a mob, broke all the windows of the house, and extinguished the transparencies with a hose.[17]

Except for three families of the 'Black' aristocracy – the Colonna, Orsini and Massimo, who claimed a classical Roman ancestry – the Roman aristocracy owed their position and fortune to the Popes of the past, who had bestowed titles, estates and palaces on their ancestors. Although as Italian subjects these 'Black' aristocrats now had to pay Italian State taxes and observe the Italian laws, while their sons had to do military service in the Italian armed forces, they avoided as far as possible any act of overt recognition of the Savoyard Government. They did not go to Court, nor have social contact with its members. Their attitude was one of abstention, passive resistance, social boycott. Of the heads of these 'Black' families, only three defected to the Savoyards after 1870: the Duke of Sermoneta, Prince Doria-Pamphili and Prince Odescalchi, the last named even flirting with socialism, thereby earning for himself the soubriquet of 'The Red Prince'. Some of the Roman aristocracy were clever enough to keep a foot in both camps. Émile Zola, who was in Rome at this time, relates that in certain patrician families which had two sons, one would go into the service of the Vatican, while the other attached himself to the Quirinale. 'The latter assured the family a retreat in that direction should the Papacy collapse completely, which then seemed a distinct possibility.'[18]

The time had now come for the greatest of the Turbolenti, Giuseppe Garibaldi, to return to Rome. He had been elected to

Parliament for Caprera, and the Government could not prevent him from taking his seat. For four years the Government had managed to keep this firebrand – who gave them almost as much trouble as he gave the Vatican – confined to the island of Caprera. As Garibaldi wrote to his friend Canzio, 'That rubbish (*rubaccia*) which calls itself the Italian Government keeps me a prisoner on Caprera – watched over night and day.'[19] The Turbolenti were naturally delighted at the thought of their old leader being among them again, and they planned a rousing welcome. Ever since he had been incarcerated on Caprera, all anyone had heard from him had been through his violent letters and denunciations in the press, in which he lambasted the Italian Monarchy and Government. The latter now took special precautions. If the Turbolenti were delighted, the Zelanti were equally pleased. They hoped that seditious acts might be committed by the Turbolenti which would give further substance to their assertion that Rome was ruled by a rabble, and that the Pope was not safe in his own city.[20]

Garibaldi arrived at the Termini station at 2.45 p.m. on 25 January 1875. An enormous crowd had gathered outside, including a large delegation from the Workers' Society of Mutual Support. Bands were playing the Garibaldi hymn, and red flags were flying. Awaiting his train on the platform were the leading members of the Municipality, including the Mayor of Rome and quantities of Garibaldian veterans. Long before the train drew into the station, shouts of '*Evviva Garibaldi!*' filled the air, reaching a paroxysm when the carriage came to a halt, a door opened and Garibaldi stood before them.

He was dressed as they had always known him, in the white cloak over the famous red shirt which had been inspired by the Montevideo slaughterhouse keeper for whom he had worked in his youth. Around his neck was the knotted scarf, over which fell his long grey locks; on his head, the famous diminutive pill-box hat. He descended with some difficulty, and it was seen, to general concern, that he walked with crutches. He was escorted to a special reception room, where the Mayor and other dignitaries made speeches of welcome. While these were in progress, enthusiasts in the crowd outside had detached the harness of his carriage, so that their hero could be drawn through Rome not by four horses, but by hundreds of his beloved 'Garibaldini'.

After the speeches, Garibaldi climbed into the carriage and stood up for a moment to receive the acclamations of the crowd, raising his right arm from time to time; but it was clearly an effort and his body was bent. He appeared exhausted, and his face was expressionless to those who remembered his robust and energetic aspect in the great days. How he had changed! How he must have suffered on that rocky island! The Government should be ashamed of itself! He was conducted to the Palazzo Baldassini in the centre of the Campo Marzio, where a crowd was waiting for him to come out on the balcony and address them. At length he appeared; but his speech was disappointingly short, and he had to deliver it sitting down.

The next afternoon he arrived at Monte Citorio to take his seat in Parliament. Owing to the enormous crowd at the main entrance, he was escorted through a side door. On his appearing in the Chamber, where a debate was in progress, the whole of the Turbolenti rose as a man, and acclaimed him with loud and prolonged cheers. The Moderates remained seated, tight-lipped and silent. Supporting himself on his crutches, Garibaldi took his place at one of the benches on the extreme left. After the cheering had subsided, the President of the Chamber turned to the Deputies and said, 'The Honourable Garibaldi being present, I invite him to take the oath.' He read the oath, whereupon Garibaldi rose, took off his little pill-box hat, raised his right arm and said, 'I swear.' The Turbolenti were hoping that he would make a speech, flaying the Government for its supine attitude towards the Papacy. But those were the only two words he pronounced. He sat there in silence listening to the debate and then, almost unostentatiously, left the Chamber.

It was the same during the remainder of his time in Rome. Instead of giving vent in public to violent denunciations of the Papacy, as both the Turbolenti and the Zelanti hoped, he refrained from opening his mouth. This was partly due to his frail health, and partly to prudence, a quality for which in the past he had not been noted. What did emerge during his stay was that he had developed an obsession with Rome, not politically but topographically. He could talk of nothing but plans for vast engineering projects – the canalization of the Tiber, drainage and development of the malarious Agro Romano, the construction of a port at Fiumincino, and a ship canal from Ostia to Rome. Before leaving Rome, he had an audience with the King, where he aired these plans to a sympathetic listener, only permitting himself at the end one political observation – that all His Majesty's Ministers were 'scoundrels'.[21]

His plans for developing the Agro Romano were regarded with great suspicion at the Vatican. A despatch from the Comte de Crouy, the French Ambassador to the Holy See, explains, 'The Cardinal Secretary of State fears that if the Government allows this, Garibaldi will have have at his disposal an army of workmen imbued with his socialist ideas. They can bring pressure to bear on the Government, and attack private property in the Agro. He has already persuaded the Government to set up a Control Commission for the project, whose members are all his nominees. And he has invited a number of our French Socialists to join him. Some of them are already in Rome.'[22]

These fears proved unfounded, on account of Garibaldi's deteriorating health. He died a year later, before the project had even begun. But his influence lingered on for decades, in the form of the 'Garibaldi Cult'. In the Vatican Secret Archives is a comment on this: 'The aim of the Italian Socialists is now to transform their hero Garibaldi into something superhuman, a half-real, half-mythical character; he is to become with the passage of time the object of a new cult aimed at replacing the religion of Christ.'[23]

4

Democracy in Rome

The Romans now had what they had been demanding for years: democracy on British lines. The word 'democracy' has become so debased in our time, interpreted in such a variety of ways, that it is now almost meaningless. Today we have the British brand, the Russian brand, the Albanian brand, the Chinese, the West German, the East German, etc., all these nations claiming the word for their own exclusive use. It has become no more than a slogan on the lips of politicians of every persuasion. But in Rome in 1870 the word had a very real meaning; it seemed to usher in a wonderful new age of peace, equality and prosperity. This was confirmed by the plebiscite for and against the new regime on 2 October 1870, two weeks after the Italian occupation. Of the ten thousand votes cast, only forty-six opposed the new 'democratic' rule.

The great expectations of a united Italy had been well summed up some decades before by the historian and patriot Vincenzo Gioberti. In his treatise, *Il Primato civile e morale degli Italiani* ('The civil and moral supremacy of the Italians), he showed that all the social elements of Italy, her artistic and literary genius, her municipal institutions, her maritime and commercial enterprise, her religious beliefs, her Popes and priests – all had contributed to her primacy among the nations of the world. All that was now required, he argued (in 1845), to restore her to her former greatness was some patriotic principle or symbol, some great national rallying-cry, such as '*Roma mater*' ('Rome, our mother') to make the city the world's capital again. Now this had come about.

The majority in Rome against the Papal rule was in part due to the nature of, and contrast with, that rule. Rome had been ruled for over a thousand years by a theocracy, benevolent but absolute. The Roman people had no voice in the selection of their rulers, who were cardinals and bishops. In 1870, the Papal States were still run on mediaeval lines. Pius IX's immediate predecessor, Gregory XVI, had even refused to have a railway in them on the ground, he said, of *'chemin de fer – chemin enfer'*. Passports were still required in the legations to move from Forlì, Ravenna or Ferrara to visit Bologna or Rome. Old laws such as the disability of a convicted political prisoner to appeal against his sentence were still in force. Refusal to follow the advice of the parish priest could entail penalties. If at Easter a parishioner neglected to attend Confession and receive the Sacraments, the priest could refuse to furnish him with the certificate stating that he was living honestly and respectably, and which he needed to obtain employment. After neglecting twice the priest's exhortation to attend the Eucharistic table, his name would be affixed on the door of the parish church, an announcement which could lead to social, and often economic, ostracism for him and his family. By 1870, with the example of the 'liberal' states of northern Europe before them, the Romans had come to regard the priest as an interfering busybody – instructing them on how to behave, influencing their thoughts, their feelings, actions, eating and drinking habits, even aspiring to advise them on their conjugal relations. In 1870, 'democracy' seemed to most Romans the millennium they had been dreaming of.

On the other hand, as the British Ambassador, Sir Augustus Paget pointed out, the Italian people are not anti-clerical in the way that word is understood in northern Europe. 'There is more tolerance,' he wrote, 'or more properly speaking more indifference, in Italy over religious matters than perhaps in any other country.'[1] Some historians, such as Maurice Pernot, attribute this to the fact that the Romans, 'having the headquarters of the Catholic Church on their own soil, tend to be less religious than other races'. He quotes the old Roman saying:

A Roma si fa la fede
Ed altrove ci si crede.[2]

('In Rome the faith is made
and elsewhere it is believed.')

Sir Augustus Paget added, 'All the people of this country ask is that they shall not be delivered bound hand and foot to a priestly Government; that the clergy shall be confined to their spiritual functions, and shall not be allowed to interfere with civil rights. Now with the Liberal Democracy of the Savoyards installed, they presumably have what they want.'

The Vatican, for its part, regarded 'democracy' with a mixture of suspicion and scorn. Its view was that the doctrine of 'the divine right of the people' was even more monstrous and fatal in its consequences than the Divine Right of Kings; because throughout history the mob had always proved to be the worst of tyrants, more capricious, more unreasonable, more destitute of moral and common sense, than the most degenerate of Oriental or Valois monarchs. The tyrant, whether possessing one head or several thousand, was always the same. Both Caesarism and democracy tended to atheism. The sovereign people – so ran the Vatican reasoning – always finished under the tyranny of some upstart demagogue who, on the pretext of executing its will, governed it absolutely, with advantage only to himself and his friends. In the words of Goethe, 'Nothing is more abhorrent to a reasonable man than an appeal to the majority. For this consists of a few strong men who lead, of some knaves who temporize, and of the multitude who follow like sheep, knowing nothing and wanting to know nothing.'

On a higher level the Catholic Church, regarding authority as derived from God, refused to countenance it in the people; authority came from above, not below. Moreover, the democratic notion of egalitarianism ran counter to the Church's tenet that natural inequalities among men were willed and sanctioned by God. For this reason, the Church preferred the French *Ancien Régime* to what replaced it in 1789; the injustices and inefficiencies of the Monarchy had been sanctioned and civilized by custom and tempered by tradition. Because the roots of the old aristocratic order went so deep, attempts to abolish it had resulted throughout the nineteenth century only in periodic bouts of anarchy in countries such as Italy and France, interspersed with continuous changes of regime. Better the old vices which people had become accustomed to than the new virtues, the consequences of which were unpredictable.

Nevertheless, the people of Rome were convinced that with the installation of democracy in their city better times lay ahead – as their vote at the 1870 plebiscite demonstrated. In particular, the Roman shopkeepers and middle classes welcomed the change.

They had observed that in the last ten years when the capital of the new Italy had been in Florence, their fellow traders there had done remarkably well. Not only had a large body of Piedmontese bureaucrats taken up residence, but curious visitors and tourists from all over the world had thronged the City of the Flower. The same, they hoped, would now happen in Rome. Trade would flourish, hotels proliferate, there would be a boom in property. In what was still a provincial city there was a shortage of accommodation, and rents would soar.

One of the special qualities of the Romans is that, although they have for so long been compelled to submit to foreign bayonets, they have never forgotten the great days when their ancestors legislated for the whole peninsula, and far beyond the Alps. Until modern times they have believed in their innermost hearts that Italian interests should be subservient to Roman ones, that Italy belonged to Rome, rather than Rome to Italy. Everything would be done on their behalf: honours bestowed and employment found, with liberal remuneration for all.

It was not long, however, before the first signs of disillusion began to appear, and they felt that the new Savoyard rulers were not bringing all the benefits they had been led to expect. The first blow came as early as 1871: a Government Decree expropriated all apartments and private lodgings described as 'not absolutely necessary for the minimum requirements of their owners – this to include haylofts, barns, granges, granaries and dilapidated buildings'. This was precisely the accommodation which the Romans had been hoping to refurbish cheaply, and let at advantageous rents. The Government had foreseen this, thereby rescuing its bureaucrats from these exorbitant increases.

The next disillusion was the tax return. That increased taxes would inevitably follow annexation of Rome to the Kingdom of Italy should have been apparent to all. But when the Roman shopkeepers were told to submit a tax return, they became highly indignant. Under the old Papal government, whose revenues came from all over the world in the form of Peter's Pence and other bounties, the Papal exchequer could afford to neglect local taxes, or at least make modest fiscal demands. Most of the Roman shopkeepers had never set eyes on an income-tax return. Now they were to be treated like the rest of Italy. Baron de Michelis, the French Ambassador to the Holy See, reports that 'Taxes under the new regime have soared from 5,000 lire to 40,000 lire overnight.'[3] He describes the new government of Rome as 'a less paternal municipality'.

The shopkeepers immediately presented a petition claiming that their case was special. They referred to the exceptional character of Rome in which, 'under the late theocratic regime, commercial activity was weak and could not flourish, as it does in the other big Italian cities. We Roman shopkeepers,' they pleaded, 'require time for recovery after the historic events of the last few months. During this period, we have suffered from an entire absence of foreigners, our principal source of income. Moreover the floods of the Tiber in December 1870, the worst in living memory, have cost us Roman citizens 40 million lire.' The petition finished by requesting that Rome should not be treated as the rest of Italy.[4]

To this the Government gave a most heartless reply. Not only did they say that Rome would not be treated as a special case, but they suggested that increased taxation would stimulate the energies of the Roman people to greater efforts. The Romans, they said, would have to work harder to pay the tax, which would in turn create new wealth. They would have to adapt their way of life to that of the rest of Italy – to get up earlier, take fewer afternoon naps, keep proper accounts, in short be more active than in the past. The Government's reply to the Roman tradesmen finished with the brazen advice: 'You will find that by working harder to pay the tax you will double your takings – so that you will be able to compete on equal terms with Italians from other cities.'

As for the floods, said the Government, Rome could not be placed in a special category here either. How about the inundations of the Po in the Veneto region? What about Pisa and Parma? Those cities had suffered severely from flooding, but they had not received special relief. And how about the cholera epidemic in Sicily? Or the plague of locusts in Sardinia? Or the earthquake in Calabria? These disasters had caused great distress to the natives; but no tax exemption had been made in their case. Rome was a special case? Yes, it was a special case, but in this sense – that it had not been called upon to make the same sacrifices in blood and treasure which for years past had been the lot of the rest of the country, in the struggle for Italian unity. Hitherto, Rome had taken no part in the forced loans or war contributions; nor had its young men been subject to conscription. And now, on the very first occasion when Rome was called upon to bear her fair share of the Italian burden – why, it should be beneath her dignity to seek an escape from her responsibilities, to appear before her sister Italian cities as a beggar! After this, no more was heard from the Roman shopkeepers; but small voices began to suggest that perhaps the old Papal times had not been too bad after all.

The Romans also began to miss the gorgeous solemnities, processions and festivities of the ancient Church, which had attracted to Rome those foreign tourists who, for at least six months of the year, had been their principal a source of income. Church projects had also provided permanent work for the artisans. Emile Zola, who was in Rome at this time, described an unemployed mason who told him, 'My father, a mason like myself, worked at the Vatican all his life. We were spoilt by those years of busy work, when we were never off our ladders, and could earn as much as we liked. If you'd only seen us in the Pope's time! No taxes, everything to be had for nothing, so to say.'[5] The French Ambassador, the Comte d'Harcourt, reported on the taxes and military conscription which followed the occupation of Rome, 'The Romans are far from pleased. They are finding that these two measures are the principal results for them of the Italian unification.'[6]

Another feature of the new Democratic rule which disillusioned many Romans was the inability of the Liberal governments to maintain order. Soon after its installation, the new Mancini Penal Code was introduced by the Minister of that name. It included the abolition of capital punishment and similar humanitarian measures. Soon the Roman Campagna was swarming with brigands and criminals of all kinds. Sir Augustus Paget reported four months after the Italian occupation:

> The condition of public safety in the Campagna is so deplorable that the Ministry of the Interior is having to apply to Parliament for extraordinary measures. People are assassinated daily in open daylight, often in the presence of witnesses who make no attempt to go to their assistance or arrest the criminal, and who cannot be made to give evidence against him in the courts. While on the other hand, judges deterred by intimidation can frequently not be brought to give a verdict.[7]

In another despatch, he attributes this to the abysmally low standard of the new Democratic Parliament:

The Roman Deputies and public men in general in the new Italy have considerable intelligence, knowledge, even culture; but they are generally wanting in firmness of purpose and character, as well as in practical sound sense. Nor have they ever learnt the lesson, 'Honesty is the best policy'. They will not venture to swim against the current of the *Piazza*, and everything appears to be decided not upon consideration of what *ought* to be done, but upon what will produce a good effect, and obtain temporary popularity with their constituents. In the Italian Parliament, every Deputy has a counter-project of his own on every subject which is brought forward, and everyone thinks himself at liberty to advocate it, as though he were the responsible Minister, and as if the rest of the Chamber was only there to attend to his suggestion. At every moment the 'personal question' is invoked. Thus it happens that days, weeks, even months, are passed in sterile discussion. But loss of time is not the only evil. Equally bad are the frequent changes of Ministry which occur in Italy today. Since the formation of the Italian Kingdom, that is within little over a decade, there have been no less than nine different administrations. In the Chamber of Deputies today there are eighty ex-Ministers.[8]

The last sentence may be explained by the generous pensions Ministers awarded themselves. As anyone who had been a Minister, even if he had held the post for only a few months, qualified for this pension, it suited these men to be involved in an almost continuous game of Parliamentary musical chairs. Moreover, everyone wanted to be a Deputy. It conferred a good salary, a high-sounding title (they all became 'Honourable'), free transport on the railways, and virtual immunity from arrest.

Of these men Queen Margherita said in 1880, 'It is impossible to believe that the country can continue to be governed by this flock of wicked men who, as soon as they are elected to Parliament, seem to be struck with a kind of madness, poisoning and debasing the life of the nation.' Strong words – but they came from one of the most intelligent consorts to sit upon a European throne. The Queen was well aware that Italian politicians often arranged 'crises' in

Parliament, because Government stocks were a highly speculative form of investment and, with their inside knowledge, they could profit during the uncertainty on the Stock Exchange. It was also well known that the politicians deliberately expanded the bureaucratic departments of the armed forces, so that friends and relations could be accommodated, and promoted to general's rank. Then there were the State railways, where lines were built in 'strategic' situations where votes could be won – the time-honoured device of bribing the electorate with extravagant public works. In the words of the scholar Gilbert Murray, who knew Italy well, 'The liberation of the *Risorgimento* lost itself in a morass of intrigue and corruption.' Pius IX expressed this sentiment in another way. In an allocution to the Consistory on 12 May 1877, he said of the new 'democracy' in Rome, 'There can never be peace, security and tranquillity as long as the supreme ecclesiastical Ministry is subjected to the passions of constantly changing political parties, the caprice of alternating governments, the vicissitudes of political elections, and to the actions of men who do not hesitate to sacrifice the interests of justice for their own ends.'[9]

In Papal eyes, the mania for parliamentary democracy in Rome could be attributed largely to the example and influence of nineteenth-century England. The English Liberals had given asylum to Mazzini, Panizzi and other anti-Papal conspirators; and it had become fashionable in the late 1860s in England to decry, traduce and misrepresent the temporal government of the Papal States. It was generally assumed that everyone all over the world aspired to the political system of the English. On this subject Pius IX had said to Odo Russell as early as 1860,

I do not doubt the good intentions of England. But unfortunately you do not understand this country, and your example is dangerous to the Italian mind. Your speeches in Parliament excite them, and you fancy that because democratic liberties and institutions suit you, they must suit everyone. Now, the Italians are a turbulent and intriguing race, and they can never learn to govern themselves. The Italians are not a bad people, but they are easily led astray by foreign agents. You English have always sympathized with and encouraged the turbulent spirits in Italy. I know the English Government has always wanted to see me deprived of the temporal power.[10]

England was then the greatest power in the world. But Pius IX's confidence was never shaken; for he finished this audience with the brave words: 'When the Italians have suffered more – and that it seems is what they want – they will repent and return to Us.'

One of the first ostensible manifestations of 'Democracy' in Rome in the decades that followed its seizure was the erection of monuments to 'the makers of the new Italy': to Victor Emmanuel II, Charles Albert of Savoy, Garibaldi, Giordano Bruno, Arnaldo da Brescia, the papal reformer Paolo Sarpi – as ill-assorted a collection as can be imagined. The Pope and the Curia from their enclave on the right bank of the Tiber could only look out in impotent fury as these monuments arose, some of them in full view of the Vatican. The Garibaldi monument was situated on the Janiculum, the highest hill in Rome, so that it was visible for miles around. (It then had the distinction of being the heaviest statue in Europe, weighing fifteen tons.) Not content with commemorating the Hammer of the Church, the Liberals insisted on a statue to his wife as well. Anita Garibaldi is some fifty yards from her husband, mounted on a rearing horse, supporting a baby with one hand and brandishing a pistol with the other.

Of all these statues and monuments, the one that gave the greatest offence to the Vatican was that of Giordano Bruno. In 1582, this renegade Dominican monk had repudiated Catholicism, first in favour of Calvinism, then of Free Thought. Such a man was naturally a hero to the nineteenth-century liberals: so early to become a freethinker, nearly two hundred years before Voltaire! After his abjuration of the Faith, Bruno spent some years wandering around Europe, inveighing in speeches and writings against Catholicism. In 1598 he was extradited from Venice to Rome, where he spent two years in gaol, refusing to recant, before being burnt at the stake as a heretic in the Campo de'Fiori.

The inauguration of his monument in this Campo took place on Sunday 9 July 1889, the Day of Pentecost and deliberately selected, the Church believed, as an insult to the Faith. A Parliamentarian, the Honourable Bovio, made the inaugural speech. 'Just as A.D. 313, the date of the Battle of the Milvian Bridge at the gates of our city,' he said, 'was regarded as the beginning of the religion of Christ in Rome, so today 1889, thanks to the courageous example of Giordano Bruno, marks the beginning of the religion of human reason.' A letter from Garibaldi was read out, in which the great man regretted that his health prevented him from being present at the ceremony, but he said he was with them in spirit; and he congratulated them on 'giving the *coup de grâce* to that nest of vipers living in sloth and idleness on the right bank of the Tiber'.

The statue which commemorated King Charles Albert I of Savoy was erected because he was a hero for the liberals, having granted a Constitution to Piedmont in 1848. The Government intended that his monument should, together with those of Garibaldi and Victor Emmanuel II, symbolize respectively the three great 'liberal' years, 1848, 1860 and 1870. The best position for it would have been on the Monte Cavallo in the piazza outside the Quirinale; but this was already occupied by the monument of the Four Horses, from which the hill takes its modern name. The best alternative site lay to the east of the Quirinale, then occupied by two monasteries, of the Capuchins and the Sacramentarians respectively. Their incumbents were accordingly evicted, and the monasteries demolished to make room for the statue. The Liberals seem to have been unaware that King Charles Albert I had been a most religious man, who would have been deeply shocked at two monasteries being demolished to make room for him.

Repeated entreaties by the Vatican to foreign governments to use their influence with the Quirinale to prevent the erection of these unsightly memorials had no effect. The Savoyard Government had commemorated their King when the capital was in Florence, by levelling the old market, the Mercato Vecchio dating from Dante's day, and replacing it by the hideous Piazza Vittorio Emmanuele II. They now proceeded to do the same in Rome, erecting on the Campidoglio the monstrous 'Wedding Cake' memorial, completely out of keeping with the old and dignified buildings around it.

In their ambition to create a 'democratic Rome' architecturally, the Savoyard Government followed the recent examples of Paris and Berlin. Paris had been transformed by Haussmann into the *'Ville Lumière'* with its wide boulevards and huge apartment buildings for the middle classes. Berlin had been enlarged and embellished in the same way after the Prussian victories of the 1860s. Rome, so went the reasoning, would not be outdone by these parvenu cities. Moreover, the fallen Papal Government must be shown what 'democratic Italy' could achieve: the splendour of the new Rome, the magnificence of its thoroughfares and modern buildings, would equal the first Rome of the Caesars, and surpass the second Rome of the Popes. This would be a worthy third Rome.

Objections were naturally made by religious bodies for whom Rome was the Eternal City, over which still hovered the spirits of Gregory the Great, Hildebrand, Innocent III, and a score of other great Popes. Their most practical objection was that such a place could not be transformed overnight into the residence of a modern sovereign and his democratic parliament; for the historic connection of *Urbs* and *Orbis* must necessarily be ruptured when a national sovereign took up his residence in the most international city in the world. Gregorovius reflects on this: 'The unparalleled fact of Rome being reduced to the head of a secular Kingdom – Rome which for 1,500 years has been the cosmopolitan city, the moral centre of the world, now descends to becoming the seat of a Royal court, like any other capital. . . .'[11]

But these objections were overruled, and a vast building programme was undertaken. It was assumed that no self-respecting European capital could number less than a million souls. Papal Rome had counted only 200,000, so an influx of four times as many had to be catered for. In the building mania that ensued, there was no question of small buildings, but only of edifices with five or six stories (then considered skyscrapers), and marble-fronted ministries. But unfortunately, no long-term plan had been envisaged; nor was there a Baron Haussmann or a Florentine Arnolfo di Cambio to co-ordinate it. In his despatch on the subject, Sir Augustus Paget writes, 'Rome is not ready to receive the many Ministries, and the whole operation of the transfer has been premature. None of the buildings selected as Ministries will be habitable for months, perhaps years. The Palazzo Valentini, which is to be the Ministry for Foreign Affairs, has not even been purchased. The Ministry of the Interior lacks windows, and is still in the hands of the masons. The Chamber of Deputies is without a roof. As for the foreign Embassies, none of us has the remotest idea when we shall find anything suitable.'[12]

The work begun out of pride was continued in an extraordinary gambling frenzy, with vast fortunes involved. A bevy of speculators descended from the North, needy, famished Piedmontese who quarried vulture-like among the Roman ruins, camping there before returning home with their fortunes. It was suddenly rumoured that land bought at ten lire per square metre could be sold tomorrow for a hundred lire. Those who were quick enough to forecast the course of a new thoroughfare, and purchased buildings on it, increased their capital a thousandfold. The fever mounted in a people naturally addicted to gambling; it infected all classes, the aristocracy, Deputies, burgesses, widows, grocers. One baker made fifty-four million lire in three weeks.

The great building programme of the new democratic Rome overreached itself, because the expected influx of half a million newcomers did not take place. The 'third Rome' remained half finished for decades. The huge ministries and mansions entered by monumental doorways flanked by lofty statues, with carved balconies upheld by caryatids, remained unoccupied. The mansions became inhabited by hordes of tatterdemalions, famished and homeless, who infested the unfinished buildings, filling them with excrement and vermin.

Although all this destruction of Papal Rome, and the erection of so many lay monuments and statues, caused much resentment at the Vatican, it was not actively harmful to the Church. Much more damaging was the Government's new law expropriating the monasteries and convents. Claiming to be an eminently democratic measure, providing accommodation for the poor and lowly, it was aimed at the very citadel of Catholic piety, the ideal of the contemplative life. The new regime argued that these Orders were all very well in the Middle Ages, but they had no place in the century of progress. The barred embrasures and casements were opened, and new windows cut into the walls. After long centuries, sun and air penetrated into the cloistered cells of the monks and nuns, who were themselves expelled like so many badgers. In a matter of months, the SS Apostoli had become the Ministry of War; the Convent of the Minerva, the Ministry of Finance; the Casa del Gesù, a military barracks; Sant'Andrea delle Fratte, the Public Security Guard; Sant'Andrea del Quirinale, the Royal Stables; Sant'Agostino, the Ministry of the Marine, and so on.[13]

Gregorovius described the last conversion:

Reading in the Library of the Sant'Agostino the other day, which is to become the Ministry of the Marine, my research was constantly interrupted by the hammering of the masons on the walls outside; they seemed to be so many hammer blows on the coffin of the Papacy. . . . A lofty scaffold had been erected for whitewashing these walls, which were encrusted with the dirt of centuries. Unfortunately a passing bus knocked into it, and the whole erection collapsed on the top of the bus, flattening it. The next morning as I was inspecting the ruin of both bus and scaffolding, an old woman sitting on the steps of Sant'Agostino said to me, '*Vedete, Iddio non vuole che si pylisca il convento!*' ['See there, God does not want the convent cleaned!'][14]

Apart from the main Orders, Benedictines, Dominicans, Franciscans and Jesuits, there were a host of lesser ones – Carmelites, Trappists, Barnabites, Lazarists, Rosicrucians, Augustinians, Theatines, Celestines, etc, to cite the male Orders alone. Certain districts of Rome were composed entirely of monasteries and convents, presenting to the outside world their silent, seemingly lifeless façades. It was true, said the liberals, that classical Rome had venerated her vestal virgins; but now there was no need of veneration for virgins consecrated to the service of a God who did not exist. The housing of the common people was more important than the habitation of nuns.

Allegations were also made by the liberals that these religious establishments were hotbeds of immorality, the Catholic school at Civitavecchia directed by the Ignorantine Brothers being cited as an example. In 1871, Mr Herries of the British Embassy reported: 'One of its teachers has been found guilty of grossly indecent practices with the boys under his charge. He has been dismissed, but a further investigation has revealed so revolting a state of affairs that the Italian Government has decided to close the school completely. This is an isolated case, but the anti-clericals have made much of it.'

In the initial stages of the Savoyard installation in Rome, there was, it was true, a shortage of accommodation. The British Ambassador, Sir Augustus Paget, reported that there was a good case for appropriating some of the religious buildings, which were often half empty. He referred to '. . . the necessity in which the Government finds itself for providing dwellings for the numerous labourers and others who are now employed in building the new Rome and who, owing to the paucity of accommodation, are obliged to sleep on the steps of the Piazza di Spagna. After toiling all day in the sun, they are struck down by typhus and other diseases.'[15]

The Government's Conventual Expropriation Bill was in its original form a relatively moderate measure, only depopulated convents and monasteries being affected, and then with financial compensation. But the Liberals and Turbolenti in Parliament introduced so many amendments as to transform it entirely, and so many offensive allusions to the religious Orders that the Pope was given a convenient pretext for condemning the whole project. One of the amendments which gave valid ground to the Pope was the following: 'When the necessities of public service require the expropriation of conventual buildings according to the Law, force will be employed if persuasion does not suffice.' This was exactly what Pius IX needed for defending the seizure of the convent of Sant'Antonio Abbate, which was required as a military hospital. The nuns had agreed to leave, had accepted money in compensation, and were about to go to a sister establishment. But then at the last moment, they changed their minds and refused to leave. The explanation was that Pius IX, having read the amendment to the Law, had instructed them to yield only to force. After repeated attempts to persuade the nuns, the Government agents had to break down the doors and expel them bodily. This caused a great outcry about the way in which the Government no longer distinguished in their brutal treatment between male and female Orders.[16]

Pius IX was deeply versed not only in the Scriptures but also in the writings of the Fathers of the Church, and could quote these to good effect. On the subject of the Orders, to defend them against expropriation, he went back to the greatest of his predecessors, Gregory the Great, and to that Pope's description of the monastic and contemplative life he had lived until he was unwillingly plucked from it to become Pope in A.D. 590. In the allegorical but expressive language of the sixth century Pius IX contrasted, quoting Pope Gregory, the lives of Rachel and Leah, the contemplative and the practical: 'The beauty of the contemplative life I have lived with Rachel . . . although by her quiet she bears less, yet she sees the light more clearly. Now I must be wedded to Leah – the active life which is more fruitful, bearing forth more abundantly, but blear-eyed, seeing less. . . .' As a poignant account of the felicities of the cloister this could not be excelled; but it was hardly likely to impress the new liberal rulers of Rome.

The French Ambassador, the Comte d'Harcourt, supported the Pope, referring to '. . . the methodical and inhuman way in which these conventual expropriations are carried out – fifty establishments suppressed in a fortnight. The authorities enter the building,' he reported, 'and demand the plans. They then take out their tapes and measuring apparatus and proceed, in the presence of the Rector or Abbess, to the measurement of their room. Their aim is to discover if the living quarters of the Rector or Abbess will be suitable for the residence of a Grade B civil servant.'[17] In a further despatch he indicated an anomaly. 'The Italian Government's proposed Guarantee Laws,' he wrote, 'make a special point of recognizing the *spiritual* power of the Pope; but the Italian Government then disavows it in fact, by dissolving the Orders which serve, assist and illumine that power. Thus by this legislation, what is at stake is this spiritual power – for the Orders are the prop of the Pope's entire spiritual edifice.'[18]

Two years later his successor, M. de Corcelle, commented even more critically. 'The Law of the Guarantees which the Italian Government offered the Pope,' he wrote, 'stipulated *textually* "the absolute respect for the spiritual institutions of the Church, for their independent administration, their goods and chattels". Yet within two years, they have flouted all these solemn engagements. By a simple law, that of 19 June 1873, they suppressed at a stroke all the religious congregations, dispersed their members and ordered the sale of their property by auction.' Then he gave the very material reason why the Government did not keep its promise: 'In spite of the principles of liberty and democracy which the new Law proclaims, the real aim of the Government in sequestering the religious houses is pecuniary – as is evidenced by their leaving untouched all religious establishments which are financially valueless to them.'[19]

5

The Advent of Leo XIII

It was the new Pope who, as Cardinal Pecci the *Camerlengo*, was summoned to rap three times on the forehead of Pius IX with a silver hammer as the dead Pope lay on his bed that morning in February 1878. Three times he called him back to life pronouncing his Christian name – 'Johannes! Johannes! Johannes!' Then, when neither divine nor human agency availed, he took the Fisherman's Ring from the dead man's finger and ceremoniously broke it [1]

The *Camerlengo* is the Cardinal who, between the death of one Pope and the election of another, is in charge of the Conclave. In this sense he is the most important Cardinal, and therefore theoretically well placed for election himself. But there is an old adage at the Vatican, 'He who goes into the Conclave Pope, comes out Cardinal.'[2] There is also a tendency for the *Camerlengo* not to be elected because, with the authority he exercises during the Conclave, he tends to arouse jealousy among his fellows. Certain *male lingue* at the Vatican even said that Pius IX had deliberately made Cardinal Pecci *Camerlengo* for this very reason. Pius IX did not wish him to be his successor because he was 'too liberal'. Nevertheless at this Conclave in 1878, the old adage was confounded and the *Camerlengo*, Cardinal Pecci, ascended to the Chair of St Peter as Leo XIII.

The word 'Conclave' for the election of a new Pope derives from the Latin *cum clave*, 'with a key'; and in the old days the members of the Sacred College who elected the Pope were literally locked up with a key, in a hall of which all the exits and entrances were walled up, save one small window for the admission of food. Lest their deliberations should be unduly protracted, and in order to help them to make up their minds, they were given proper meals only for the first three days. If no decision had by then been reached, the ration was reduced to one fish dish daily for the next five days. If after this, they still had not decided, they were further restricted to a diet of bread and wine. In the ironic words of Gregorovius, 'If as the Church asserts, the Papal election is the work of heavenly inspiration, then hunger and thirst appear a curious means of attracting the Holy Ghost. . . .' By the Papal Conclave of 1878 after the death of Pius IX, these stringent measures had been much abated, although the Cardinals were still locked up.

In the old days, until the nineteenth century, the ambassadors of the big European powers possessed considerable influence in the Conclaves, which they exercised to obtain the election of the candidate most acceptable to their respective monarchs. For this they also possessed considerable means, in the shape of the royal treasury. Great families of France, Spain, the Empire (the Guises, Borgias, Hohenlohes) numbered among their members cardinals, archbishops, abbés, and high-ranking prelates of all kinds, who were paid by their ambassadors in return for their support at the Conclave. The French Ambassador at the Vatican at the time of the 1878 Conclave, the Baron de Baude, lamented the passing of those good old days. 'Today,' he said, 'not the smallest vestige of monarchical influence remains. For years now, this Embassy has disposed of no pecuniary means whatsoever for obtaining information from the Vatican, or exercising any influence there. He further regretted the venue of the Conclave, which took place in the Vatican, instead of as before in the Quirinale. The Vatican, he said, is a fortress isolated and surrounded by high walls, which lends itself much less to the exchange of information (by this he meant finding out what is going on in the Conclave) than did the Quirinale, which was easily accessible to foreign diplomats. He suggested to his Government that he might be given permission to have the French cardinals who had gathered in Rome living under his roof in the French Embassy – and not in private habitations. 'This,' he ended his despatch pathetically, 'is about all I can do.'[3]

However, his fears of a protracted Conclave and a pro-Austrian Pope proved unfounded. In 1878, the Sacred College quickly came to a decision, after only two ballots electing Cardinal Pecci, who was well known for his pro-French sympathies.

After Cardinal Pecci's election the British Ambassador, Sir Augustus Paget, reported to London:

We may glean something about the new Pope from a pastoral

letter he recently published from his previous post as Bishop of Perugia. . . . The contrast between the spirit of this document and the tone which usually characterizes documents of a similar nature emanating from Pius IX is most marked. . . . Leo XIII would seem from it as likely to adopt a much more reasonable attitude towards the civil power. . . . It is said that immediately after his election, he wished to give the benediction *Urbe et Orbi* from the balcony of St Peter's, and was deterred only by the frowning countenance of most of the Cardinals. . . .[4]

This 1878 Conclave was the first in which almost the whole College of Cardinals was present. They came from the ends of the earth with unprecedented despatch – for which the Conclave could thank those novelties of science, the steamship and the railway. It was also the first occasion when the College was – at least compared with earlier times – a body of no great aristocratic rank, but typical of the new middle-class society of the late nineteenth century. No Medici, Farnese, Este, Guise, Lorraine or Habsburg graced its portals, overawing the Conclave with their noble presence.

Before the Conclave, the College had been divided into two factions. The first, and slightly smaller, was in favour of a relatively inactive Pope. They had seen the failure of the militant policies of Pius IX and his Secretary of State Antonelli, and they thought it wiser for the moment to have no policy at all. The fact that human efforts had achieved so little surely implied that God wished to work on his own. It would be impolitic to elect a highly intelligent or active Pope, or one who was a man of the world; better to elect a man who would spend his time in prayer, lifting his arms to Heaven from time to time. This would be the best way of co-operating in a work Providence had clearly reserved for itself.

The other group took the opposing view that, because Italian and European society was in a state of flux, moving towards a new order, the shape and scope of which could not be foreseen, the barque of St Peter required a skilled pilot, able to negotiate the political shoals ahead. Here they were encouraged by most of the lay Catholic states of Europe, who indicated that they hoped that whoever was the new Pope would appreciate the changing social conditions, and adapt himself to them.

At most Conclaves there is generally an officious cardinal, a kind of self-appointed 'kingmaker', who busies himself with canvassing votes for the candidate of his choice. On this occasion it was Cardinal Randi, who proudly announced, 'I shall cast my vote only for a great nobleman, or for a great Saint.' He believed that in this, the first Conclave since the loss of temporal power, the new Pope would have to possess exceptional qualities, of social prestige or of saintliness. At the outset, he was against Cardinal Pecci, on the ground that he was 'too liberal'. Moreover Pecci was sixty-nine years old, of frail physique and in poor health. It seems, however, that these very qualities contributed to his election. Many people regarded the election of an elderly valetudinarian to the Papal throne as no more than a stopgap measure.

When Cardinal Pecci was informed of his election he objected, 'But I am advanced in age, and none too strong in health. I cannot accept such a burden. I shall collapse under it. It is not the Papacy that is offered me, but Death.' It took an hour of arguing and the joint efforts of five cardinals to persuade him. 'My Pontificate will be short,' he warned them. 'The Conclave will soon have to be held again. My Pontificate will be like that of Marcellus II.'[5]

'Your Eminence,' they said, 'that depends on God. If God in his glory wishes you to be Pope, even for a few days, that is all that matters.'

'So be it! I will only quote from what Alexander VII said when he was in the same dilemma as myself: " Jamque dies ni fallor adest quam semper amaram semper honoratam sic Di voluistis habeo." ["Already unless I am mistaken the day is come which, as Thou willest O God, will be for me one of both honour and distress."]'

Cardinal Pecci then proceeded to the Sistine Chapel, where the *Sedia Gestatoria* (the inaugural chair, in which the Pope is carried) was placed in front of the high altar. The Cardinals returned to their stalls and lowered their *baldacchini*. Cardinal Pecci went to the robing-room where, as is customary, were three chests, each containing a set of white Papal robes – one for a tall man, one for a medium-sized man, one for a small man. He donned the second of these.

Cardinal Randi had said that the new Pope must either be a great nobleman or a great saint. Gioacchino Pecci was neither; he was something in between, a great gentleman. Born in 1811 at Carpineto, a remote, somewhat neglected hillside town in the southern part of the Papal States, he was the sixth son of the eleven children born to Lodovico Pecci, a colonel in the local militia and commander of Prince Aldobrandini's guard. After a conventional education in the Jesuit College of Viterbo, the young Pecci graduated to the Ecclesiastical College in Rome. Here after ordination, he so impressed his superiors that he was allotted, at the early age of twenty-six, a task of a most forbidding nature. He was appointed Papal Delegate to the province of Benevento, which was teeming at the time with brigands who terrified the local population. The government of the Papal States was so paternal, and at the same time so light that it verged on the casual, and criminals of all kinds were in the habit of taking refuge from the Neapolitan police in Benevento, from where they continued their activities more or less unhindered. The local Benevento nobility, far from attempting to suppress them, often connived with them, and occasionally appeared themselves at the head of these ruffians on the highway. They also brought pressure to bear on the law courts to mitigate the sentences passed on brigands who were caught. For this, the latter gladly paid them tribute money. The unfortunate public cried out for a strong hand.

Immediately Mgr Pecci arrived in Benevento, he obtained the fullest information about the districts in which brigandage flourished, and despatched columns of Papal troops whose officers he had carefully selected. The robber chiefs and their gangs were hounded down and brought to justice. In order to restore public confidence, Mgr Pecci had them loaded with chains and paraded through the streets of the town. When one of the local nobles came to him arrogantly announcing that he was overstepping his powers, and that he, the Marquis, was going to Rome to make representations to the Pope to have the Papal Delegate removed, Mgr Pecci replied, 'Well, before you leave for Rome, I shall put you up in gaol for three months, where I will keep you on bread and water with your brigand friends.' He was as good as his word, and the people blessed him for his resolution.[6]

So successful was he in Benevento that he was transferred in 1841 to Perugia, to restore the Papal influence which had been much reduced by the revolutionary activities of the Camorra. Again he was successful; which led to his most important formative experience, that of Papal Nuncio in Belgium in 1843. Here he came into contact with the industrial revolution which was convulsing Transalpine Europe, creating on the one hand fortunes for the few, and on the other abject poverty for the many, the new industrial proletariat. He was the first Pope to become aware of the dehumanized masses engendered by the industrial revolution; and to realize that the Church's mission must be to bring them back to Christianity, rather than simply to admonish them for their soullessness. As the newspaper *L'Italia* wrote on 18 February 1872:

> Unlike his predecessor, Leo XIII cannot ignore the political and religious conditions in Europe today. As Papal Nuncio in Belgium – a constitutional monarchy – he has been able to see for himself the new political institutions being forged all over Europe. He has seen how democratic administrations come to power – and how they fall. He has seen how good Catholics can live under a liberal regime, and take part in public life.

In view of all this, it would not be true to say that Cardinal Pecci was elected simply as a 'stopgap' Pope. At the Conclave, the cardinals had realized that he was the most representative of a growing body within the Sacred College in opposition to the Zelanti who had surrounded his predecessor. A few of these cardinals even went so far as to desire immediate conciliation between Church and State. But most of them demanded no more than a less hostile atmosphere, an acceptance under protest of existing conditions, as long as they could not be changed. This was broadly the attitude of the new Pope: that he had in his official position been gravely wronged by the Italian State, but that he personally bore no grudge against it.

It is said that the Papal name which a new Pope assumes is significant, an indication of the policies he intends to pursue. It was known that both as Bishop and Cardinal, Gioacchino Pecci had had a special admiration for Leo XII (1823–29), the Pope of the period following the French Revolution. As Nuncio in a number of countries Leo XII had acquired wide and intimate knowledge of Europe. He had seen the changing face of the continent, and realized that the Church must adapt itself to a newly emerging society, that it could not ignore what had happened between 1789 and 1815. By taking Leo XII's name, the new Pope indicated that he intended to follow this course, which had been abandoned by the two intervening Popes, Gregory XVI (1830–46) and Pius IX (1846–78), both of whom were Ultramontane.

He expressed this in one of his first Encyclicals, in which he asked Catholics to demand through their prayers 'a cessation of the conflict between Church and State'. The language of this Encyclical, although periphrastic in the usual Vatican manner, was no longer hostile in the style of Pius IX's *Non Possumus*. Sir Augustus Paget reported, 'It constitutes a remarkable contrast in both tone and spirit with those which have habitually issued from the Vatican under the Pontificate of Pius IX. It would appear to indicate almost the abandonment of the passive attitude towards temporal affairs, in favour of a more active policy in political matters.' The Ambassador added, however, 'There is of course no renunciation of the claim to the temporal power. But on the other hand, the Encyclical contains no positive reaffirmation of it. As an indication of the spirit of the new Pope, the omissions in this Encyclical are perhaps more important than anything it says.'[7]

In it Leo XIII also asked Catholics 'to pray that those who direct public affairs in Italy may listen to the counsels of the Supreme Pontiff'. He requested 'our adversaries to remember that we too love our country, and desire to see it strong and prosperous'. He indicated that he would in no circumstances accept foreign armed intervention to restore the Papacy to its former state. Instead of confining himself to regret at the loss of temporal power, and to delivering anathemas against existing institutions, as Pius IX had, Leo XIII discussed in his early Encyclicals the problems of modern society, warning against the evils which threatened it, socialists, communists, nihilists and other revolutionary sects under various guises and denominations.

Pius IX had died with the prestige of a martyr, and under him the Papacy had been as powerful as it had ever been, but *only among Catholics*. Leo XIII had seen that elsewhere in the world it was at its lowest ebb. When he ascended the Throne of St Peter, his aim was to become not a martyr but a statesman, and to restore the power and prestige of the Papacy throughout the world. He has been depicted as a liberal, but in fact he was only liberal in contrast with his predecessor. The difference between the two men was not that one was a liberal and the other a conservative; but that one was a diplomat and the other was not. Leo XIII was also a man of his time, of the coming twentieth century.

It is surely significant that he early announced that his chief mentor in theological and philosophical matters was Thomas

Aquinas. Now, Aquinas's principal work, *Summa Theologica*, although a product of the thirteenth-century schoolmen, deals not only with theology, but with all known science. Although one of the most authoritative and devout Fathers of the Church, the 'Angelic Doctor' – as Aquinas was called – contended that a scientific knowledge of the universe, as then conceived, was an essential part of the Beatific Vision for all Christians. Of all the mediaeval schoolmen, he is the most intelligible to us today; and it is understandable that he should have appealed to Leo XIII. Both Aquinas and his great teacher, Albertus Magnus of Cologne, deeply impressed and influenced Leo XIII.

Albertus Magnus left twenty-one folio volumes on every subject known in the thirteenth century: logic, metaphysics, psychology, natural science, ethics, theology, chemistry, botany. He applied himself to physical science, and advocated experimental methods of research.

Leo XIII's analytical mind had much in common with these two men. In Milman's words, 'Aquinas approaches more closely than most philosophers, certainly than most divines, to pure embodied intellect. He is absolutely passionless, displaying not a shred of polemical indignation, nor any of the churchman's jealousy and suspicion. He shows no fear of the result of any investigation; he hates nothing, hardly even heresy; he loves nothing, unless perhaps naked abstract truth.'[8]

Leo XIII fully subscribed to Aquinas's attitude towards human reason – in that Aquinas reconciled human reason with religion, maintaining that reason is as essential to a man as is religion (in contrast to Luther, who contended that faith alone matters, and that human reason is nugatory). On the contrary, said Aquinas, reason is necessary, for it precedes faith and prepares the way for it. Reason he described as 'the light of God shining in the natural mind of man'. However, he made this important proviso – that human reason must be supplemented by the supernatural light of faith; for there are certain truths of revelation which are inaccessible to human reason. He who lives by human reason and logic alone, said Aquinas, must be a very narrow-minded and cold-hearted man; and he utterly condemned those who believe they are self-sufficient, 'men without God'. In his *Contra Gentiles* ('Against the Heathen') he wrote, 'There are many who are so presumptuous of their own genius as to believe that they can measure all things with

74

their intellect . . . unaware that there are certain things proposed to man from God which altogether exceed his understanding.' Aquinas was, in short, the great 'bridge-builder', bringing revealed religion (that is, the supernatural) into association with human reason, showing that they are not – as so many of the Zelanti believed – mutually antagonistic, but mutually beneficial. On the philosophy of such a man, Leo XIII was to base his own throughout his long reign of twenty-five years.

Although Leo XIII was deeply versed in classical, and above all Latin, literature, he was always open to contemporary thought. His official biographer, Eduardo Soderini, says there was no important contemporary book, review or newspaper in French or Italian, that Leo XIII did not read. He had a member of his staff prepare for him a daily résumé of the Italian and foreign press, excerpts from which were pasted into his book of cuttings. 'His study,' said Soderini, 'was like a reading-room, the desk littered with papers and newspapers, which were often scattered on the floor around him as he sat, no one being allowed to touch them. Sometimes when there was no longer room for them, he laid them on the bed – to the despair of his faithful servant, Centra.' As a young priest, Giocchino Pecci had often been seen in the company of poets and writers in the Caffè Greco, that meeting-place of minds in the Via Condotti. His greatest intellectual interest since early schooldays had been Latin. That language became almost his mother tongue, and throughout his life he would take time off for his favourite pastime, the composition of Latin verses, at which he was highly skilled.

One of the best descriptions of his appearance and manner is given by Émile Zola in *Rome*. Although like all self-respecting French intellectuals of the time, Zola was anti-clerical, he was also too much of an artist to allow politics to colour his literary approach. He even expresses a certain grudging admiration for this Pope who was bent on restoring the Papacy to its former influence.

When Pierre entered the presence, Leo XIII was seated in an armchair before a small table littered with newspapers, on which a lamp was burning. His face and figure seemed shrunken, the neck very slender suggesting that of a small, aged, white bird. The face had the pallor of alabaster, transparent to such a degree that one could see the lamplight through the profile of the large commanding nose, as if the blood was entirely withdrawn from that organ. . . . But this impression of age and debility was completely belied by the eyes – superb eyes, brilliant like black diamonds, with the penetration you felt to lay souls open. Owing to these, you forgot the simian ugliness of the face, the long, thin slit of the mouth, the vastness of the ears. In the waxen countenance you saw only the brilliant, flashing eyes, beaming with eternal youth, with an extraordinary intelligence and penetration.

At the end of his reign, twenty-five years later, Leo XIII was to be compared with another Pope, Pius IV of the sixteenth century. That great Pope of the Council of Trent achieved his successes less as a priest than as a jurist; less by masterful authority than by pliant diplomacy; less by forcing, but by following, the current of events. Leo XIII, in his contest with the *Kulturkampf*, the campaign which Bismarck had been waging for the last six years against the Catholic Church in Germany, and which he now inherited from Pius IX, was to display these talents and methods to the full.

6

The Fallacy of Prince Bismarck –the *Kulturkampf*

The main source of Catholic strength in Germany extends along the valleys of the Rhine and the Mosel, broadening out in the south into the fertile plains and mountains of Bavaria. In 1870 this region contained some of the most devout and intelligent Catholics in the world. The character with which their great Apostle, St Boniface, stamped these people in the eighth century can still be seen in the sincere attachment of German Catholics to Rome, to which they look constantly in time of affliction. The Pope is venerated with an affection which is almost personal and – Germans being Germans – they actually read his Encyclicals, and try to follow the instructions contained in them.

On the occasion of Pius IX's fifty-year jubilee of priesthood in 1869, the German Catholic Union sent him an address of homage with a million signatures appended, contained in seventeen morocco-bound volumes. Every diocese in Germany supplemented this with financial and artistic contributions, the whole value amounting to about a million *thalers*. According to Gregorovius, 'Pictures, mosaics, golden goblets, reliquaries, hangings, are arriving in profusion at the Vatican. What lay monarch could ever vaunt such a tribute at his Jubilee!'[1]

When Rome was occupied by the Italians eleven years later, Archbishop Ledochowski of Gnesen-Posen sent an address to the Kaiser supported by thousands of German Catholic signatures stating: 'Because the Papal States are the possession of Christendom, no one may lay hands on them without an atrocious violation of the rights of 200 million Catholics all over the globe.' A month after the proclamation of the new German Empire in the Hall of Mirrors at Versailles in November 1870, the Kaiser received a further address from his Catholic subjects, expressing the hope that one of the first acts of the Imperial wisdom and justice would be to restore temporal power to the Pope. As the Italian Ambassador to Germany reported, 'Even in the working classes, the feeling of belonging to the Catholic Church is stronger than their class consciousness.'[2] It is understandable therefore that Germany should occupy a high place among the countries whose welfare concerned the Holy See.

The troubles which now beset the Catholic Church in Germany appear, at least superficially, self-inflicted, the result of Pius IX's Dogma of Infallibility. In the last decades of the nineteenth century, a body of devout Catholic opinion had been growing in Germany opposed to the central control imposed by that Pope, and seeking a return to the old days of primitive Christianity. For this reason, they called themselves 'Old Catholics'.

This was no isolated phenomenon. Throughout the Church's history, such groups have arisen from time to time – Arians, Erastians, Albigensians, Patarenes, Jansenists, to name only a few; as well as, after Luther, the various brands of Protestantism. Most of them, like these Old Catholics, did not wish to break away from Catholicism, which they revered and respected, but to return to the simplicity and purity of the primitive faith. The only difference in this case, which makes this name sound anomalous, was that the Old Catholics also wished to bring Catholicism up-to-date, into line with the new scientific discoveries. It is significant that at this time the greatest discoveries in science were being made in Germany, to such an extent that the nineteenth century has often been called 'the German century'. The Old Catholics' aim was expressed in their programme published in Munich on 23 September 1871: 'With the co-operation of theological and canonical *science* [italics author's], we are working for a reform of the Catholic Church which, in the spirit of the early Church, will cleanse the abuses and vices of the Church today. We consider that instruction in science is indispensable for the education of the clergy.'[3] One of the Old Catholic leaders, Dr Döllinger, Rector of the Munich Catholic University, gave a sermon in which he said that Rome was adopting the same attitude towards modern science as it had towards Galileo.[4]

Not content with this, and referring to the 'abuses and vices of the Church' – they added a suggestion calculated to displease Rome even further: 'We hope to reunite with the Greek Orthodox and Russian Churches, whose separation from Catholicism was unnecessary and based on no irreconcilable differences. And also with the Protestant Churches of England and America.' They also objected to the Pope's Dogma of Infallibility which, at a meeting in Munich on 13 June 1871, a number of them condemned as 'despotic pretentions which exceed even those of Islam. Both the Sultan of Turkey and the Shah of Persia recognize the limits of Divine Right and the Laws of the Koran. But they do not overstep them as does the Pope with his Infallibility.'[5]

This was an open declaration of war, as well as a personal attack on Pius IX. One of the Old Catholic leaders, Professor Friedrich, demanded a special Church of their own in Munich;[6] he said, 'The Catholic clergy who follow the Pope are little more than slaves of the Jesuits.'[7] The ex-priest Hyacinthe Loudon made his notorious statement in Munich: 'If twelve simpletons [the Apostles] could regenerate the world, what can we not do – we who have science on our side?'[8] The Nuncio reported sarcastically from Munich in April 1872 that the leader of the new movement, Dr Döllinger, was now pronouncing 'the wildest calumnies against the Church. In one dissertation in the Aula of the Museum, he went back in history to Pope Pius V, whom he accused of plotting the assassination of Queen Elizabeth I of England. In another learned lucubration, he showed that all the ills which afflict suffering humanity emanate from the Jesuits. And this luminary of German Science has after 73 years of his life arrived at this wonderful conclusion!'[9] It will be seen from all this that the name 'Old Catholics' was something of a misnomer, and that a more appropriate title might have been 'New Catholics'.

Prince Bismarck, a Lutheran and no lover of Catholics, saw the possibilities in the Old Catholic movement of reducing Papal power in Germany. He believed that German Catholics were on the whole hostile to the Dogma of Infallibility; now was the moment to wean them from the Papacy and to incorporate them in a German National Church. In the words of the French Ambassador to the Holy See, the Comte d'Harcourt, 'Prince Bismarck regards the Papal power in Germany as one of the principal obstacles to the unification of his new State. He has decided to disparage it by supporting and fomenting the theological agitation known as the Old Catholic movement.'[10] This was the beginning of Bismarck's famous *Kulturkampf*.

Kulturkampf means literally 'struggle for culture', a term which, as applied against the oldest body of culture in Christian Europe, the Catholic Church, is something of a misnomer. It had little to do with culture, but was a campaign by Prince Bismarck to eliminate Papal influence from the Catholic community in Germany. His dominating thought in the 1870s was to preserve the united Germany which he had just created, and which he considered the Catholic Church might disunite. Here again, from a Lutheran point of view, his reasoning was at least logical.

During the nineteenth century, the populations ruled over by Prussia had increased considerably – *and the increase was all Catholic*. At the Congress of Vienna, victorious Prussia had been rewarded with the Rhine from Trier to Düsseldorf, a riparian zone so Catholic in population that it came to be known as 'the street of the priests'. By the later decades of the nineteenth century, after further victories in the Franco-Prussian War, Prussia continued to expand, and its new Empire now comprehended the exclusively Catholic lands of Bavaria, Württemburg, the principalities of Hohenzollern-Sigmaringen, a part of the Grand Duchy of Baden, German Poland, a part of Silesia and Alsace-Lorraine. Within half a century, the Catholic population of Greater Germany had increased tenfold (to thirty million), so that the small Lutheran state of Prussia which ruled over this new Empire seemed swamped.

Moreover, the lay side of the Catholic Church in Germany was extremely powerful and well organized. Apart from Catholic Church schools and Youth Organizations, there were Catholic Journeymens' Guilds, Catholic Mercantile Guilds, Catholic Female Employees' Guilds, Catholic Guilds for Officials, and a great network of Catholic hospitals, asylums, and charitable institutions.

Bismarck feared that these Catholics were so numerous and powerful that they could form a 'state within a state', their allegiance or a large part of it – particularly after the proclamation of Papal Infallibility – being accorded to a 'foreign potentate'.[11] That his fear was at least partially justified is revealed in a sermon delivered by a high Catholic prelate. The Vatican Secret Archives have this report of Mgr Suttner's address to his flock at Eichstatt, Bavaria, on 12 December 1871:

It is true that we Catholics have our civic duties – as Germans. But we also have our religious duties – as priests. It is true that we swear allegiance to the German Emperor. But we are also bound by our vows of obedience to the Catholic Church. It is true that we recognize a fatherland on earth – Germany. But we also have a fatherland in Heaven – our Church. We are ready to sacrifice our lives for the Kaiser. But our honour and conscience belong to God.[12]

Bismarck may have read his *Lives of the Saints*, and become aware of a convenient precedent for the chastisement of such men professing dual allegiance. In the third century, the Roman commanding officer Mauritius, when instructed to renounce his new-found allegiance to Christ by the Emperor Maximinian, declared: 'O Caesar! We are thy soldiers – but we are also soldiers of Jesus Christ. To thee we owe service – to him obedience!' For this dual allegiance, he was put to death.[13]

An additional reason for fear of Rome was that many German Protestants believed that the Franco-Prussian War of 1870 had been contrived by the German Catholics, who hoped France would overthrow their lay ruler, Lutheran Prussia (a supposition which appears to have been quite unwarranted, for the German Catholics in the army fought most loyally against France). They also believed that Napoleon III's declaration of war on Prussia in 1870 had been urged on him by his devout Catholic wife, the Empress Eugénie and her Ultramontane 'clique'. Because she was known to be close to the Vatican, a facile deduction was drawn: that the Vatican was responsible for the war.

That the Catholics were considered at least partly responsible for the Franco-Prussian War is revealed in another document in the Vatican Secret Archives, drawn up by the German Catholic Episcopate in Fulda (the fount of German Catholicism), entitled *The Present State of Affairs in Germany*. 'If we are to counter Prince Bismarck's measures,' it commented, 'we must understand his reasoning. He contends that when the King of Prussia became Emperor of Germany, the sentiments and conditions of the German Catholics changed, becoming hostile to the Empire. The German Catholics – such is his reasoning – oppose the Imperial Crown being worn by a Protestant.[14] For this reason, the Emperor can no longer treat the Catholics as leniently as he did, when he was only King of Prussia. Having defeated the foreigner in 1870, the Emperor now considers he has an equally dangerous *internal* enemy. He and his Chancellor must therefore declare war on Rome.'[15] This is a balanced piece of reasoning by the German Catholic bishops, and an accurate assessment of the situation when the *Kulturkampf* began.

The Comte d'Harcourt confirmed this. 'Bismarck,' he wrote, 'having failed to attract the Catholics to his policies, now intends to intimidate them. The Prussian Ambassador in Rome, Graf von Taufkirchen, has told a number of persons here that if the German Catholics resist, it will be the end of Papal influence in Germany.'[16] On much the same lines is the assessment by Sir Augustus Paget, the British Ambassador to the Quirinale: 'Bismarck, having crippled France in the late war, is determined to prevent her from reviving by allying herself with other powers. To ensure that Italy's friendship inclines to Germany and not to France, he is trying to attract Italy by attacking her enemy, the Vatican.'[17] Bismarck calculated that after the Italian seizure of Rome, the Papacy was as weak as it was likely to be for some decades, and that now was the time to strike. Thanks to the Prussian victory over Austria at Sadowa in 1867, the hegemony in the Teutonic world had passed from Catholic Austria to Protestant Prussia, and the last traces of the Holy Roman Empire had been extinguished. Bismarck's Minister for Cults, Dr Falk, now introduced the laws named after him, which legally enshrined the aims of the *Kulturkampf*. Among his first measures was the expulsion of the Jesuits, who were strongly represented. With the departure of these unbending arch-educators of Catholic youth, the way was open for controlling religious education on Prussian lines. Falk introduced legislation by which each candidate for the priesthood (of any denomination) had to attend a three-year course in a State school where, before he was allowed to undertake his ministry, he had to pass an examination in 'Germanic culture'. This would explain to some extent the term *Kulturkampf*, a movement back in time to the origins of 'Germanic culture', in some dark Teutonic wood before Boniface came in A.D. 743 to Christianize them. It is as if the English were to maintain that they were more 'cultured' before the arrival of St Augustine than after him. Further, these candidates for the priesthood had first to be approved by their *Oberpräsident* (the Prefect of their Land, or district), who could veto their candidature if he thought they might be 'hostile to the State'. Thus the State was made the sole judge of the fitness of priests for office. Other measures included compulsory civil marriage, introduced in 1875 and, in the same year, a law excluding from the Prussian kingdom all Orders and Congregations except the nursing ones. All seminaries were closed. Ecclesiastical students, and even priests, were subject to military service. Episcopal authority was to be reduced to a minimum, under the pretext of granting the subordinate clergy greater administrative freedom.

All these measures were incorporated in the new Penal Code, which seems to have been directed almost exclusively against the Catholic Church. They were reported on indignantly by the Papal Nuncio in Munich, as they were successively introduced. There are too many of them to concern us here; but one, Article 174, may be quoted as typical of the equivocal language employed, so that they could be interpreted in a variety of ways against the Church. It enacted. 'A priest shall be punished by a prison sentence of up to two years if, with the moral force of his Ministry, he disturbs the peace of the family.'

In his report to the Vatican on this, the Nuncio complains;

But what is meant by *the peace of the family*? It can be interpreted in many ways. A priest is liable to disturb the peace of the family if, for example, he refuses absolution to a man who has brutally repudiated his wife, and is in the arms of another woman. If a priest refuses absolution to a public official who has defrauded the state of several million, a barrator, he disturbs the peace of the family. If a priest refuses Christian burial to a person who has led a thoroughly irreligious and scandalous life, he disturbs the peace of the family. There is nothing that a Catholic priest wants more than to *preserve* the peace of the family. But sometimes he *has* to disturb it, to bring a person back to the good life. . . . At the very origin of our religion, the preaching of Jesus Christ and his Apostles greatly perturbed families, and disturbed their peace of mind, when their sins were pointed out to them. But that perturbation, which was transitory, was necessary, because it was followed by great peace of mind and a knowledge of glory.[18]

With these laws, Bismarck seemed to have effectively put an end to Papal influence in Germany, and in 1874 he withdrew the

German Embassy from the Vatican. But in one respect he had miscalculated, not as to Rome, but as to his own people. He had seriously underestimated the resistance of the Catholic priests and their parishioners. The bishops refused to apply the Falk laws in their dioceses, and denounced them from the pulpit. In a collective letter to German Catholics the bishops, gathered at Fulda, exhorted their flocks '. . . to resign yourselves to every form of suffering and oppression. Only remain resolute in your faith in the Church.' For such public pronouncements six of them, the Archbishops of Cologne, Gnesen-Posen, Breslau, Limburg, Münster and Pader-born, were haled off to prison. The priests followed their example, to such an extent that they were escorted to prison from their very altars and pulpits, amid the protests of the congregation. Seven hundred parishes were deprived in this way of their pastors, of whom many fled the country to escape imprisonment. Numerous German Catholic priests, both regular (under monastic vows) and secular, were soon to be seen roaming in foreign lands, homeless and penniless. Those that remained, thrown out without pay, would, it was calculated by the Government, either starve or capitulate. But the German Catholic population came to their aid. As one priest said, 'I have no fear of the *Hungerkur* ["remedy through hunger"]. I have faith in my parishioners. They will provide me with a porringer into which I can dip my spoon.'[19] And so it was. For the next eight years, as the *Kulturkampf* increased in severity, the devout Catholics of Germany fed and supported their evicted priests (those, that is, who were not in prison).

The principal result of all this was that Catholic life in Germany – in the Church associations, missions, reunions, pilgrimages, literature, etc. – only flourished more actively, while the devotion and attachment of German Catholics to the Church increased. It confirmed the old adage about the Church thriving on persecution: 'The Catholic Faith is like a nail. The more you hit it on the head with a hammer, the more it sinks in.' In 1875, the Pope was handed an address of homage with 1,200,000 German signatures. In 1877, the festivities for Pius IX's jubilee were celebrated in Germany with such wild enthusiasm that special police forces had to be called in to control the crowds.[20] To members of the Catholic Circle of German Youth who visited Rome in 1872 the Pope said:

The German Chancellor is the principal culprit of the present persecution of our Church in Germany. He does this because he is confident after his military triumphs. I say this to him – success on the battlefield is not enough. His persecution of the Church will render all his victories vain. I say to you German Catholics – lift up your eyes to the Heavens whence cometh your strength! Have confidence in God! Remain united! Then the stone will surely fall from the mountain and break the feet of the colossus. But if the Lord should ordain that we must undergo more persecution, we will do so without fear. Persecution can be a cleansing, a purifying action. Persecution can only strengthen our Church.[21]

Pius IX appeared to have no fear of the man before whom all Europe trembled, describing Bismarck publicly as a 'boa constrictor', 'the great sorcerer', 'Satan in a helmet'. In an allocution to another group of German pilgrims, he said Bismarck was 'the new Attila, the scourge of modern times'.[22] 'Sometimes,' he said, 'God sends a scourge deliberately to awaken men from their sloth. Just as many centuries ago, he sent Attila to reawaken the people to religion, so today he sends this modern Attila. And this modern Attila who prides himself that he is destroying – he does not know that he is really creating. This modern Attila who thinks he is eliminating the religion of Jesus Christ in Germany, in reality he is reinforcing it. . . .'

These apostrophes infuriated Bismarck – all the more because Pius IX combined them with an air of tolerant derision. Mr Jervoise reports on an audience with him, that the Pope said laughingly of Bismarck, 'So, the poor fellow has lost his head again! He is so carried away by all his military successes in France that he has lost all generous feelings. He now talks openly of the next Conclave – after my death, if you please! – and how he intends to have his say in it. But the Catholics of Germany will not let him. Look how stalwartly they are standing up to him on my behalf! The poor fellow has blundered again! (*Il povero ha fatto un altro fiasco!*)' He then recalled, says Jervoise, with much satisfaction how Bismarck had thought he could persuade the schismatic Armenian Bishop to support his *Kulturkampf*. But the Bishop had refused, saying that his difference with the Pope was one not of doctrine but of privilege. 'The Bishop still looks on me as his spiritual head,' said the Pope chuckling and pulling out his snuff-box. 'So you see the poor old Bismarck has made another fiasco!'[23]

The principal form of political defence which the Church employed against the *Kulturkampf* was the Catholic Zentrum ('Centre') Party in the new Parliament, which had been founded in 1871. The German Catholics possessed something which was lacking in most Catholic countries – organization. The tendency to organize, and the faculty for doing it thoroughly, seems innate in the German character. On this occasion, it proved the best defence of the Catholic Church in the new German Empire. Both in the Prussian Chamber and in the all-German Reichstag, the Zentrum Party was at once so compact, so well led, and so disciplined that it immediately made itself felt as a third power between the Government under Bismarck and the growing Socialist opposition.

Although the Vatican in principle does not favour Catholic political parties, here an exception was made. As early as 1870, Antonelli had been urging on Pius IX that henceforth, after the loss of temporal power, it would be better not to try to deal directly with foreign heads of state, but rather through a political party within the state, which was sympathetic to the Vatican. Hence the formation of the Zentrum Party.

The word 'party', as indicating a body of men elected to achieve certain well-defined political ends, hardly described the Zentrum. It represented no particular class or interest, but existed solely to further the affairs of Catholics, be they employers or employees, landlords or peasants. As well as feudal landlords and farmers, it included bishops and priests, a cross-section of the bourgeoisie and the Catholic trades union leaders, whose ideas about social progress were almost indistinguishable from those of the Socialists. All these men sat together in the Reichstag and voted in unison, not because they necessarily thought alike, but because they had a common goal, to promote the interests of Catholics. In their leader, Windthorst, they possessed an outstanding orator who countered all Bismarck's anti-clerical measures in Parliament with speeches of such scathing wit that on several occasions Bismarck lost his temper. In the words of Georges Goyau, the French historian of the *Kulturkampf*, 'For twelve years Windthorst fought against this formidable foe. "I and my friends," he cried in the Reichstag, "will if necessary suffer and fight for another twelve years. We will never give in." '[24] And he did not. In Parliament, in public assemblies and meetings all over the country, in international congresses, he ceaselessly attacked the Bismarck-Falk Laws. As a result the Zentrum became known among the Bismarckians as *Reichsfeind* ('enemy of the Empire'), one of the most disparaging epithets in the German language. But whether Bismarck liked it or not, he had to take the Zentrum into account because, in common with other European countries in the new 'liberal' age, Germany was governed through its Parliament. Iron Chancellor though he was, Bismarck could not govern without it, and to pass his laws he had to command a majority in that Parliament. The Zentrum party had until 1871 been insignificant and, although vigorously opposing the Falk Laws in Parliament, it had insufficient votes to make any impression on them.

But then at this moment when the *Kulturkampf* was at its height, a volte-face occurred. In the elections of 1878, to everyone's astonishment, the Zentrum obtained 103 seats, making it the second largest party in the Reichstag.[25] Bismarck's large majorities which had voted in the Falk Laws were over. The Zentrum could not yet unmake these laws, but it could prevent further legislation of the kind being passed. Moreover, its support in the Reichstag would be required against the rapidly expanding Socialist Party. Pius IX had said to the German pilgrims, 'Who knows when the stone will come down from the mountain and break the feet of the colossus?' That stone came down with the 1878 elections.

The new Pope Leo XIII, who had acceded in the year of these elections, had the advantage over Pius IX of having lived for some years as Papal Nuncio in a country under constitutional parliamentary rule, Belgium. He had learnt something about Parliamentary majorities and how they are manipulated. Here he perceived Prince Bismarck's Achilles heel. Although diplomatic relations with Germany had been suspended under Pius IX, one of Leo XIII's first acts as Pope was to write a personal letter to the German Kaiser announcing his accession, and referring to the Kaiser's 'mighty and glorious sceptre'.[26] It also referred to the *Kulturkampf*, but in measured terms: 'I appeal to the magnanimity of Your Majesty that Catholics in your land may be permitted to return to the peaceful conditions of old. I can assure Your Majesty that our religion enjoins them always to behave as loyal subjects of

Your Majesty and their country. For this I can vouch personally.'
He ended with a prayer that God might endow the Kaiser with
heavenly grace and unite all his subjects around him.[27]

Here too it seemed that Bismarck had miscalculated. He had
assumed that the new Pope would continue the *Non Possumus*
policy of his predecessor, namely of having nothing to do with
states which persecuted the Church, as instanced by Pius IX's total
repudiation of the new Italian State. Pius IX had adopted much the
same attitude to Prussia on account of the *Kulturkampf*, confining
himself to fulminations against it and its Chancellor. This had
played into Bismarck's hands, for he had used them as a pretext for
declaring that the Pope was clearly setting himself up as a rival for
the loyalties of German Catholics, and a superior authority to the
Kaiser in his own domains. Bismarck hoped and assumed that the
new Pope would continue this kind of spiritual warfare against the
Government of Prussia. He wanted a Pope who refused to
compromise and would not listen to reason.

At this point two assassination attempts were made on the life of
the Kaiser in Berlin; and when it was discovered that 'anarchists'
were behind them (one of the would-be assassins was a Socialist)
the Kaiser, who was a religious man, publicly announced that
God's providence had protected him against the anarchists. This
confirmed Leo XIII's calculation that the Socialists were becoming,
in the eyes of the Prussian Government, a greater danger than the
Catholics; and he followed up his letter to the Kaiser with another
congratulating him on his escape, and assuring him of his best
wishes for the continuance of his reign. With these letters, which
were given full publicity, Leo XIII disappointed Bismarck's hope
and frustrated his wishes.

Leo XIII now bided his time, on the age-old Vatican principle
Cunctando regitur mundus ('The world is ruled by delaying'). For the
next three years he could do little more than negotiate through his
Nuncio in Munich with Bismarck, who was now faced in the
Reichstag with a greater adversary, the rapidly growing Socialist
Party. Leo XIII abominated socialism as much as Pius IX did but,
unlike his predecessor, he had seen that in modern industrial society
socialism had arrived; it was with them for the foreseeable future.
The selfish greed and avarice of the big capitalists and industrialists
in the late nineteenth century had rendered the advance of socialism
among the proletariat inevitable. More than this, he realized that he

could use the growing strength of the Socialists in Germany for his own ends.

It was not long before the Iron Chancellor found that the easy majorities in the Reichstag which had enabled him to govern absolutely for two decades were over. It now appeared that if he was to keep the Socialists from power and pass his legislation, he must obtain support from other parties than his own Conservative cartel. The Zentrum was of course hostile to him. He looked round for a way out of the labyrinth he now found hmself in, without losing face. All Europe was watching him. In connection with the *Kulturkampf* he had once unwisely announced that he could never 'go to Canossa';[28] Rome must come to him. There being no diplomatic relations between Prussia and the Papacy, he sent one of his Ministers, Count Holstein, to sound out the Nuncio in Munich, Mgr Aloisi-Marsella. Count Holstein told the Nuncio that the whole matter of the *Kulturkampf* could be settled in a quarter of an hour, if the Church so desired. Mgr Aloisi-Marsella, sensing that such haste implied weakness, replied that so grave a matter as the lot of thirty million human beings, the Catholics of Germany, could hardly be dealt with in such a peremptory manner. After the interview, he reported back to Rome his impression that Bismarck did not wish to abrogate the Falk Laws completely but he was looking for a way of reaching as quickly as possible some form of *modus vivendi* which would satisfy the German Catholics and also obtain the support of the Zentrum Party, without which he could not pass any of his legislation.

This impression was enhanced by Bismarck's next move. He suggested that he personally should meet the Papal Nuncio in Kissingen, where he would be in attendance on His Majesty, who was taking the cure there. It would thus appear to the outside world as purely fortuitous and – as the Nuncio commented tartly – certainly not a 'Canossa'. Leo XIII gave his consent, but he instructed the Nuncio in no circumstances to accept anything less than the complete abrogation of the Falk Laws.

At the meeting, the Nuncio reported, Bismarck was extremely courteous, and it was clear that he wanted some form of 'armistice', so that he could draw up new plans and wait on events. 'He is still intent,' reported the Nuncio, 'on eliminating, or much diminishing, Papal influence in Germany.' What Bismarck offered was that some of the deposed bishops should be reinstated in their dioceses.

On the advice of these German bishops themselves, Leo XIII refused to accept these terms, declaring that the Church had no confidence in promises so long as the Falk Laws remained on the statute books. His Secretary of State, Cardinal Franchi, wrote to Bismarck on 11 August 1878, 'We are not disposed to conclude with Germany what would be no better than a truce which, because it makes no reference to the Falk Laws, can only be ephemeral and a source of new and graver conflict. We desire a real and durable peace.'

At the same time Leo XIII, aware of the weakness of the other side, spoke up more forcibly than was his wont, comparing Germany unfavourably with other European powers. 'No other Government in the world,' he said, 'whether in France, Austria, Spain, or even England or America, has ever thought of interfering with the education of the Catholic clergy. In all these countries, that education has always remained in the hands of the Church. Even Russia recognizes this.' He was here referring of course to the notorious Article 174 of the Falk Laws prescribing a three-year course in 'Germanic culture' for all candidates for the priesthood.

At this point the Kaiser himself made an intervention, which modified the *Kulturkampf*. Referring to the two assassination attempts which had been made on his life by embittered workers, he said to his Minister Falk, the introducer of the Laws, 'If you would only leave the workers their religion, these things would not have happened.' Falk, it is said, took the hint and resigned.

Bismarck prevaricated for another year, but during this time he gradually repealed the Falk Laws, one by one, in return for increasing support in Parliament from the Zentrum, to keep the Socialists out. The Socialists had become for him a greater enemy than the Catholic Church. Leo XIII's policy was bearing fruit, and by 1888 all the Falk Laws had been repealed. The year 1888 also marked another new era in German history – the death of William I, followed three months later by that of his son Frederick III. The new Emperor was William II, who was to dismiss Bismarck a year later. The Catholics of Germany were back where Leo XIII had requested in his first letter to the old Kaiser, 'to the peaceful conditions of old'.

The whole controversy, lasting nearly two decades, is a remarkable example of the power still wielded by the Pope. In the words of the French Ambassador to the Holy See, Comte de

Bourgoing, while the *Kulturkampf* was in progress, 'With the loss of the temporal power, it was assumed in some circles that Rome was weakened for ever. But this weakness is only apparent and superficial. Beneath the surface, the Pope disposes of very great power. . . . The Papacy is giving Bismarck sleepless nights. The victor of Sadowa and Sedan would not be attacking it so ruthlessly, if he considered it infirm and powerless.'[29]

To sum up in the words of Goyau:

If only the *Kulturkampf* had achieved some of the results expected by its authors. . . . But no! Religious Germans deprived of the support they looked for from the Catholic faith – because its churches were closed – did not, as Bismarck and Falk had expected, take refuge in a Protestant form of Christianity, nor in the schismatic groupings such as the 'Old Catholics', thereby replacing obedience to the Pope by obedience to Caesar. No, the Catholic Church continued its work undeterred on behalf of these people. Expelled from its sanctuaries, it maintained close contact with its faithful – in the factories, mines, shops, workshops of Germany. The Abbé Mitze built up in Prussia and the Rhineland, where the persecution was at its height, a vast Catholic organization of working men and women, some 170,000 of them in over 800 centres.[30]

It was typical of Leo XIII that he did not parade his victory. He could have demanded, and obtained, the reinstatement of the more refractory German bishops, who had spoken up against Bismarck using the language of Pius IX, in terms which the Chancellor could hardly forget – Bishops Ledochowski of Posen and Melchers of Cologne. Leo XIII did not wish to provoke the unpredictable temper of the Iron Chancellor by making him take the full 'road to Canossa', thereby perhaps losing what the Church had gained. Leo XIII's principal goal had been achieved, and he preferred to yield on this point, even at the sake of appearing disloyal to his bishops. For the sake of the longer-term interests of the Church, he asked these bishops to resign.

Leo XIII's flexibility during this time, an essential part of his character, is well expressed in the words Émile Zola puts into his mouth in his book *Rome*: 'Oh, in matters of form, we will do whatever we are asked. We are ready to adopt the most conciliatory courses if it be only a question of resolving certain difficulties and weighing expressions in order to facilitate a solution.' There is a well-known saying in German about a reed, *sich beugen um nicht zu brechen* ('to bend so as not to break'). Leo XIII had demonstrated to the Germans the truth of their own aphorism.

In this way in 1888, the *Kulturkampf* ended. During it, both the higher and the subordinate clergy of Germany had remained undaunted in face of Prince Bismarck's assault. In the words of that notable Englishman Cardinal Manning, 'The German Empire defended by a million bayonets and with a legion of public and secret policemen at its disposal, celebrated, sung and idolized by an innumerable court of panegyrists as the First Power in the world, was forced to bow before 200 defenceless priests!!' Pius IX's forecast had been vindicated.

In fact, Bismarck's persecution had proved ill-timed, because when he initiated it, a division in the Catholic ranks was already opening in Germany, owing to the Ultramontane pronouncements of the Vatican Council, and the unpopular Dogma of Infallibility. But Bismarck's persecution effectively healed this breach before it could broaden. As so often happens in the history of the Catholic Church, persecution was responsible for a renewal of faith; in the words of Machiavelli, '*Persecuitatemi se volete farmi regnare!*' ('Persecute me if you want to make me reign!').

It was at about this time, when the *Kulturkampf* was in its last stages, that Pope Leo XIII's diplomatic skills were employed in another way, on behalf of one of the traditional roles of the Holy See throughout the centuries – that of mediator between great powers on the point of war. Here again Bismarck and Germany were involved, this time in a dispute with Spain over the Caroline Islands in distant Oceania, to which both powers laid claim.[31] Petty as the dispute appeared initially, as national tempers inflamed it might have led to a general European war.

At the end of the sixteenth century Spanish navigators had discovered a large island archipelago in Oceania rich in spices and, as they believed, metal mines, but whose inhabitants were reputed to be cannibals. They gave it the name of Carolines in honour of their King, Charles II. Spain's overseas adversary in those days was not Germany, but Portugal; and Pope Alexander VI had made his famous act of mediation between these two maritime powers, his

Bull of 1493, *Inter Caetera* ('Among other matters . . .'), defining all territory discovered by Europeans west of a line through the Azores as Spanish, and that to the east as Portuguese. The Caroline Islands thus became, at least in European eyes, Spanish. They were difficult of access, surrounded by treacherous currents, shoals, and rocky promontories. It was not until the eighteenth century that, under the Spanish Jesuits, any serious attempt at *de facto* possession was made.

We should remember that in those days the navigators who risked their lives in these unknown regions on the other side of the globe – and the governments who sponsored their enterprise – were not concerned exclusively with commercial profit. The immediate aim, the driving force, behind these expeditions was generally religious. Nor did they hesitate to declare it openly. In the commission which Francis I of France granted to Jacques Cartier, he announced the aim as, '*D'induire les peuples d'iceux pays à croire à notre saincte foi, de faire chose agréable à Dieu et qui fût à l'augmentation de son sainct nom*' ('To bring the peoples of those lands to believe in our holy faith, to do something pleasing to God and such as may magnify His holy name').

In 1705, two Spanish Jesuit Fathers, Serrano and Medel, set off for the Caroline Islands with the intention of taking possession in the name of God and Spain, and converting the natives to the Catholic faith. They had with them the Brief of Clement IX, and the financial aid of Philip V. They made two attempts at reaching the archipelago, but each time had to return, owing to the treacherous currents and storms. At the third attempt, they reached the island of Sonsoral on the periphery of the Caroline archipelago, and decided – against the advice of the captain of their vessel – to go ashore in a longboat. They were never seen again, and it was generally believed that the local inhabitants had eaten them.

Such setbacks have never deterred the Jesuits, who sent another expedition in 1711. This was shipwrecked and the entire crew perished. In 1731, Father Cantora, also of the Society of Jesus, and three companions tried again. They were more successful, and established a foothold on the island of Falasep, from where they set about extending their missionary activity to the entire archipelago. But a year later, the natives rose and massacred them.

So much for the early Spanish attempts at colonization. It was not until the late eighteenth century, when methods of navigation had much improved, that the Spaniards managed to establish themselves in a small way on these islands, and then not as traders – for the Spanish Hidalgos despised trade; they were concerned principally with spreading the Faith and extracting metals, preferably gold. They did not even bother to install an administration, and their military garrison was diminutive.

At this point the Germans appeared for the first time on the world maritime scene. Until the nineteenth century, this European inland race hardly knew what an ocean-going boat was. But they quickly made amends for their late start in the European colonization movement. By 1885, they had established themselves at several points in the Caroline archipelago, where they founded flourishing plantations and trading posts. They never contested that in the Carolines they were on Spanish soil; they simply observed that there were virtually no Spaniards there, no governor, no administrative system, no defence forces. Spanish sovereignty, they observed, did not exist. Henceforth, the Germans formed the majority of the European population in the Carolines, bore the costs of colonization and protected other European traders against attack by natives.

Somewhat earlier, in 1861, Bismarck had declared with more candour than foresight, 'We want no colonies. For us Germans, distant possessions are exactly what a fur-lined sable coat is for a Polish nobleman who doesn't own a shirt.' He now changed his mind. With the advent of the German Empire which he had created, he became aware of the importance of overseas possessions, in particular of the Carolines.

The gradual and insidious German trade invasion appears finally to have made the Spaniards aware that the Caroline Islands, to which they had hardly given a thought for three hundred years, belonged to them. Absentee owners though they were, they possessed the *de jure* right; even if the Germans, in much greater numbers, were the *de facto* owners. By August 1885, Spanish pride had been stimulated to such an extent that they sent a ship, the *Velasco*, with a provincial governor to take possession of the islands. Whereupon, four days later, the Germans sent a gunboat, the *Iltis*, whose Captain proclaimed that he was taking possession *de facto* of the Caroline Islands, in the name of the German Emperor. A crisis was at hand.

The German captain of the *Iltis* now invited the local native king,

Abathul de Korro, on board, and after entertaining him royally, dilated on the benefits which would accrue to him and his people if a German Protectorate were established in the archipelago. It appears that the King spoke a little English. He was much impressed, and commanded the tribal leaders on all the isles to put their mark to a declaration stating that they had never seen the Spanish flag, that they had never entered into relations of any kind with Spain, nor signed any agreement with that country. The declaration finished, 'We saw the German flag hoisted yesterday. Henceforth, we recognize a German Protectorate of our interests.'

This was virtually a declaration of war. Spain was suffering at this time from the delusion that she was still a great European power. Her popular masses still believed that she was one of the first nations in the world. They now descended into the streets of Madrid, attacked and sacked the palace of the German Ambassador, tore down the German arms, and burned the German flag. The Spanish Ambassador in Berlin was instructed to take back his letters of credence. Yet the Spanish army was ill organized, the navy almost non-existent, and the national exchequer more or less bankrupt.

Hostilities would undoubtedly have broken out, had not the Pope's mediation been summoned. He was at this moment involved in the final negotiations for terminating the *Kulturkampf* with Bismarck, and in almost constant contact with that statesman. The Pope suggested, not very hopefully, that rather than go to war, the two countries might look for a mediator to settle their differences. After some hesitation, the two sides agreed, and the Spaniards asked the Pope to act as referee. To general surprise, neither the Protestant German Kaiser nor his Lutheran Chancellor objected to this proposal. (The French biographer of Leo XIII, J. de Narfon, says that an Italian journalist was responsible for this. Having been expelled from Germany by Bismarck, he bore him a grudge which he expressed in a practical joke. He sent a telegram to a Berlin newspaper announcing that the Spanish Government was about to ask the Pope to mediate in the Carolines dispute. Bismarck intercepted the telegram and took it seriously. Believing that he was about to accomplish a diplomatic master-stroke, he resolved to anticipate Spain, and proposed the arbitration himself.)[32]

The Pope refused to act as *referee*: he foresaw the complications for the Church if he decided, as a referee must, in favour of one side or the other. He insisted that his role should be no more than that of *mediator*. Whereas the referee is virtually a judge who adjudicates which party is in the right, the mediator does no more than attempt to conciliate the parties. The first gives a final judgement, which is obligatory; the second only offers his good offices and advice, which both parties can if they wish repudiate.

Both Germany and Spain agreed and Leo XIII, after studying the question in detail, suggested proceeding on these lines. The priority for the discovery of the Carolines belonged *de jure* to Spain, even if it was not a real title, because it had not been followed by formal physical possession. It was nevertheless *the beginning of a title*. In the Papal letter of 22 October 1885 to both parties, Leo XIII suggested that the Spanish Government should establish as soon as possible a regular administration in the archipelago, supported by sufficient military force to maintain order. At the same time Germany, which had done so much for the islands, should be allowed to have a plantation and agricultural settlements.[33] Spain would offer and guarantee Germany full liberty of commerce, navigation and fishing, and the right to a naval base on the Carolines.

The terms were accepted and both parties expressed their satisfaction. The Kaiser William II wrote a letter to the Pope: 'At a moment when it appeared that relations between Germany and Spain were deteriorating, it was thanks to the wisdom of Your Holiness, joined with the authority of Your great office, that passions were calmed and good relations restored between the two nations. I beg Your Holiness to accept this pectoral Cross in token of my appreciation. William II.'[34]

It might be supposed from this that the Zentrum Party in Germany, which had played such a part in defeating the *Kulturkampf*, would have expressed satisfaction. That the Head of its Church had returned to the age-old role of mediator and peacemaker, was surely matter for congratulation; surely it was a sign that the prestige of the Papacy, at its lowest ebb in 1870, was reviving. But this was not the view taken by the Zentrum Party. In the Vatican Secret Archives is a despatch from the Nuncio in Vienna, Mgr Serafino, in which he said that the leader of the Zentrum Party, Herr Windthorst was 'extremely jealous of His Holiness's success in dealing with Bismarck over the Carolines';[35] for during the negotiations the Pope dealt directly with Bismarck, going as it were over the heads of the Zentrum Party leaders, with whom he had been closely associated during the *Kulturkampf*. The Nuncio added that Bismarck encouraged this, because he found it easier to deal with the Pope direct than with Windthorst, who 'wishes to be more Papal than the Pope'. Moreover Windthorst, said the Nuncio, saw 'in the successful conclusion of the *Kulturkampf* and the Carolines affair also the conclusion of his own Parliamentary career. It is with rancour,' he continued, 'that the *Zentrum* has been made to stand aside while the Emperor and the Pope deal directly with one another, as they did in the old days before Parliamentary government was the rule.' To make matters worse, Leo XIII then bestowed on Bismarck the highest honour of the Catholic Church for laymen, that of Cavaliere del Ordine di Cristo ('Knight of the Order of Christ') a distinction not accorded to Windthorst; while in return, the Kaiser gave the Pope a golden mitre to wear at his jubilee in 1888.

The bestowal of decorations has long been a source of jealousy in human relations, and so it proved on this occasion. Not only were Windthorst and his colleagues aggrieved, but the Spanish Prime Minister, Canovas, expressed his indignation that he, representing Spain in the Caroline negotiations, should not have been treated as Bismarck had been, and made a 'Knight of Christ'. In a despatch from Madrid (17 February 1888) the Apostolic Delegate, Mgr Mariano, urgently recommended that this honour should be bestowed immediately on Canovas who was, unlike Bismarck, a devout Catholic. He added that one of Canovas's senior Ministers, the Count of Toreanaz, the Minister for Justice, had let it be known that he too would like a Papal decoration, the Grand Cross of St Gregory. Mgr Mariano commented, 'Although the Count is respectable in his religious conduct towards the Church, this I cannot recommend. He had absolutely no part in the Caroline Islands negotiations, and I do not see what claim he has to a Papal decoration.' The whole Caroline Islands episode was an eloquent, and somewhat ironical comment on the 'vanity of vanities'. Bismarck, Pius IX's 'Satan in a helmet', was now Leo XIII's 'Cavalier of Christ'.[36]

7

The Need for Reform

Under Pius IX the Zelanti had been all-powerful, and had effectively resisted any movement among the hierarchy for accommodation with the Italian State, and other reforms. Officially for them that State did not exist. But as the reign of Leo XIII continued into the 1880s and 1890s, their dominant position was challenged by a growing number of the episcopate, who advocated a less intransigent attitude. Prominent among these bishops was Mgr Bonomelli, the young Bishop of Cremona, who in 1894 published a book entitled *Roma, l'Italia e la realtà delle Cose* ('Rome, Italy, and the Reality of Things') in which he argued that in the twenty-five years since the Italian occupation of Rome, the situation had changed entirely. A new generation of Italians had grown up, accustomed to the idea of Italian nationality. 'In 1870,' he wrote, 'the Romans were saying, "But what have we to do with these Piedmontese? We have no need of Piedmont." But today you will never hear them talking like this. Nor indeed do the Neapolitans and Florentines. In other words, the notion of *national* Italian unity has become rooted in the public mind all over the Peninsula in these last twenty-five years. All Italy today regards with pride and affection her national army and navy. A nation knows it exists, when it knows it can defend itself.' He added that all eminent Italians in the field of the arts, philosophy and science as well as in industry, business, banking and the professions – in short, all the men who *directed* the country – did not support the temporal power of the Pope. His book had a considerable effect, not only in Italy, but beyond her frontiers.[1]

The Bishop of Cremona made various prognostications:

Let us assume [he wrote] that a foreign power attempts by force to restore the Pope to his temporal position. The whole of Italy will rise as a man to resist it. A cry of fury will go up from a million throats, particularly from the young, a cry of hatred for the Papacy which has once again called in the foreigner. We should not forget that when in 1792 the people of Paris learned that the Allied armies had been summoned in by the expelled Bourbons, and were about to invade France to restore them, the battlecry was, 'Let us free ourselves first from our internal enemies! Then we will defeat the external ones!' It was then that the Reign of Terror began. Should this ever happen in Rome – because the Pope has summoned in the foreigner – we shall witness similar horrors. Much priestly blood will flow. Should this take place, I pray God that he will by then have gathered me – so that I shall not witness the massacre of my native land and, what is dearer to me, my religion.

The Bishop followed this with a remarkable forecast of what the Vatican should strive for in its relations with the Italian State. It should be satisfied with the right bank of the Tiber, and a zone of a few square kilometres behind St Peter's, where a new Papal city could be constructed. 'It would be a kind of Principality of Monaco, or a small republic on San Marino, Andorra lines, with no more than 10,000 souls. On account of its exiguousness, it would not excite fear or jealousy in either the Italian or foreign governments. With the Ambassadors accredited to the Holy See within its walls, it would form an ornament to the Roman municipality, and would be the prodigy of Europe.'

Leo XIII would probably have let the Bishop's book pass unnoticed, had not its author forced his hand. On 28 October 1896, the Bishop gave a lecture on his book in a church in the Borgata S Martino in Cremona, which had been turned into a lecture hall for the occasion. Only one priest was present, and the Bishop was surrounded on the rostrum by what the official Vatican newspaper, the *Osservatore Romano*, described as 'the flower of the local liberal intelligentsia'. One of these liberals referred to the Bishop in most adulatory terms, congratulating him on 'joining the ranks of those who possess the modern spirit, whose conscience is dictated by the principles of Reason'. In the company of such a churchman as the Bishop of Cremona, liberals like himself could at last feel comfortable. All this was published in the press, and the liberal *Provincia di Cremona* wrote, 'We have here reached the point when the cultivated and educated classes who do not wish to abandon religion can find an alternative – in the religion of Bishop Bonomelli.'

The possible effects of the Bishop's book had been followed closely in the Vatican, which now felt that this consorting with liberals had gone too far. The *Osservatore Romano* came out angrily, 'The Liberals talk of "the religion of Bishop Bonomelli" as if it was some kind of alternative to Catholicism! They openly announce that they find themselves "comfortable" in the company of the Bishop's ideas!'[2]

The Pope was now forced to act. In April 1896, he officially condemned *Roma, l'Italia e la realtà delle Cose*, and placed it on the Index. The result was that on Easter Day 1886, the Bishop of Cremona in his Cathedral, in front of his own clergy, recanted completely. 'Yesterday,' he announced, 'I received an instruction from Rome that my book had been placed on the Index. I wish not to delay even by twenty-four hours announcing my complete submission to the Holy Father, and my withdrawal of the book. I profoundly regret that I caused him sorrow. May my act of recantation serve as an example to the clergy of the manner in which they should pledge their complete obedience to the Holy Father.' The local Cremona papers reported that the Bishop burst into tears, and 'many of the people with him'. A week later the *Osservatore Romano* commented, 'The noble gesture of the Bishop of Cremona recalls that of the illustrious Fénelon in an earlier age, and marks another triumph for the Church, another defeat for its enemies.'[3]

Surprising as it may seem that a Bishop should pronounce this criticism of Papal policy, no one would have imagined that a member of the Jesuit Order could do the same, and in even stronger terms. The Jesuits are normally regarded as the Ultramontanes par excellence. Yet a Jesuit father, C. M. Curci, now published very much on the lines of the Bishop's book his *L'Italia nuova ed i vecchi Zelanti* ('The New Italy and the Old Zelanti'), in which he advocated that the best policy now would be for the Church to occupy itself exclusively with spiritual matters and abandon its temporal claims.[4] His book was also widely read and attracted attention abroad. In it he argued that as the temporal power could not be restored without destroying the unity of Italy, as long as the Vatican claimed that power it followed that Italy must regard the Vatican as an enemy, and do all she could to weaken and destroy the

Church, on the principle *mors tua vita mea* ('your death is my life'). He therefore recommended reconciliation between Church and State, by the former's renunciation of the claim to temporal power. He also said that Pope Pius IX's *Non Expedit* ('It is not expedient . . .') forbidding Catholics to vote in political elections was a grave error, because as half of the population followed this ruling, their electoral weight in opposing the Liberals and Socialists was wasted.

When this document was shown to Leo XIII, he had some difficulty in believing that a Jesuit could have written it. According to the Vatican Secret Archives, he wrote on it, *'È una vera impertinenza . . .'* ('It's a real impertinence . . .') and added that he expected the Vicar General of the Company of Jesus to take disciplinary action. Leo XIII insisted that it should be the Jesuits themselves who corrected this errant member. A prominent member of the Jesuits, Father Becker, was accordingly entrusted with the task. But he appears to have been unwilling and suggested that it should be undertaken by another Jesuit, Father P. Boero. The latter also evaded the responsibility, excusing himself on the ground that he was suffering from bronchitis and had only one eye. A number of others were approached, and it was some time before a responsible member of the Society could be found, in the person of Father Bardinelli of Florence. He agreed that if he could 'work in conjunction with his colleagues', he would do what was required. Father Curci's writings were then carefully examined; after which they were condemned, and their author expelled from the Society.

The reluctance of these Jesuit Fathers to undertake the task supports a theory of the British Ambassador, Sir Augustus Paget, who reckoned that Father Curci was almost certainly encouraged to write and publish his book by the Society of Jesus itself. Sir Augustus suggested that when a serious crisis occurs in the Catholic world the Society, wanting to sound public opinion, would detach one of its members, and instruct him to adopt a certain attitude towards the crisis. If the line pursued by this Jesuit were successful, and the ideas set forth by him supported by an educated Catholic public, the Society would take the credit for having initiated the theory. If, however, the contrary happened, and the new theory found no favour – as was the case here, for Curci's opinions were premature in the Catholic world – the Society would quietly drop the author, condemn his aberrations and denounce his doctrines. In a few years, the miscreant would 'see the error of his ways', retract what he had said or written, and be received back into the fold. This is the purely personal opinion of Sir Augustus Paget; it was at least confirmed on this occasion, because Father Curci now withdrew his book, recanted, and was in due course received back into the Society of Jesus.

It would appear from this that in matters of dogma, Leo XIII did not differ from his predecessor. This was so. But over social matters he differed considerably from Pius IX, principally because during the Pontificate of the former Pope the 'social question' had not become acute; the effects of the European industrial revolution were then barely perceptible. But in the last two decades of the nineteenth century, the condition of the newly industrialized working classes was becoming a question of prime importance. Such a preoccupation did it become with Leo XIII that he had by his death in 1903, earned the popular sobriquet, 'the Pope of the working classes'.

The first indication of his concern for the proletariat can be read in the Italian State Archives for 1891, in a despatch from the Italian Ambassador in Brussels. He referred to the Catholic Congress which had just taken place in Malines. 'What has emerged overwhelmingly from it,' he said, 'is the new tendency of the Vatican to take possession *at any cost* of the social question, to support and guide the demands of the working classes.'[5] Here the Ambassador discerned a subtle move by the Pope to gain popular support in his struggle with the Quirinale. He warned the Italian Government to be on its guard against this.

Dated the same year is a similar despatch from the Italian Ambassador in Munich, Conte Cuva, relating a conversation he had with the Bavarian Foreign Minister, Baron von Crailsham.[6] The latter told him that the Vatican was now actively supporting a Bavarian body called the Association of Catholic Workers, a form of trade union. Conte Cuva commented sharply, 'But in spite of all the Vatican's fine words about its interest in the lot of the workers, this is really a skilful political move to beat the socialists at their own game.'

There was some truth in this. Leo XIII had observed the effects of industrial capitalism on the lower classes, who were gradually being reduced to a condition little short of servitude and, as a result of this oppression, the great advances made all over Europe by socialism. There were then broadly speaking two brands of socialism: the idealistic, based on the teaching of Saint-Simon, Proudhon and Louis Blanc; and the materialist, dominated by the theories of Marx and Engels. The second was rapidly gaining the ascendancy in the public mind, and Leo XIII realized that if the Church was to combat this materialism it must present an alternative.

For the last two decades there had been a feeling all over Europe of imminent revolution, an almost 1789 atmosphere, manifested in the increasing assassinations of prominent people: President Carnot of France; the Empress Elizabeth of Austria; the Prime Minister of Spain, Canovas; and King Umberto of Italy. After the two attempts of 1878 on the life of the Kaiser William I, the German socialist August Bebel gave a sinister warning that unless the lot of the working classes was improved, 'a tidal wave of blood will engulf and wash away both Throne and Altar'.

Leo XIII's first social Encyclical *Inscrutabile* indicated the direction of his thought:

The eighteenth century destroyed the old corporations and guilds which had provided protection for the poor and lowly; and it substituted nothing in their place. Henceforth, the workers found themselves defenceless, delivered to the greed of their masters. The concentration of power and resources in the hands of a few is a distinctive feature of the economy today, the result of unbridled competition. In this battle, only the strong can remain on their feet – which generally means the least susceptible to the promptings of a Christian conscience.

Leo XIII's greatest Encyclical, the one by which he will be remembered, was issued in 1891: the significantly entitled *Rerum Novarum* ('Of New Things . . .'). It has often been called 'the workman's *Magna Carta*'. In it he reprobated 'those who regard work as the supreme end of human endeavour, and man as a kind of machine, valuable only insofar as he produces material goods. Labour must not be considered a commodity subject solely to the law of supply and demand. It is a human act by which man, in obedience to Divine command, earns his bread in the sweat of his brow.' Some of his recommendations sound obvious, trite even,

103

today, but they did not at the time. Thus, the workman's wage should, he said, be sufficient to enable him to support himself and his family! Similarly, what we take for granted today: 'It is right and proper that some of the results of labour should belong to those who have provided that labour.' Trade unions were then only in their infancy, and powerfully opposed by the ruling classes. But in *Rerum Novarum* Leo XIII recognized them, even recommended them, as a necessary defence against the voracity of the proprietors. The only distinction here was that he envisaged *Christian* trade unions which differed from the socialist brand, in that an ecclesiastical superior or referee would exercise persuasive power in resolving the conflicts between capital and labour. Two other economic reforms recommended in the Encyclical were that, although private property should be maintained, it should be diffused on a much wider scale; and that monopolies should be suppressed.

Rerum Novarum is full of practical advice rarely to be found in Pontifical documents. Most of its recommendations have long been put into practice, but in 1891 it seemed – coming from what was generally regarded as one of the most reactionary bodies in the world – to conservatives almost treasonable. That only the liberal press approved it was surely proof of this; the liberal Parisian *Le Pays* wrote, 'This Encyclical marks the beginning of the twentieth century.' On the other hand the French socialists, who saw the ground cut from beneath their feet, condemned it as 'Marxism with rosewater'.

It is true, as some critics pointed out, that much of the Encyclical appeared only to repeat in more orthodox language what Marx had said ten years before (*Das Kapital* was published in 1881). But there was a fundamental difference in the attitude of the two theses towards the modern State. Leo XIII repudiated the Marxist and socialist apotheosis of the State, with its abolition of private property, to be transferred to the State. His Encyclical postulates the family, not the State, as the basis of society; and the family, he insists, involves the possession of private property. Leo XIII starts from this premise. Man is bound by the laws of Nature to found a family (here his Encyclical quotes Matthew xix.5: 'For this cause shall a man leave father and mother, and shall cleave to his wife . . .'); and as head of the family he must make provision for it, which inevitably involves the possession of property. Leo XIII refuted the socialist theory that the State can provide this. The State's duty is relatively simple; to protect and defend the family when it is threatened, from thieves within the country, and enemies without. In arguments between families the State may adjudicate, but it can never assume the role of *paterfamilias*.

Unlike Marx, who attributed the exploitation of the workers solely to the capitalist system, Leo XIII contended that although this exploitation did arise in certain cases through the greed of *individual* capitalists – whom he severely condemned – the capitalist system itself was not bad. The postulate of private property was essential for the production of wealth; and wealth was essential in a good and healthy society. The Encyclical abounds in phrases emphasizing this: 'The right to own private property is necessary for the interests of the working classes themselves. . . . Private property is the principle and foundation of social order. . . . Private property in regulated quantities makes a man free. . . . The right of property is established by natural law. To transfer it to the State is theft. . . .'

This was theory, but Leo XIII soon introduced practical measures to implement these views. Four years after his accession, he founded the Roman Circle of Social Studies under Mgr Dominico Jacobini in the Palazzo Odescalchi. Its students examined a wide range of social problems concerning the working class in different countries: minimum salaries; the curbs that should be placed on the abuses perpetrated by property owners; the legality of loans at interest, and of usufruct (the use and profit of a thing not owned). Under the stimulus of *Rerum Novarum*, the Catholic hierarchy in other countries also entered the social arena. In Germany, Mgr von Ketteler, the Archbishop of Mainz, denounced from the pulpit the abuses practised by certain factory owners. In Austria, Baron Vogelsand instituted a Catholic Social Centre, studying and enumerating the duties towards society owed by those privileged by birth and fortune. In France, after the excesses of the Commune, the Governor of Paris asked one of his officers, the Catholic Comte de Mun, to conduct an enquiry into the origins of that insurrection by the working classes. De Mun was given an office in the Louvre, where he interrogated hundreds of workers who had been involved in the uprising. He made friends with a self-educated worker called Maignan, who had conceived the idea of an Association of Workers to press for the betterment and re-Christianization of the proletariat. This working man's insistence on religion particularly interested the devout de Mun. In this way, under the patronage of these two men, was born the famous *Oeuvre des Cercles Catholiques d'Ouvriers* ('Organization of Catholic Workers' Circles'). Branches were established throughout the provinces, and soon there were some four hundred, with a membership of fifty thousand. Inspired by the Encyclical *Rerum Novarum*, de Mun now devoted his life to this cause, to making Catholics, particularly upper-class Catholics, more aware of the social problem, so that they might use their influence with their rich industrialist friends. Thanks to de Mun, Social Catholicism also made its appearance in Parliament. When he was elected Deputy for Pontivy in 1891, he supported measures for legalizing trade unions; for providing relief for victims of accidents sustained in the course of employment; for limiting female and child labour to a working day of eleven hours (considered a great advance at the time); on arbitration in labour disputes.

In the Protestant countries, the Catholic social movement also played a prominent part. In England Cardinal Manning announced: 'The purpose of life is not simply to produce endless yards of cotton. Work is a social function, and not simply merchandise. The maximum hours of work and a minimum salary must be stipulated by law.' In the United States, Leo XIII gave support to the Catholic Knights of Labour, regarded by many American industrialists as a dangerous Marxist organization.

Leo XIII was known to grant audiences sparingly; but he was always prepared to receive workers' delegations. When a pilgrimage of French workers came to the Vatican in 1885, he received them in state, seated on his throne and surrounded by ten Cardinals, to demonstrate how important he considered the visit.

8

Leo XIII and the French Republic

The sufferings of the Popes in the nineteenth century were considerable. They affected 'the two Piuses', Pius VI and Pius VII, under Napoleon; and the third, Pius IX, in 1848, when he was forced to flee for his life to Gaeta. The dignity and fortitude with which these troubles were borne greatly increased the respect and affection which people all over Europe felt for the Papacy. Nowhere was this feeling deeper than in France, as if the chief instigator of modern Papal miseries, which had begun with the French Revolution, felt remorse for what she had done.

The Revolution had proclaimed that all forms of oppression, including that of the Catholic Church, would be swept away in a millennium of order, harmony and brotherly love. But these grandiloquent hopes had not been fulfilled. On the contrary, the French people had seen the promised age marked by murder and tyranny at home, and the invasion of the entire continent abroad, in the bloodiest wars that had been waged in Europe since Attila.

A consequence of this volte-face in French public opinion, was that, when between 1815 and 1870 the Popes had required material or military aid, it had been provided by France. During that period the French Catholic party – or it might be truer to say, the Catholic social hierarchy – dominated French politics. In these conservative circles, the Pope became the object of a veritable cult; after the Italian seizure of Rome in 1870, he became a martyr. French bishops headed a new 'spiritual crusade' for the liberation of the imprisoned Pope, and French priests collected thousands of signatures petitioning their Government to do something practical for His Holiness. The Catholic journal *L'Univers* asked its readers, 'Who is the Pope?' It gave the simple reply, 'He is Christ on earth.'

107

The most important French supporter of the Papacy between 1850 and 1870 was Napoleon III. During his time Rome had become almost a French city, with a French garrison at the Castel Sant'Angelo, the Antibes Legion occupying the Piazza Barberini, and the Papal Zouaves, officered by the French and Belgian aristocracy, prominent at all important official and social occasions.

After the abdication of Napoleon III and the Paris Commune of 1871, it seemed that the Revolution had returned to France. Churches and religious buildings were looted, and during the 'week of blood' at the end of May 1871, the Archbishop of Paris was murdered on the twenty-fourth, and fifty priests done to death in various ways. The Tuileries Palace was burnt down. But as so often in the past, such excesses only strengthened the Church. They sickened most Frenchmen and, after the Commune was suppressed, the ensuing governments in the 1870s were all conservative, headed by men such as Marshal MacMahon and Louis Adolphe Thiers, whose sympathies lay with the Vatican. So strong did the clerical party become in France in these years that five new Catholic universities were opened. Thiers instructed the French Ambassador at the Vatican, the Comte d'Harcourt, to take the Pope's side in all his dissensions with the Italian Government. On the twenty-fifth anniversary of Pius IX's reign, Thiers wrote him a personal letter of congratulation, referring to 'your melancholy and glorious Pontificate'. 'I can assure Your Holiness,' Thiers declared, 'that whatever political institutions France may adopt, she will preserve in the depths of her heart the highest regard and veneration for Your Holiness.' Earlier, in the summer of 1870, Thiers had offered a French frigate, the *Orénoque*, to wait in the roads off Civitavecchia to convey the Pope, should he so desire, to Corsica.[1] When Victor Emmanuel's troops occupied Rome on 20 September 1870, Thiers recalled the French Ambassador to the Italian Government on indefinite leave.

The French National Assembly which met in 1871 was predominantly Catholic and Legitimist (royalist). More than five hundred Deputies sat on the right, and less than half that number on the left. So Catholic was it, that it granted privileges to the Church which would not have been accorded even in the days of Charles X. The Papal Nuncio was consulted in the nomination of bishops, who were virtually all Vatican nominees. The Chambre (lower house) approved that prayers should be said in all the churches of

France for its good government; and it voted public credits for the great new basilica on Montmartre, the Church of the Sacré Coeur. Bishops sat on the Conseil Supérieur de l'Instruction Publique ('Superior Council of Public Instruction', dealing with education), and priests on the Committee of Public Assistance.

As for the Legitimist element, its Pretender, the Comte de Chambord, announced that one of the first acts of a restored French monarchy would be an expedition to Rome to reinstate the temporal power of the Pope – just as a thousand years before another French (or rather Frankish) King, his ancestor Pépin le Bref, had routed the Lombards besieging Rome, and re-established the Pope on his throne.[2] The sentiment that throne and altar still went hand in hand in these royalist circles, as they had immemorially, was expressed by the French Cardinal Bounechore on a visit to Rome, when he invited the Pope to come to Paris to bless the foundation stone of the Sacré Coeur. Sir Augustus Paget, the British Ambassador to the Quirinale, explained this invitation as an ingenious pretext. 'What Cardinal Bounechore and his Legitimist friends really want,' he reported, 'is that His Holiness, once in France, will be persuaded to place the crown of St Louis on the head of his descendant, the Comte de Chambord, who will take the title Henry V.[3]

Most of the French bishops were opponents of the Republic, and some like Cardinal Pie made no secret of their Legitimist sympathies. Mgr Veuillot contended that there was no salvation for France save in a monarchy, and that no form of republic could be good, because a republic would always be irreligious. The Bishop of Lucon so detested the tricolour that he had it removed from all the churches in his diocese.

What was the Papacy's attitude towards these French Legitimists? If the French Monarchy supported the restoration of the Pope's temporal power, surely the Papacy would reciprocate in favour of a restored Bourbon Monarchy? Yet this was not so. The Pope's attitude is described in a remarkable despatch from Mr Herries to Lord Derby on 26 August 1874. He reports on '. . . a long conversation I had with a member of the Diplomatic Corps who is exceptionally well informed. Contrary to what might be expected, the Pope is not well disposed towards the French Pretender, the Comte de Chambord. Although the royalist movement in France has announced that if it achieves power, it will support the re-establishment of the Pope's temporal power, the Pope believes that in the long run the Legitimists have no chance. He believes the Church must wait.'[4]

This was due primarily to certain blunders of overconfidence committed by the Comte de Chambord and his followers. They insisted, for instance, that at the coming restoration, the revolutionary tricolour flag should be removed from every town hall in France, and replaced by the white and gold fleurs de lys of the Bourbons. 'Frenchmen!' cried the Comte de Chambord, 'The King of France will never abandon the flag of Henry IV and Joan of Arc. No one shall make me consent to become the legitimate King of the *Revolution!*' This question of a flag seemed in itself of small account; but it meant a great deal to the growing body of Frenchmen who, after the humiliation of Sedan and Metz, recalled the Napoleonic glories associated with the tricolour. The Comte de Chambord was also unwise enough to identify his cause so closely with that of the Church that, for him and his followers, it was enough for a man to be a practising Catholic to be automatically a Legitimist; just as for them a Republican was automatically a freethinker. Such was the simplification that the struggle for the faith was between religion represented by the Monarchy, and irreligion represented by the Republic.

Had the Comte de Chambord shown more political flair, the Papacy might have stood behind him; but when he died prematurely in 1876 without an heir, most people in France realized that the Legitimist cause in France was lost, at least for the immediate future. Nor was the next Pretender who followed him, the Orleanist Comte de Paris from the non-Legitimist branch, an attractive royalist candidate. He was the son of that Duc d'Orléans who had described himself as 'passionate servant of the Revolution'; grandson of the Citizen King, Louis Philippe; and great-grandson of the regicide Philippe Egalité. Moreover, he had been brought up by his mother, who was a Protestant.

As for the Bonapartists, the Pope had made it clear as early as 1876 that the Papacy did not support their cause. When the ex-Empress Eugénie and her son, the Prince Imperial, visited Rome in that year, they were received after some delay by the Pope. The French Ambassador at the Vatican, the Baron de Baude, reported back to Paris; 'The Pope has been at pains today before a numerous audience to emphasize that he has informed the Empress that the

Church cannot be linked with any dynasty – nor with any specific family.'[5]

Although Pope Leo XIII had a personal preference for monarchy over republic, he did not allow this to interfere in any way with practical politics. His aim was to restore the power and prestige of the Papacy, and he believed that the Catholic Monarchists in France were more disliked by their opponents for being monarchist than for being Catholic. He also considered that there was little chance of a real union among the monarchical parties in France. Even if the Legitimists, the Orleanists and the Bonapartists were to unite for a while and overthrow the Republic, they would soon quarrel among themselves as to the nature of the restored monarchy. To the Bishop of Besançon he said, 'Because the Monarchist cause in France seems in abeyance, people who are truly religious should not adhere to it, but seek their form of government elsewhere.' He expressed himself even more strongly in a letter to the French Cardinal Lecot on 3 August 1893, in which he said that the restoration of the French monarchy could now be considered a chimera, and that any alliance with its representative would only embarrass the Church. That he did not approve of the Comte de Chambord's intransigence was clear from a remark he made after Chambord's death. The intransigence had, as was common knowledge, been much encouraged by the Count's wife. After her husband's death, this lady announced that she was about to take the veil. Leo XIII remarked drily, 'A pity she didn't take it earlier.'

Leo XIII knew that to restore the prestige and fortunes of the Papacy he required allies in Europe. Already before his accession, he had decided that the most likely friend, whatever government was in power, was France. According to the French historian Dansette, he said in 1878, when he had just become Pope, 'France needs a solid government, it doesn't matter what kind, provided it's Christian.'[6] Where elsewhere should he turn? Not to Germany, whose *Kulturkampf* was in full swing. Not to Austria, which had joined Italy in the Triple Alliance, a clause of which specifically recognized Rome as the capital of Italy. This Triple Alliance, with Prussia as the third party, was clearly directed against France. Thus France and the Vatican shared a common enemy, the new State of Italy. At the time of the signing of the Triple Alliance, Leo XIII remarked, 'As long as this Alliance lasts, Rome is guaranteed to Italy.'[7] His foreign policy was therefore directed first at establishing a close relationship with France, and then persuading France to heal her quarrel with Germany. In the longer term, he hoped thus to detach Germany from the Triple Alliance and so isolate Italy, who would then be forced by the great powers to settle the 'Roman question' in his favour. Immediately after his election, he wrote to Marshal MacMahon, then the French Premier, of 'my admiration for your noble nation, in which the Apostolic See has always found its firmest and most constant supporter'. His first Encyclical, in 1884, was significantly entitled *Nobilissima Gallorum Gens* ('The most Noble Nation of the French').

That the Italian Government was well aware of this is revealed in the Italian State Archives in an assessment of the European political situation; it refers to '. . . the marked Francophile policy of the new Pope, Leo XIII . . . a distinctive trait in Vatican policy is now a condescension towards France *which knows no bounds*.'

By a quirk of fate, and unfortunately for him, Leo XIII's attempt to come to terms with Republican France coincided with the eclipse of the Conservative pro-Papal cabinets, and the beginning of the Socialist and Radical domination of the French Parliament. Leo XIII became Pope in 1878; the last Conservative Government of Marshal MacMahon fell a year later.

Leo XIII knew that he could not come to terms with France, which was inhabited by the cleverest race in Europe, a people all thinking and reasoning individually, if the Church continued to proclaim, as his predecessor had, the Papal Infallibility, the absolute sovereignty of Catholic doctrine over all others. He intended to compromise; and the Nuncio he sent to Paris at the opening of his reign, Mgr Czacki, was ideally adapted to that task. A member of an old Polish family, he combined a lively intelligence with easy manners and knowledge of the world. It did not take Mgr Czacki long to realize that there was little immediate hope in France of a Legitimist restoration. When the Comte de Chambord learnt of the Nuncio's views, he cried despairingly, 'But I thought the Church forbade suicide!'

Not content with this, Mgr Czacki frequented Parliamentary circles and met the Republican leaders, including Gambetta. The latter was the *bête noire* of the Legitimists and the French Episcopate; it was he who had coined the expression: '*Le cléricalisme, voilà l'ennemi!*' ('Clericalism, that's the enemy!'). This did not alienate Mgr Czacki, who realized that Gambetta was the most powerful

French politician since Thiers. He accordingly cultivated him, and soon could report to Rome:

> Gambetta's intellectual culture hardly corresponds with his present powerful position. He is today, it is true, a priest-eater; but he will not be a priest-eater tomorrow. I am teaching him his Cathechism. A self-made man, he has acquired most of his political education in cafés, and he has a number of erroneous ideas about the Church. He suffers from the result of having arrived as it were by leaps and bounds, without proper preparation. But his heart is not bad; it is in the right place.[8]

That Mgr Czacki knew exactly with whom he was dealing is revealed by his comment on the Republican leaders in general: 'It is impossible to overemphasize the ignorance of these men in the French Government on religions matters. Not only do they know nothing of Christian doctrines but they cannot, so to speak, even make the sign of the Cross.'

Prominent in the new left-wing Government as Minister of Public Instruction was a Freemason called Jules Ferry. He was an intellectual and icy doctrinaire with the stamp of Saint-Just (who, under Robespierre, had proposed that boys should be separated from their parents at the age of seven and brought up by the State). Ferry was, indeed, described by the Nuncio in such terms: 'Of a most ferocious aspect, he calls to mind those creatures of the French Revolution who could send hundreds to death in a single day.' This man now drew up the first anti-clerical bill of 1879, which forbade members of the religious Orders to teach in public or private schools, or to direct educational establishments. This does not sound very drastic; but as we have already seen in Bismarck's *Kulturkampf*, lay education is the first essential of any anti-clerical campaign, for it undermines the very foundation of the Church, the religious education of youth.

In its reference to 'religious Orders' the law was directed first, as always, at the Jesuits, to whose schools the upper classes and the army families sent their sons. Ferry contended that the Jesuit schools inculcated ideas hostile to the 'modern spirit'. He charged them with ignoring the State, and taking their orders directly from Rome. His long-term aim was to expel the Jesuits entirely from France; and he quoted Voltaire, who a century before had said that to destroy the Catholic Church, it was first necessary to destroy the religious Orders, in particular the Jesuits. 'The Jesuits,' Voltaire said, 'are the advance posts, the Janissaries of Rome. Destroy them, and Rome will fall.'

The twenty-eighth of June 1880 was chosen as the day when Ferry's Education Bill was to be implemented, and the teaching Orders ejected from their schools and institutions all over France. Both parties prepared for it with almost military measures. The teaching Orders placed locks, bolts, bars, and chains on the doors and windows of their religious houses, and posted sentries outside; while the civil authorities equipped themselves with boarding-gear, scaling-ladders, axes and ropes. Almost everywhere, the public supported the Orders. At Nîmes, Solesnes, and Frigolet the population, recalling the benefits they had received from the Fathers in the past, took sides openly with them. A number of magistrates resigned rather than authorize the sequestrations, as did certain army officers, to avoid having to carry out orders. In Paris, a commission of police demanded entry to the Jesuit house in the Rue de Sèvres. When the Fathers refused and shut themselves up in their cells, the police employed locksmiths to open the doors. The Fathers were ejected into the street, where they blessed hundreds of the faithful kneeling on the ground in front of them.

One of the anti-clerical measures on which Ferry was most insistent in his bill was the emancipation of women from clerical education. He regarded the influence of the Church on the female as even more baneful than on the male. For here the Church was fully entrenched. As early as 1860 Catholicism had renounced its claim to be the *exclusive* source of education for boys; but it still retained it for girls. Ferry was well aware that there was more to this than simply the question of the girls acquiring a lay education, for he said, 'He who holds the female holds everything. She can make life intolerable for the husband, if he flouts a religion in which she believes. That is why the Catholic Church is so zealous in keeping her for itself. And it is precisely for this reason that democracy must wean women from Religion.' That she could make 'life intolerable for the husband' was demonstrated in the domesticities of his friend, Edmond Jaurès. When taken to task by a fellow Socialist for allowing his daughter to attend First Communion, Jaurès pleaded the harmony of the hearth. 'My friend,' he said, '*You* can no doubt do what you like with your wife. *I* – no!'

With a large majority in the Chambre, the Socialists and Radicals now set about exterminating religion entirely from the school-rooms. The crucifix which had hung above the blackboard was replaced by the 'Republic', a device bearing the figure of Voltaire lifting up a drapery covered with masonic symbols depicting the victory of Truth over Superstition and Ignorance. The latter were represented by two monks being strangled with a silken cord. The Catechism was replaced in the schools by the French State Instruction Manual.

The Socialists discovered, however, that the Church in France was, as it had been in Napoleon's day, extremely resilient. The priests were perfectly capable of giving as good as they got. They visited private houses and instructed parents not to allow their children to attend the lay schools. They warned them that voting for any Republican candidate in the national elections was a mortal sin. On this subject, a Jesuit priest in Lourdes expressed himself eloquently, 'Take the sword!' he cried to his congregation, 'the electoral sword which cleaves the good from the bad! In the next elections, there will be only two candidates – Jesus Christ and Barabbas. Do you intend to vote for Barabbas?' A number of French bishops directed that the sacraments were to be withheld from all teachers, parents and pupils who used the French State Instruction Manual. In some places the *curés* made a public bonfire of these manuals.

Had the Education Laws been imposed during the reign of Pius IX, his fulminations would have descended in all their fury on the French Government; and the French bishops now awaited such a condemnation from Leo XIII. It did not come. On the advice of Mgr Czacki, his Nuncio in Paris, Leo XIII had come to the conclusion that open opposition to the French Republic would only worsen the situation for the Church. He therefore did not oppose the suppression of the Jesuit schools. To Mgr Lavigerie he said, 'The Jesuits are, I fear, lost for the time being. So let us concentrate on saving the others.' It was the beginning of his policy, later to be known as *le Ralliement*, in which he instructed French Catholics to 'rally' to the support of the French Republic. This proved extremely difficult for many prelates, inveterate enemies of that Republic, to stomach. When the Superior of the Assumptionists, Father d'Azon, was told of the Pope's decision, tears came into his eyes. 'So, I have to break with all my past! With tradition and all my friends! But if that is the Holy Father's will – so be it!'

Leo XIII then took the unprecedented step of giving a press interview on the subject (unprecedented in that, whereas in our own times it is perfectly normal for heads of State to announce their policy through press interviews, it was then unheard of, particularly for a Pope). Moreover, he did not give the interview to one of the more reputable papers, but to a popular Parisian, *Le Petit Journal*, claiming to be 'the most widely read newspaper in the world'. By this means his policy of '*Ralliement* to the French Republic' reached a far greater audience than it would have if announced in the normal way through an Encyclical.

In his interview with *Le Petit Journal* (17 February 1892) Leo XIII drew a parallel between the present Government in France and that of the United States of America:

I am of the opinion that all French citizens should unite in supporting the government France has given herself. A republic is as legitimate a form of government as any other. Look at the United States of America! There you have a Republic which grows stronger every day – and that in spite of unbridled liberty. And the Catholic Church there? It develops and flourishes. It has no quarrel with the State. What is good for the United States can be good for France too.

In this interview he urged French Catholics to co-operate with authorities, making his famous distinction between, on the one hand, constituted authority which, being ordained by God, was good and must be respected; and, on the other hand, bad *legislation* emanating from that authority, which it was the duty of Catholics to oppose and modify. If legislation was bad, he said, Catholics should unite and, by using all legal means, change that legislation. 'Catholics do not lack the means,' he said, 'on the electoral and political platform for obtaining the reform of bad laws.' These views were later more formerly expressed in his Encyclical *Diuturnum Illud* ('The long-lived Entity'), announcing that the Church recognized all forms of constituted government, monarchy, empire, dictatorship, republic – but with the clear proviso: 'The peoples may give themselves whatever political form is best adapted to their genius, tradition and customs. The Church does not condemn the *form* of government. What it does condemn are unjust laws passed by governments which violate Divine and natural laws. When the French Government passes laws repudiating the religious cult, we condemn them.'

Here Leo XIII was only following an established principle of Church policy. Throughout history, the Catholic Church has always adapted itself to whatever form of socety prevailed, to serfdom at the opening of the millennium, to feudalism in the Middle Ages; to centralized monarchy after 1600; in modern times, to bourgeois capitalism, and in this case to French Republicanism. When the laws of any of these societies are at variance with the tenets of the Catholic faith, the Church does not attempt to destroy the society, but to *transform* it, by continuous internal action. For example, the Church was by no means opposed to serfdom, when that system was the accepted form of society; but the Church continually preached its conception of Christian living within that society, thereby mitigating its more objectionable features.

The French Monarchists and the Conservatives were naturally incensed by this attitude, which they regarded as a piece of Papal juggling. 'The Pope is badly informed about France,' wrote their journal, *L'Autorité*. 'Political affairs do not come within the Pope's province,' wrote another, the *Gazette de France*. The Monarchical publicist, Édouard Drumont, went further. 'Where today,' he cried, 'can we find those French cavaliers like Nogaret capable of donning the iron glove in the face of Boniface VIII?'[9] The Monarchists asserted that the Pope had been duped by the Nuncio in Paris, Mgr Czacki, who hobnobbed with the Republican politicians. They also attacked the Papal Secretary of State, Cardinal Rampolla, well known for his *Ralliement* sympathies; in Faubourg circles he was described as '*cette canaille*'. Prominent Catholic politicians such as the Comte de Mun, who had followed Leo XIII's ruling and 'rallied' to the Republic, were ostracized by their own class.

It should not be supposed however that Leo XIII made no objection to the anti–clerical and education measures *as such*. He made it perfectly clear that if these laws were not repealed, or at least attenuated, the Papacy would revise its attitude towards the *Ralliement*. The new Education Law, he said, 'goes far beyond any possible definition of State neutrality in religious matters. What it amounts to is that every teacher is permitted – except the Catholic Church.'

In his policy of *Ralliement*, Leo XIII was supported whole-heartedly by his Secretary of State, Cardinal Rampolla. After 1888, when Italy joined the Triple Alliance (which was directed primarily against France, and which contained a clause recognizing Rome as the capital of Italy), Rampolla's sympathies lay unreservedly with France. He was the greatest Secretary of State since Consalvi,[10] possessing knowledge of men, adroitness, learning, and political insight. Beneath his calm and frigid exterior burned the fire of religious fanaticism, and he was said by the Italians to wear a hair-shirt. He became the *bête noire* of the Italian Government, and its State Archives for the years during his secretaryship from 1885 to the death of Leo XIII in 1903, are full of invective against him: for example, 'This tall and bigoted Sicilian who is extremely pious, who wears the hair shirt beneath the purple robe, who works sixteen hours a day for his master . . . he is as precious to Leo XIII as Berthier was to Napoleon.'[11]

A later memorandum in the Italian State Archives on Rampolla's foreign policy commented bitterly on '. . . the present Francophile attitude of Cardinal Rampolla who, now that the Pope is over ninety, has taken complete control. He exhibits a condescension towards France which knows no bounds. . . .' The writer refers to Rampolla's 'hypocritical affection for a Republican Government which can hardly be called one of *curés*'.[12] In the stronger words of the Italian Ambassador in Paris, 'There is something repulsive in the spectacle of the Pope's Secretary of State flirting with a pack of French atheists.'[13] Another Italian State report expressed repugnance that Rampolla should have 'accepted with effusive thanks, from the last batch of French pilgrims to the Vatican, a medallion they had struck to commemorate their visit – on one side of which was represented the Pope wearing his tiara, and on the other *La France Républicaine* wearing her Phrygian bonnet!'[14] The Italian Government's antipathy towards Rampolla is also expressed in an extraordinary allegation that he is an, 'outright Republican'. A report in the Farnesina files states that he had threatened that if the Crown of Italy did not restore the temporal power of the Pope, the Church would throw its weight in favour of a Republic in Italy, and repudiate the Monarchy: 'Such is the admiration which Rampolla has for the Republican form of government – as seen in his beloved France.'[15]

At this point in Leo XIII's conciliatory approach to the French Republic an incident occurred in Rome which was trivial, even ludicrous, in itself, but which had international repercussions. In September 1891, the French Catholics mounted a pilgrimage to Rome which included some ten thousand members of the Catholic Workers' Association, together with various Catholic Youth organizations. Among them were a number of devoted admirers of the late Pius IX. Most of them arrived in Rome on the anniversary of the Italian seizure of the city (20 September), and then proceeded immediately to the Vatican, a fact which was considered something of an insult by Italian patriots. But worse was to follow. On this historic date, hundreds of eminent Italians had gathered in the Pantheon to do homage at the tomb of 'the father of Italian Unity', King Victor Emmanuel II, by signing their names in the Book of Honour. While they were thus engaged, a score or so of the newly arrived French pilgrims entered. It was assumed that they, too, had come to write their names. Instead, they wrote in the book a number of anti-Italian slogans, including 'Death to the King of Italy!' and 'Long live the Pope-King! [il Papa Re]'.[16] The authorities immediately ordered them to leave, but they only began shouting these slogans. Mr Dering, the British Minister, wrote in his despatch, 'Words even more insulting to Italian national feeling were pronounced, and I understand that some of the French pilgrims spat on the tomb of the King.'[17] A number were arrested. The others returned to their hotels in carriages, besieged by the Roman mob, shrieking 'Down with France!' 'Long live the House of Savoy!' 'Down with the Pope!', etc.

That evening a patriotic demonstration of some twenty thousand Romans took place in the Piazza Colonna, where a vote of loyalty to the King of Italy was passed. The more unruly elements called for a march on the Vatican, shouting that the Pope had encouraged the behaviour of the French pilgrims. Being turned back at the Borgo, they proceeded to the French Embassy in the Piazza Farnese, where they threw stones, broke a number of windows, and burnt the Pope in effigy. They spent the rest of the evening marching about the streets with a brass band playing the 'Garibaldi March'. Mr Dering concluded his report: 'The news of the Pantheon demonstration has quickly become known throughout Italy. Anti-French and anti-Papal demonstrations are being held everywhere. Thus a somewhat insignificant incident has caused a

119

great deal of excitement in this emotional people. It is bound to produce a public reaction in favour of those Italian politicians who are always inveighing against Leo XIII's pro-French policy.'

This proved to be the case; and as he forecast, it was not the end of the affair. The French pilgrims had a stormy passage home along the Mediterranean coast. Demonstrations were waiting for them all along the railway line, at Pisa, Chiavari, Sestri, with cries of 'Death to the Pope!' 'Long live Sedan!' 'Down with the temporal power!'[18] In Paris M. Fallières, the Minister for Justice and Cults, sent a circular to the French bishops suggesting that, after this incident, all pilgrimages to Rome should be suspended, for they 'can easily lose their religious character, and cause breaches of the peace'.[19] Although mildly worded the circular was perhaps clumsy, because it could be construed as placing responsibility for the incident on the French episcopate. Most of them accepted the suggestion; but not the Archbishop of Aix, Mgr Gouthe-Soulard, who replied to M. Fallières, 'We do not require your instructions. We decide such matters on our own, and have already suspended the pilgrimages. When they start again is our affair. It will depend entirely on the interests of my diocese. You talk of "breach of the peace". Peace is on your lips, but persecution and hatred are in your hearts. For Freemasonry, the eldest daughter of Satan, governs and dominates you.' As this letter was widely published in the press, M. Fallières had to defend himself by going to law against 'this flagrant libel on a Government Minister exercising his legal functions'. This incident and its international repercussions brought Leo XIII to such a state of despair that he seriously considered leaving Rome.[20]

In the latter part of his Pontificate, Leo XIII's policy of *Ralliement* to the French Republic was further impaired by two episodes of French domestic history which, properly, should not have concerned the Church at all – the Boulanger and Dreyfus affairs.

In 1886 General Boulanger was Minister of War in the Freycinet Cabinet. He had distinguished himself in the Tunis expedition; but apart from this, his only qualifications appear to have been his military bearing, a certain *panache*, and a popular song which had been composed about him. The French were now becoming tired of the frequent changes of government in the Third Republic – eight in fifteen years – and, when Boulanger founded a party which he called, significantly, the League of Patriots, he became almost overnight a popular hero. He demanded a return to authoritative government, if not as under Napoleon I, at least as under Napoleon III. The Monarchist and Conservative forces under the Orleanist Pretender, the Comte de Paris, saw in General Boulanger a force to overthrow the Republic, and pave the way for a return to an Orleanist monarchy – a French General Monk. They supported him liberally with funds. Unfortunately for the Church, General Boulanger now made overtures to the Papacy, assuring Leo XIII: 'When I hold the sword of France, I shall recognize the rights of the Church.' This was taken to mean restoration of the Pope's temporal power. So popular did Boulanger become that throughout France revisionist committees sprang up, and the land was covered with posters bearing the name of the new 'saviour of the country'. Boulanger also expressed a desire for revenge against Prussia, which increased his popularity among a people tired of the pacificism of the Third Republic.[21] In the frenzied period of 1888-9, political parties in France appeared to be reduced to two, Boulangist and anti-Boulangist, insulting one another in public and taking their war-cries from popular songs. In the Paris by-elections of 1889, Boulanger won a resounding victory, and he seemed destined for supreme power. At this point a number of French bishops came out openly in his favour, and their priests engaged in propaganda on his behalf. It seemed that, as was said in former days, *le sabre et le goupillon* (the sabre and the holy-water sprinkler) were held by the same hands.

Leo XIII thought otherwise. He refused the overtures of both the Boulangist Monarchists and the Boulangist bishops, who were expecting a proclamation of Papal support. His judgement proved sound, for the Boulanger bubble burst as quickly as it had grown. Had Boulanger marched on the Elysée immediately after his Parisian electoral success, he might have obtained power. But at the decisive moment he hesitated, and three days later when he gave the order to move, it was too late. The Government had acted with unusual promptitude. It had outlawed his League of Patriots whose members, when ordered to disband, wavered like their leader, and then complied. The Government ordered Boulanger's immediate arrest, but he had fled the country – which was exactly what the Government wanted. A few months later he committed suicide in Brussels.

This short *opéra comique* episode had a disastrous effect on the Monarchist cause, on account of the backing it had given to

Boulanger. It also seriously retarded Leo XIII's *Ralliement* policy, owing to the support given to it by the French clergy. It took some years for Leo XIII to regain the lost ground in France, and by then the French Socialists and Radicals were firmly in the saddle.

Leo XIII might well have felt that Providence did not bless his *Ralliement* policy: for the *Affaire Dreyfus* which followed closely on the Boulanger episode was even more damaging to the Church. Here again, the Church should not have become involved in what was really another aspect of the Monarchist–Republican struggle. But it so happened – entirely by chance – that while the friends of the Church were anti-Dreyfusards, the enemies of the Church were Dreyfusard. The former included a large section of the aristocracy and the Académie française, the army, and the more *bien pensante* bourgeoisie; while the latter comprised all shades of socialists and freethinkers, the university professors, the Jews, the Protestants and the lower middle classes. The struggle thus added to class bitterness, which again should not have concerned the Church. The army officers came from the upper classes, while the socialists and university intellectuals were mostly *petits bourgeois*. The provincial professors in their tight-fitting black tail coats felt a grudge against the military caste which ignored them. Thus to be a Dreyfusard – that is a person demanding a revision of Dreyfus's trial – was, to oversimplify greatly, to be Republican, lower middle class and anti-clerical; while to be an anti-Dreyfusard, was to be Royalist, upper class and Catholic.

This is not the place to analyse the ramifications of the Dreyfus affair – only to assess how the Church became involved in it. In December 1898, a Parisian Conservative newspaper, *La Libre Parole*, opened a subscription list on behalf of the widow of Lieutenant-Colonel Henri, the officer who had allegedly forged the documents incriminating Dreyfus, and who had since committed suicide. She contended that her husband's name had been besmirched and libelled by a Jew, Joseph Reinach, whom she intended to sue. Again, this had nothing to do with the Church; but some three hundred secular priests and thirty regulars unwisely answered her appeal. Had they simply sent the money, nothing more would probably have been heard of them; but several of them openly announced their sympathy with the widow and her late husband. The Abbé Cros announced that Dreyfus, who was now in prison on Devil's Island, should be 'trampled on morning and night'. A young priest wrote to a newspaper that 'The Jew Reinach should have his nose bashed in.' Three curés wrote that they would like 'to get our thirty thumbs and fingers round the dirty neck of the Jew Reinach'. A member of the clerical hierarchy, the Archbishop of Toulouse, referred to the proposed Dreyfus retrial as 'this attempt to rehabilitate a traitor'. The Assumptionist paper *La Croix* entered the fray on behalf of Lieutenant-Colonel Henri and the anti-Semites. Its editor, Père Bailley, wrote, 'In the dock today with Dreyfus stand all the freethinkers, Jews, Freemasons, Protestants and enemies of the Church. . . . Against such people it is the duty of the Army to open fire.' Unwisest of all was the Roman Jesuit journal *Civiltà Cattolica* which, most uncharacteristically, wrote: 'The Jew was created by God to act the traitor everywhere.' The paper added that the French nation must regret the Act of 1791 which had granted French nationality to Jews, because the Jews were now obtaining financial aid for reopening the Dreyfus trial from France's enemy, Germany.

These clerics and journals represented only an inconsiderable proportion of French Catholic opinion, but their statements, and many like them, were given great prominence in the socialist press. In the *Dépêche de Toulouse* Georges Clemenceau wrote, 'Now we see who leads the campaign against the Jews! It is the whole Jesuit clan!' Georges Sorel wrote, 'The Dreyfus affair has caused divisions in every social class. But not among the Catholics! The whole Catholic world has marched as one man against Dreyfus and the revision of his trial.'

As is known, the Dreyfusards were triumphant when, on 20 June 1899, at the retrial Dreyfus was found not guilty, and was rehabilitated and his army commission restored. That day in France signified the humiliation not only of the army and the Royalists, but also of the Church. But owing to the hardening of attitudes among the extremists of both wings, the Ultramontane clergy and their sympathizers on the one hand, and the radical socialists on the other, Leo XIII's policy of *Ralliement* was so weakened after the Dreyfus affair that it failed to extenuate the extreme policies of the violently anti-clerical Waldeck-Rousseau and Combes governments which took office. Their Association Laws of 1901 were even more Draconian than those of Ferry. Finally, in 1905, they were able to break entirely with Rome, and complete the separation of Church and State.

Leo XIII seemed to have failed in France. With his *Ralliement*, he had envisaged a Republican Party combining both Catholics and moderates, which would reconcile Church and State. This had not occurred. The moderate Republicans, frightened by the royalists and such incidents as the Boulanger and Dreyfus affairs, moved ever closer to the Socialists and Radicals, thereby ensuring the anti-clerical coalitions of the years 1900-22. The *Ralliement* might have succeeded in Leo XIII's lifetime, had there not been ranged against it most of the French bishops, the two extremely powerful religious Congregations of the Assumptionists and the Jesuits, and all the royalist-Catholic elements; men who were, in short, more in sympathy with the ideas of Pius IX than with those of Leo XIII.

But did he really fail? There are, in the words of Montaigne, 'Triumphant defeats which are often worth more than Pyrrhic victories.' In 1925, two decades after Leo XIII's death, the French Socialists and Radicals had to admit the failure of their attempt to eradicate the Catholic religion from France, and the Third Republic was obliged to come cap in hand to the Pope, and request the re-establishment of diplomatic relations. The Catholic Church became again the official Church of France, and nearly all the anti-clerical legislation was dismantled. It was the story of the *Kulturkampf* all over again, a generation later. However, this was still far in the future.

9

The American Crucible

The English colony of Maryland was founded in the seventeenth
century as a political haven for Catholics who had been driven out
of England by a persecution so bitter that they had even been
deprived of the right to dispose of their own property by sale or
will. In 1632, the Irish Catholic peer Lord Baltimore, who had
emigrated there with one priest and some two hundred families,
obtained the concession of the territory which he named 'Land of
Mary' in honour of Henrietta Maria, the Catholic wife of Charles I.
Here, then, in the early days was a small Catholic island surrounded
by a sea of Protestants. In those colonial times under the rule of
Protestant England, the Catholics in the rest of the thirteen colonies
became a beleaguered minority, at once feared and despised,
repressed with cruelty only a little less than in the mother country.
A few English, Irish and German Catholics penetrated into the
Protestant centres, but not many survived the repressive measures.
In 1700, there were only seven Catholic families in New York.

Until independence was wrested from England in the last quarter
of the eighteenth century, Catholics were disenfranchised,
excluded from public life, forbidden to teach in schools, and
hampered in conducting religious services. The only Protestant
state in which they enjoyed any degree of toleration was the Quaker
colony of Pennsylvania. At the time of the Declaration of
Independence in 1776, they numbered thirty thousand, with
twenty-six priests. Almost to a man they fought on the side of
Washington and, when the war was won, they received their
reward. For with victory came the proud tradition of religious
tolerance enshrined in the new American Constitution, Article 6 of
which states: 'No account shall be taken of the *quality* of religion
professed by any individual, when applying for employment or
public office.' Henceforth in the new United States of America, all

religious creeds and forms of worship were to be permitted. This religious toleration has continually surprised Europeans. Even as late as 1910, the Italian Ambassador in Washington expressed his amazement that 'At a banquet offered by Cardinal Gibbons, I saw sitting up at the high table with him and President Taft – a Protestant bishop and a rabbi! All apparently in perfect harmony.'[1]

The great increase in the Catholic population of the United States took place, understandably, after independence. Then, a decade later, came the French Revolution, when thousands of Catholics found a haven there. After that, the nineteenth century saw Catholic immigration from almost every part of Europe, in particular from Italy, Germany and Ireland. So great was this immigration that the predominantly Protestant population of America felt itself threatned; because the Catholic immigrants, mostly from the European lower classes, were prepared to work for low pay. In the mid nineteenth century The New York Protestant Association organized public meetings revealing 'the true character of Popery'; and anti-Catholic journals such as *The Protestant Magazine* and *The Anti-Romanist* were founded. These made a certain headway, but in a fundamentally tolerant society there could never be religious persecution as there was in Europe.

Leo XIII was the first Pope to appreciate the potential importance of the United States to the Catholic cause. In 1886, eight years after his accession, he sent a special legate, Mgr Germano Straniero, to make a detailed study of Catholicism in the North American continent. He realized that these ten million Catholics, most of them devout and rapidly increasing in number, could become a Catholic community of the first importance. Mgr Straniero's detailed report is in the Vatican Archives where, since February 1979, it has been available for consultation.[2] He treated the Catholics in America according to their various ethnic groups, starting with his own countrymen, the Italians. Numerically, he reported, the Italians were by far the biggest foreign Catholic element in the States, hundreds of thousands, most of whom had taken part in the Carbonari and other revolts against the Papal authority in the years 1830, 1848, and 1859. Most of them came from the lowest, often the criminal, classes of southern Italy and Sicily, and were the least religious of all the Catholic ethnic groups. He referred to '. . . the insatiable appetite of the Italian Catholic community for lucre. It makes them forget all else.' He made a sharp distinction between the Italians and the other groups, Germans, Irish, Poles, French; for whereas these latter all came generally to settle in America, the Italians came to make a quick fortune and return home. 'The Italian Catholics thus have,' he said, 'little reason for contributing to the prosperity and well-being of the developing continent.' Here his words have been confirmed by the American Catholic historian, Henry Brann, who described the Italian Catholic immigrants in the United States as 'more familiar with the assassin's knife than with the Cathechism'.[3] 'Moreover,' added the Papal Legate, 'the Italian priests who have accompanied these immigrants – in theory to minister to their spiritual needs – have mostly been suspended from their dioceses in Italy, and taken refuge in America for reasons which are anything but holy.'

The only part of the United States where any considerable Italian settlement took place was, as might be expected with persons of Sicilian and southern Italian extraction, the far South, particularly in Louisiana. That these Italians were more respectable and God-fearing was revealed at this time (1886) by the visit of the Italian prelate, Mgr Martinelli, to report on the situation in New Orleans.[4] But it led to a most unfortunate incident.

As he was Italian, it was natural that the local Italian language paper *Picayone* should ask for an interview with him. He readily agreed, and the paper sent one of its lady journalists, a Miss L. Points. Among other questions she asked him was what was his opinion of his Catholic compatriots who had emigrated to the United States. He gave his opinion, and the next day she reported him as saying, 'The Italian immigrants here are the dregs of American society. They came solely for the dollars, to make a fortune and go home as soon as possible. Some of them are even criminals and *banditti*.'

The next morning Mgr Martinelli – who had not yet read this report in the paper – said Mass in the church of St Anthony, the principal Catholic church of New Orleans, in the heart of the Italian quarter. After the service, he was informed that an Italian delegation was waiting on him in the sacristy. He said he would be delighted to meet them – only to be greeted when he entered the room by the scowling countenances of some twenty-five men, who demanded point-blank that he should retract what he had said about the Italian immigrants. This he refused to do – for the simple reason that what he had said was not what had been reported.

What had happened at the press interview was that the lady journalist had asked him, among other questions, what was his opinion of the education of women in Italy. She said the general impression in New Orleans was that Italian women lacked education. Mgr Martinelli had replied that this was not true at all; women in Italy went to school and attended lectures, some even gave lectures themselves. They were well educated. It was now that the misrepresentation took place. He went on to suggest, politely, that she had perhaps formed her impression about female education in Italy from the Italian women who had emigrated to the United States. He said it would not be fair to judge the ladies of Italy from those who immigrated here, as the latter were nearly all members of the lower or working classes. This was perfectly true. But unfortunately the lady journalist travestied and embroidered his words, including this offensive 'criminals and *banditti*', which he had not used.

Naturally the Apostolic Delegate, not knowing this, refused to retract what he had said about Italian womanhood. Whereupon the Italians in the sacristy became abusive and violent, threatening him and shaking their fists. After receiving a blow, he had to beat a hasty retreat, to find outside a large and vociferous mob waiting for him. They followed him down the street baying for his blood.

He managed to reach the haven of the house where he was staying, that of the local Bishop, Mgr Janssens. The Bishop had seen the report in the paper, and he gave the Papal Legate a lecture on the exemplary nature of the Italian colony in New Orleans, implying that the Pope had no business to send such an irresponsible representative to make his work more difficult. 'On the contrary,' the Bishop said. 'our Italians in New Orleans are sober, industrious, good fathers and obedient sons. And as for the womenfolk, their wives and daughters are remarkable not only for their piety, but for their purity. . . . They are good Catholics and they venerate the sovereign Pontiff of whom you, most reverend Excellency, are the representative.'

That afternoon more Italians came to the Bishop's house, this time carrying copies of the offending article. When Mgr Martinelli read it, he was appalled, and insisted that he had said nothing of the kind. He had only used the words 'poor people' in connection with the Italians because he had every sympathy with them. Bishop Janssens now suggested that the best way to make amends would be to address these people in terms of eulogy. And this the Apostolic Delegate immediately did. He told them he had heard about them from their Bishop, and this was exactly what he had expected from his own knowledge of their sturdy character. Although many of them were poor as far as the goods of this world were concerned they had, he said, what was better than riches, their Catholic faith. 'Wealth,' he said, 'is not everything. But I am glad to learn that you are striving to improve your material condition. I pray to Our Heavenly Father that you may prosper in worldly goods.'

It appears that the incident was not closed until Miss Points admitted that her reporting had not been all that it should be. She apologized, and her apology was printed in the newspaper, together with the Apostolic Delegate's glowing tribute to the Italians of New Orleans. All was forgiven and the incident closed. Nevertheless, the very fact that it had taken place revealed how sensitive were members of the Italian Catholic colony about their bad reputation in the United States.

The next numerically important Catholic group after the Italians was the Irish, who emigrated after the potato famines of the late 1840s. They arrived in large steamers accompanied by flocks of priests.[5] The Papal Legate, Mgr Straniero, reported, 'They distinguish themselves, together with the Germans, among the Catholic ethnic groups in this country by the tenacity of their faith.' He speaks very favourably of their devoutness, but then makes this qualification: 'In the United States there is one terrible abuse, worse perhaps than in the northern cities of Europe – that of spiritous liquors. More than any other class the workman, particularly the Irish workman, drinks every Saturday evening his entire weekly earnings. All who have the welfare of the unfortunate worker at heart, and of the Irish Catholics in particular, are aware of the need to discover a means of removing this temptation from them.'

For this reason, he acclaimed the recent foundation of the Catholic League of the Cross which – though this was not apparent from its name – was concerned almost exclusively with Irish intemperance. While on the subject, Mgr Straniero had a sharp word for an Irish prelate, Mgr Caspel, who '. . . sets an extraordinarily bad example. I shall limit myself to saying that on account of this abuse of alcohol, he has been suspended by his Archbishop. He is now living in a house in San Francisco with a Protestant woman who has been separated from her husband. It is said that the Protestants are hoping to inveigle him into joining their camp. Such are the fruits of intemperance.'

There was a further aspect of the Irish Catholic immigration to America which concerned not America but the motherland itself – the influence which the Irish who had settled in the United States exercised on the land of their origin. In the Vatican Secret Archives is a report by the Papal Legate, Mgr Persico, whom Leo XIII sent in 1888 to Ireland to report on the 'troubles' there.[6] It is concerned largely with Anglo-Irish Catholic relations, but there is a section on the influence of America on the explosive Irish situation. The Legate deprecated the influence of America in Irish affairs, on account of their 'socialistic bias'. He wrote:

> The excessive liberty in the United States, as well as its anti-social and revolutionary principles, constitutes a continuous and very potent incentive to the Irish, who maintain close and intimate relations with the American people. The Irish immigrants in the United States have absorbed the revolutionary and socialist spirit of North America, and communicate it back to their relatives at home. America forms the most important recruitment centre for the Fenian movement, whose emissaries are despatched to Ireland to foster violence. The American Irish send back large sums of money to build churches and alleviate the lot of the poor; but a large part of it, I fear, finds its way into the pockets of the Fenians and Home Rulers.

It is well here to recall that the United States, regarded today as the bastion of conservatism was, only a hundred years ago, considered almost revolutionary, its republicanism in sharp contrast with the monarchical regimes of Europe.

In spite of his strictures on the Italian Catholics, Mgr Straniero's overall picture of the Catholic community in America at the end of the nineteenth century was favourable. He explained that the future prospects for Catholicism in America were bright – for a somewhat unusual reason. Numerically, the Catholics were the largest of all the religious groups, in a country which was eighty-five per cent Protestant – but whose Protestants were divided into a host of sects, some fifty of them. He enumerated these sects meticulously but with, one suspects, his tongue in his cheek. First came the Baptists, with two million souls; then the Episcopalian Methodists, with one million; then the Non-Episcopalian Methodists, with 300,000; then the Southern Episcopalian Methodists, with 800,000. The Congregationalists, he said, had 300,000; the Presbyterians 500,000; the Lutherans 600,000; the Brothers in Christ 150,000. There were also the Mormons with 110,000; the Quakers and another thirty-eight smaller sects numbering in all some 150,000 souls. 'If all these Protestants were to unite,' he wrote, 'they would completely swamp the Catholics. But they all bicker among themselves. We thus see that the Roman Catholic faith is the largest and most powerful individual religious community, with four times as many faithful as in the largest of the Protestant sects. It is also a most efficient organization, a quality to which great consideration is accorded in America. *For Americans admire efficiency above all else.*'

The steadily increasing growth of Catholicism in the United States was confirmed by the French Ambassador in Washington, M. Jules Cambon. He made a significant comment about the nature of American Catholicism as contrasted with Catholicism in Europe. 'Since my predecessor's last despatch on the subject in 1892,' he wrote in 1898, 'the number of Catholics here has much increased; at present just under ten million. Bearing in mind that religious sentiments are not the same in this country as they often are in Europe, *of outward appearance only*, this is a considerable figure. Catholics in the United States – particularly in respect of the indissolubility of the marriage bond – are of a severity in doctrine and practice which puts them in a class apart.'[7]

He added that this growing power of the Catholic Church had so perturbed the Protestants that they had formed an American Protective Association (A.P.A.) to combat it, and to oppose all nominations of Catholics to high office in the State. But in this last design, he said, they had not succeeded. In spite of their vigorous opposition, Mr McKenna, a practising Catholic, had just been nominated to the nine-man Supreme Court, the most august body in the land. This appointment was made by the President of the United States, Mr McKinley, because '. . . although religion and politics are theoretically strictly segregated in the United States, religion exercises a great influence over the public mind; Mr McKinley has certainly not forgotten that most Catholics, among them the notorious Archbishop of St Paul, Mgr Ireland, supported most actively his candidature for the Presidency in the last elections.'

131

On the subject of 'the notorious Archbishop of St Paul', Mgr Straniero had this to say: 'Archbishop Ireland perfectly understands the American admiration for efficiency. He is one of the greatest exponents in the Catholic hierarchy of the example of "Martha rather than Mary", of active rather than contemplative religion. Archbishop Ireland has advised his flock to stop regarding money as something evil, and to set about acquiring it. His words to a Catholic congress in St Louis last week were, "It is energy and enterprise that win everywhere. They win in politics, they win in business, they will win in religion." ' Although the Papal Legate had related this without criticism, there is an underlying disapproval in his comment.

This American attitude towards religion was even more emphatically expounded by a certain Miss M. T. Elder, a devout Catholic lady who preached 'the Gospel of Wealth'. She pointed out to American Catholics that the three men Christ restored to life were all rich; and that it had required the funds of a rich man to give Christ a proper burial. She deplored the relatively small number of rich American Catholics. 'Most Catholics here are poor, ' she said, 'not from love of holy poverty – but from aversion to holy industry.' She therefore recommended this prayer to Catholics: 'Oh Lord, give me good sense! Give me hard, practical, everyday gumption! If I had a little of that, I shouldn't make such a fool of myself, and might make money with which to help the Church.'[8]

On the subject of wealth among the Catholics, Mgr Straniero also made a revealing comment in his report on 'The Social Status of Catholics in America'. 'The Catholics come mostly from the European poorer classes,' he says, 'so it is generally considered that a Protestant who marries a Catholic lowers him or herself. In general, these mixed marriages are unsatisfactory. But an exception must be made in the case of southern States like Louisiana, or St Louis, Missouri, where the reverse is generally the case. They have an organized French Catholic population, many of whose families belong to a higher and richer stratum. So here, Protestants by marrying Catholics often improve themselves. They often become Catholic for this reason. Here is an area where our efforts may well be directed.'

With every year of Leo XIII's reign relations between the Vatican and the United States improved. For the Pope's silver jubilee, President Cleveland sent him a luxuriously bound copy of the

American Constitution.[9] This curious gift, which in other times might have appeared almost an affront, was received by the Pope with every expression of pleasure. In his dealings with France, Leo XIII had already shown that he fully understood republicanism and constitutional government as practised there, as well as in the United States. In 1893, he appointed the first Apostolic Delegate in history to the U.S.A.

The only incident which ruffled Papal relations with the United States occurred when ex-President Theodore Roosevelt visited Rome. He committed the solecism of first giving a lecture at the Methodist Church in the Via Venti Settembre, and then requesting an audience with the Pope. The Italian Methodists had been vociferously abusing the Pope, as 'The Harlot of Babylon', 'Anti-Christ', 'the new Lucifer', etc. To make matters worse, Roosevelt also took part in a Masonic ceremony, in which he was invested with one of its Orders. In these circumstances, the Pope could hardly receive him, and an excuse was found for refusing the audience.

How did the Americans regard the Papacy in the last decades of the nineteenth century? A fundamentally Protestant and egalitarian nation, the Americans still believe deep in their hearts that the Pope should not live in a palace, keep up a court and be surrounded with pomp and circumstance; but rather go about the world with staff and scrip, and preach at street corners. In spite of this evangelical approach, the Americans at this time showed a much greater interest in, and esteem for, the Pope than did most Europeans. The Italian Ambassador in Washington commented indignantly on this:

> It is due to the fascination which the antiquated and pompous ceremonial of an ancient court *sui generis* can exercise on a new people. The Americans are more interested in the nomination of a Cardinal than in that of an Italian Prime Minister. The news in the American press about Rome is seldom about the modern Italy of Victor Emmanuel II, and its unification, but about the Pope and his Court. When foreign monarchs or delegations visit Rome on official occasions, the reports in the American press are not about receptions given for them at the Quirinale, but about those at the Vatican.[10]

He explained this as '. . . largely due, I fear, to the Vatican habit of bestowing titles of nobility on rich Americans who help the Church financially. Because they have no aristocracy, the Americans are particularly susceptible to this form of flattery.' He added bitterly, 'The rich Protestant Mellon of Philadelphia has just been made a Papal Marquess.'[11]

To American Government circles, the Catholics became with every year that passed more important electorally. It was simply a question of numbers. In 1870, there were three and a half million Catholics in America; by 1914, there were sixteen million. By the latter date, the city of Boston, which had once been exclusively Protestant, had become seventy-five per cent Catholic. The Italian Ambassador reported in 1903 that the American President was taking the greatest interest in the Catholic community '. . . because election time is approaching, and there are ten million Catholics in the United States. He is trying to get the purple for Archbishop Ireland. He has even taken a Catholic into his Cabinet, Charles Bonaparte, as Attorney-General. The President is caressing the Catholics for political purposes.'[12]

Some time before this, in the early 1890s, the first signs had begun to appear that the Catholic hierarchy of America, loyal as it was to the Pope, was acquiring a quality of its own, distinguishing it from its European counterpart. This was, as already seen, centred on Archbishop Ireland's putting of 'Martha before Mary', the belief that the active life was more important than the contemplative. Archbishop Ireland represented that element in the Catholic Church which has always existed in all ages, but which each century sees as something new: the call for Church reform, to bring the Church 'up to date', 'into line with modern thought, progress, science', etc. In the case of Mgr Bonomelli, the Archbishop of Cremona, it was called 'Liberal Catholicism'. In America it was given the ill-sounding name of 'Americanism'.

Its ideals were not the loyalty, obedience and uniformity prescribed by Rome, but freedom for every man to act according to his own conscience. The argument appears to be that God bestows his grace in strict proportion to a man's physical efforts in this life. He expects a good American to show above all initiative and enterprise. The exponents of 'Americanism' observed that American secular civilization was growing apace and flourishing, because it encouraged man to act freely in political and economic life. The Church in America, they said, must follow suit. They warned Catholics against regarding the Sacraments as a substitute for personal effort, or regarding the attainment of Heaven after death, where there would be no more striving, as the supreme felicity. One of their leaders, Bishop Keane, said, 'In Heaven, a man should feel every muscle of his body swelling with strength, every fibre eager for a day's work.'

The position of 'Americanism' in contrast to the more traditional attitude of the rest of the Catholic priesthood was summed up in a despatch from the French Ambassador, M. Jules Cambon, referring to '. . . this movement which has deeply divided the Catholic clergy of the United States into two camps. In one are Mgr Ireland and Cardinal Gibbons, the Archbishop of Baltimore, intent on giving Catholicism a flavour more in keeping with the egalitarian and rational nature of this great American democracy. In the other are the traditionalists, whose standard-bearer is Mgr Correghan, the Archbishop of New York, and who follow closely the rulings of Rome.'[13]

'Americanism' stood in opposition, as these liberal Catholics saw it, to 'feudal Europe', where so many Catholics believed that man was not safe unless he was provided with the greatest possible amount of guidance by the priest. They condemned the practice in European Catholic churches of erecting chancel- and rood-screens and heavy railings, which placed the priest in a position of supremacy. Their journal *The Catholic World* advocated in American churches 'a simple democratic platform down almost to the level of the people, instead of speaking to them from a formal aristocratic [sic] pulpit'. A Catholic called Alfred Young waged a campaign to increase contregational singing, as opposed to choir singing. A choir, he argued, relegated the community to a passive role, while general singing would allow each individual to praise God in his own voice, and in his own spirit.[14] This was something very akin to Nonconformism.

It is understandable that the energetic period of expansion through which this race of pioneers had just passed could hardly have been conducive to those states of contemplation and reflection which are an essential part of Catholic doctrine. Many American Catholics regarded their Church more as a system of organized benevolence than as a repository of sublime moral teaching and transcendent belief. To quote Archbishop Ireland again, 'The religion we need today does not consist in singing beautiful anthems in cathedral choir stalls vested in cloth of gold – while the nave and aisles are empty of people, and the world outside is dying of spiritual starvation.' On another occasion he said, 'It is better today to study works of social economy than those of Bourdaloue.'[15] This active and intelligent people without the old European traditions, but in whom the principles of Christianity were deeply rooted, who said plainly (and often loudly) what they thought, aroused a deep feeling of apprehension, even fear, among the traditionalists at the Vatican. In what direction was this powerful Catholic community moving?

Partly responsible for this fear was the latitudinarian attitude adopted by the American Catholic bishops towards the International Congress of Religion, which was held in Chicago in 1895. Here all the religions of the world were represented, and each was asked to announce its particular contribution to the welfare of mankind. Cardinal Gibbons of Baltimore, the Primate of America, accepted the invitation on behalf of the Catholic Church; and during the two weeks of the Congress his prelates were to be seen in conversation and earnest discussion with Protestant clergy of all kinds, Orthodox Archimandrites, and those of more exotic faiths: Brahmanists, Buddhists, and others. In those days, the word 'ecumenical' had hardly been coined, and the Vatican strongly deprecated this consorting with heretics. The Vatican has never subscribed to the liberal view that 'one religion is as good as another.'

Nevertheless, as long as all this was confined to America, the Vatican was not unduly disturbed. Important as these ten million Catholics might be, they could not be compared numerically with those in Europe. It was only when, at the beginning of the twentieth century, many Catholic prelates and laymen in Europe, particularly in France, became influenced by 'Americanism', seeing in the young and robust Catholic Church of America a pattern on which 'progressive European Catholics' might be modelled, that the Vatican became apprehensive. Many of the French clergy were now contending that the American churchmen, Gibbons and Ireland, were the true prophets of Catholicism, on whom all Christians should model themselves. A French Catholic priest, Father Naudet, advocated educational reform on the American lines to fit the clergy for 'energetic action in the world'.[16] At this time France and the United States, both proud of their new form of republican government, were much closer than they are today; and the Vatican feared that France could easily come under the latter's baneful influence. The French Ambassador in Washington, M. Jules Cambon, pointed this out: 'It is probable that the Holy See has kept silent until now, as long as only American Catholics are involved; for in America, whatever may be the effect on Catholic discipline, their Faith remains as solid as a rock. But I am now beginning to suspect that what Rome fears above all is the contagion of these American ideas in other countries – particularly in France, where they could have consequences very different from those in the United States.'[17]

At all events, Leo XIII now decided to speak up, and warn the Catholic world of the dangers of 'Americanism'. He could do this because he was personally very popular in the United States. Thanks to his great social Encyclicals such as *Rerum Novarum*, he enjoyed an acclaim there unrivalled by that of any of his immediate predecessors. Liberal American Catholics pointed to his concern for the working class, as evidence that he understood the twentieth century. Mgr Ireland described him as 'the greatest Pope since Ganganelli' (significant because Ganganelli was Clement XIV, whose principal achievement was to dissolve the Society of Jesus in 1773). Even American Protestant leaders were flattered by his calling them 'our brothers separated from us'.[18] The American press continually published articles about his exemplary life, praising his personality and tastes. They even published his Latin verses.

In order not to offend American susceptibilities – for all these Liberal American prelates were sincere and devout Catholics – Leo XIII did not express himself in the time-honoured form of an Encyclical, but in a personal letter to Cardinal Gibbons: *Testem Benevolentiae* ('A Witness to the Benevolence . . .'), on 22 January 1899. Its principal recommendations were again summed up by the French Ambassador:

His Holiness states in this letter that over matters of dogma there can be no question, even in the name of science and progress, of attenuating or modifying to the slightest degree the principles of Catholic belief. Against this, His Holiness says that in matters of *discipline*, the Church is the first to adapt its laws to the conditions of time and place, to the customs and habits of different peoples and countries – provided that these adaptations are not the work of isolated individuals acting on their own, but are drawn up by the responsible hierarchy. The Church, His Holiness insists, is far from repudiating the conquests of progress and science; on the contrary, the Church is only too willing to use them for increasing the patrimony of the human spirit, and promoting the public good. . . . But His Holiness emphasizes that the Church will not tolerate, in America or elsewhere, any Catholic organization which does not partake of the Church's universal character, nor recognize the absolute authority of the Roman Pontificate.[19]

Politely but firmly, the Pope censured certain aspects of 'Americanism': first, 'the desire for a Catholic Church in America different from that in the rest of the Catholic world'; second, the notion that the Church should 'adapt itself to civilization' and show more indulgence to modern theories and methods; and third, that the extent of the Church's powers should be limited, so that each individual might act more freely in pursuance of his natural bent and capacity. 'Hence,' concluded the Pope in his letter to Cardinal Gibbons, 'from all we have said, Beloved Son, it is clear that we cannot approve the opinions which are comprised under the heading of "Americanism".' However, he softened his censure by adding a tribute to American Catholicism in general: 'While the vicissitudes and failings of almost all the traditionally Catholic nations fill us with concern, the state of your churches and their flourishing youth rejoices Our soul.'

The Ambassador went on to say that the Pope's letter was originally much more vehement, but that it had been considerably toned down:

It was originally prepared at the Vatican by Cardinals Satolli and Mazzella, both of whom are uncompromising enemies of Archbishop Ireland. As such, it was an absolute condemnation of 'Americanism'. But the Pope and his Secretary of State, Cardinal Rampolla, cut and expurgated it to such an extent that it was almost unrecognizable to its authors. . . . It was at first received by Mgr Ireland with deference, in a letter he wrote to the American press, in which he admitted that there had been certain 'errors' in Americanism. I doubt however if it will make much difference to him in the long run. He is an Irishman, self-confident, noisy and for ever travelling all over the place making speeches. . . . If proof is required, it can be seen in the interviews he is always giving to the press. In these he still emphatically asserts the rights of the American clergy against the interference of the Orders – which is simply another way of saying *Rome*. Neither side is really satisfied, although both say they are. I should say the real victors are the 'Americans'.[20]

Nevertheless, the Pope's letter was gratefully received by the traditionalists, who saw in it a condemnation of Americanism. Mgr Correghan, the Ultramontane Archbishop of New York, expressed his satisfaction in a letter to the Pope, in which he referred to Americanism as 'the Monster': 'We can now truly say that the Monster which, in order to obtain a lasting abode among us, assumed the fair name of America, has been struck dead. It is thanks to you, Holy Father, that this felicitous result is due. Your Holiness has rooted out at its first appearance this tare from the fields of wheat.'[21]

The Pope was in any case so respected and admired throughout the United States that his letter was sufficient to discourage, if not to halt entirely, the more extreme forms of Americanism.

There was one other aspect of American Catholicism in the late nineteenth century which disturbed the Vatican: its suspected involvement in secret societies. Between 1880 and 1895, there were some five hundred of these, mostly in the industrial eastern States. They used a variety of high-sounding names which, it was alleged, concealed their true nature: The Noble Order of the Knights of Labour, The Knights of Pythias, The Knights of Maccabeus, The Militia of Christ for Social Service, The Catholic Order of Foresters. The Catholic Church has always disapproved of secret societies, not only because of their subterranean nature, but because many of them have a quasi-religious character, and they tend to demand total allegiance from their members.

Leo XIII's view was expressed to Bishop Keane, Rector of the American Catholic University, when that prelate visited Rome.[22] The Pope said that these secret societies with their general hostility to constituted authority tended towards socialism, and as such were pernicious. The American Bishop argued that they were an integral part of American life, and should not be regarded as they would be in Europe. There, for the time being, the matter was left.

In Europe, the only secret society of any importance was Freemasonry, which was openly anti-clerical, and as such easy for the Church to identify and condemn. As early as 1738, Clement XII had condemned Freemasonry in his Bull, *In Eminenti*, as a quasi-religious cult based on Deism.[23] The American episcopate followed his ruling and officially condemned Freemasonry in the United States. But they could not condemn the many other societies, because the nature and purpose of these was so cloaked in secrecy that it was impossible to know what were their aims, some of which – those for example concerned with the relief of poverty – were eminently laudable. The Ku-Klux-Klan was easy to condemn, because of its open and ludicrous anti-Catholicism. It accused the Vatican of having installed in Washington a concealed artillery battery trained on the White House; and of having prepared a secret palace to house the Pope when he arrived to govern the United States.[24]

Then there were the Irish societies, with which the United States teemed. The Fenians, with their avowed violent aims, proved easy enough to detect. But hardly had they been condemned, than a host of other Irish secret societies sprang up, with occult names such as the Ribbonmen, the Emeralders, the Ancient Order of the Hibernians, the Molly Maguires – this last, an organization for fomenting discord in the coal-mining districts of Pennsylvania. It would be impossible to condemn them all. Moreover, Bishop Keane's argument against condemning them was that in general they were beneficent. In an age when the working classes were virtually defenceless, these societies provided a kind of trade union when that movement was proscribed. This was the era when the great monopolies were beginning to dominate the lives of millions of Americans, the so-called 'Gilded Age', which was in fact no more than unrestrained capitalism. With each succeeding year, the number of Catholic immigrants to the United States increased, and most of them found employment in the expanding factory system, which was transforming the United States into one of the leading industrial nations of the world. These poor people, often speaking little or no English, soon became victims of the capitalist system at its worst. The Archbishop of Baltimore, Cardinal Gibbons, well known for his sympathies with the working classes, referred in a sermon in the early 1890s to the plight of the men and women working in the 'sweatshops' owned by the clothing manufacturers. He described how in one of these the unfortunate people had to work ten or twelve hours a day for six or eight dollars a week. He condemned the 'sweat-shops' as 'exiguous, ill-ventilated and poorly lit'. Of the streetcar employees, he deplored that they should have to bargain to achieve a reduction from a seventeen- to a twelve-hour working day.

As this capitalist society pullulated and flourished in America in the second half of the nineteenth century, these underpaid people had only one recourse: to secrecy, in order to protect their attempts at achieving some degree of working-class unity when faced with the owners, who were powerfully opposed to any form of trade unionism. On a completely different level, it also gratified the conceit of many obscure Americans, by enabling them to dress up in elaborate regalia on ceremonial occasions.

For the Church in the 1880s, the most disturbing of these societies was – owing to its size, as well as to its claim to be 'holy', and to the involvement in it of a well-known prelate – the Noble and Holy Order of the Knights of Labour. This had been founded in Philadelphia in 1869, and was virtually a trade union; it possessed a Masonic element, its membership being closely guarded by a ritual handshake and a password. Its precise aims were hard to divine, but what troubled the Vatican most was that over half its members were Catholics. Its first 'Master Workman' (president), Uriah S. Stephens, was a declared Freemason, as well as a Knight of Pythias; and both of these societies were reprobated by the Church. Owing to the depression of the early 1880s, the membership of the Knights of Labour had greatly increased; by 1888 it numbered 700,000, and it was the largest secret society in the land.[25]

Most of the American episcopacy under the leadership of Cardinal Gibbons did not share the Vatican's fears; they regarded the Knights of Labour as beneficial to the working classes. Mgr Straniero, the Pope's envoy, also wrote favourably of them in his report to the Vatican, already quoted.[26] 'A society about a million strong,' he said, 'at least a half of whom are Catholic. Their movement appears to have no political significance, its aims being to procure by legal and constitutional means an equitable reward for their members' labour.' He then used a strong term, *despotico*, in

141

connection with the capitalist factory owners, and refers to '. . . the injustices which the proprietors commit against the indigent sons of toil. It is alleged that the Knights of Labour harbour secret and malevolent designs on society in general, and that they should therefore be condemned by the Holy Office. . . . I strongly advise against this. I have ascertained that in the view of the American Bishops, led by Cardinal Gibbons, condemnation of the Knights of Labour by the Holy Office would only give them more importance.'

Mgr Straniero was here influenced by a remarkable man, Cardinal Gibbons, of Baltimore. Born and bred in the United States, Gibbons perfectly understood the psychology of his countrymen, and was aware of their innate repugnance for orders given in the form of a fiat – the customary and traditional procedure of the Vatican. He was not afraid to criticize the growth of the colossal private fortunes being amassed in his country, and the spirit of greed which distinguished its rapidly expanding 'free economy'. Although condemned for this by the capitalist classes, as 'a Red Revolutionary Bishop', he was far from being a socialist. For instance, he vigorously condemned any form of nationalization – of the railroads or other public utilities –as likely to be inefficient. He also condemned other socialist weapons, such as the strike and the boycott. His remedy for the 'sweat-shops' was equally far from socialist. He recommended the public to take their custom to the clothing-house proprietors who treated their employees best. 'In making your purchases,' he said, 'you can discriminate in favour of these establishments. You will thus exercise a moral pressure on the oppressors by appealing to their self-interest.'

On the subect of the Knights of Labour, Gibbons explained to Rome that, 'Since the Government does nothing to protect the workers, the latter, many of whom are good Catholics, look elsewhere for help. . . . If certain objectionable features, such as the excessive secrecy, are eliminated, the Knights of Labour are not a pernicious body. Moreover, if we condemn them, a worse secret organization will replace them, *over which we may have no control*.' He then quoted his English colleague and fellow Cardinal, Manning, that the Church in the coming twentieth century would 'no longer have to do with Princes and Parliaments, but with the masses', and this would be even more true in democratic America. 'To lose the heart of the masses,' he said, 'would be a misfortune for which the friendship of the relatively few rich and powerful can in no way compensate.'[27]

During this debate, Cardinal Gibbons's position was complicated by the conduct of one of his priests, a fiery Irishman called Father Edward McGlynn, the incumbent of St Stephen's Church in New York, and a vociferous supporter of the Knights of Labour. His was one of the most populous parishes in the country, where he came into direct contact with the unemployed and the sufferings of the poor. He took up their cause whole-heartedly, and every Sunday supported the Knights of Labour with eloquent pleas from the pulpit. In Mgr Straniero's Report in the Vatican Archives is this comment on Father McGlynn:

What is particularly distressing is that a New York priest who was educated in Rome, Father Edward McGlynn, has departed from the established practice of the Catholic clergy of abstaining from politics, by supporting the candidature of a socialist for Mayor of New York. Father McGlynn has openly announced his sympathy with socialism, and with the Knights of Labour. The Archbishop of New York, Mgr Correghan, has instructed him to desist from this political activity, but he ignores the order. On the contrary, it has turned him into an open rebel against Episcopal authority.

Contrary to the directions from Rome that priests should abstain from politics, Father McGlynn now became President of the Anti-Poverty Society, an overtly political body. On its behalf, he toured the eastern States propagating socialist views, maintaining that they alone could alleviate the suffering of the masses. This was too much for Rome, and the Holy Office announced that attendance at Father McGlynn's political meetings by Catholics would be regarded as 'an open and public sin'.

Having ignored the instructions of his Bishop, Father McGlynn was summoned to Rome on 6 December 1886 to explain his conduct. He ignored the summons, and so was removed by Mgr Correghan from the pastorate of his church in New York. In Mgr Correghan's words, 'His is no longer the case of a wound that may heal under the soothing influence of a poultice; it is an ulcer that needs the knife.' Far from moderating Father McGlynn's conduct, this removal only goaded the Irish priest to more outright statements. In Brooklyn, he delivered an address on 'The New Know-Nothingness and the Old', in which he referred scathingly to his ecclesiastical superiors both in the United States and in Rome.[28]

The Father McGlynn affair was soon doing considerable harm to the Catholic cause in America. In the opinion of Cardinal Gibbons, his removal from the pastorate of St Stephens had been a mistake, because it had stimulated his more fanatical friends. Open demonstrations in his favour took place in all eastern cities. Not only did the laity take sides, but the American Catholic clergy themselves had become divided. The majority supported Mgr Correghan, but a powerful and articulate minority favoured Father McGlynn. What had started as a small incident threatened to lead to a schism in the American Catholic Church.

It was now that Cardinal Gibbons decided again to take a hand in the matter. His recommendation to the Holy See not to condemn the Knights of Labour, because this would only increase their intransigence, had borne fruit. The Knights of Labour were already declining in face of the growing trade unions, which had begun to offer greater advantages to the working classes. By 1887 the Knights of Labour had declined from 900,000 to 500,000. Cardinal Gibbons gave similar advice to the Holy See in the case of Father McGlynn: not to condemn him publicly. He said that in a land like the United States, doctrinaires and visionaries abounded, but they never got very far; it was better to leave them alone to die a natural death.

It was fortunate for the American Church that Leo XIII had a high opinion of Cardinal Gibbons's judgement. The Pope had long been aware that in dealing with Americans, he was dealing not with a nation composed largely of Europeans, and second-class Europeans at that – as many prelates at the Vatican still seemed to think – but with an entirely new people possessing a character and psychology of their own. In the matter of Father McGlynn, he therefore followed Cardinal Gibbons's advice. In 1892, he sent a Papal Legate, Archbishop Satolli, to America to enquire into the matter, and to enlist the help of four professors from the Catholic University of America. After careful examination, the professors reported that they found nothing 'contrary to the Faith' in Father McGlynn's teachings. 'Economically,' they said, 'his proposals may be censured; theologically, they contain no false principles.'

On 23 December 1892, three years after the ban, Archbishop Satolli accordingly received Father McGlynn back into the fold, informed him that he was free from ecclesiastical censure, and restored to the exercise of his priestly functions. In the summer of 1893, Father McGlynn made his much-delayed visit to Rome, where he was received in audience by Leo XIII, and the past was forgiven. It was typical of this Irish-American priest that during the audience, he could not resist a Parthian shot at his old enemies in the American hierarchy. He congratulated His Holiness on establishing for the first time on American soil a permanent representative, an Apostolic Delegate, 'for this will put a stop to the tyranny exercised by some of your Bishops in governing our priests and people'.

The episode of the secret societies such as the Knights of Labour, and of the socialist priests, was the first occasion when the American Catholic Church, far from playing the traditional secondary role to the Catholic Church in Europe, set the example for the whole Catholic world. Leo XIII's social Encyclical *Rerum Novarum* owed more to the social and economic developments in America at the end of the nineteenth century than to events in Europe; and Cardinal Gibbons, by averting the Papal condemnation of the Knights of Labour and of Father McGlynn, exercised considerable influence in the preparation of that famous Encyclical.

10

The Irish Bane

The despatch of a Papal Legate to report on the affairs of any country – as when Mgr Straniero was sent to the United States in 1888 – is not undertaken lightly. Papal Legates tend to be unwelcome guests among the bishops and clergy of the land they visit, because some of the spiritual honours and prerogatives of the local bishops devolve on them. Any service at which the Legate officiates, however small, be it a Mass or a Benediction, tends to be regarded by the people as virtually performed by the Pope himself. Froude[1] maintains that on the few occasions when the Holy See has sent a Legate to Ireland, it has regretted it. The last one, in the seventeenth century, perished mysteriously in the bogs. Indeed, caution has always marked the dealings of the Holy See with Ireland, a caution based not only on secular traditions of prudence, but on contact with a mentality which, if a mystery to Englishmen, is no less opaque to the closer reasoning of the Latin. It is not only here that lay rulers have disapproved of visiting Legates. Some eight hundred years before, William the Conqueror announced to Gregory VII, 'I am a dutiful son of the Church, but if you send your Legate into my domains, he will be found hanging from the tallest oak in my forests.'

Nevertheless, Mgr Straniero's visit to America had been successful, and Leo XIII now decided to repeat the process in Ireland. The British Government was complaining bitterly that the Irish Catholic clergy were encouraging the Fenian movement[2] and fostering violence. Reports from Ireland, where religion and politics are always related, were so conflicting, depending on whether the source was Irish or English, that Leo XIII felt he must have a report from his own observer.

Largely through historical accident, the Roman Catholic Church in Ireland had for long been the Church of the People – not the

146

Church of the State, as in other Catholic countries. Its clergy were poor, sharing the trials and tribulations of their flock. In other Catholic countries, wealth and close alliance with the throne and the aristocracy had combined to make the Catholic Church a pillar of the existing order. The same would probably have been true in Ireland, had not the English conquest taken place, and with it the imposition of the Anglican religion, to which the Irish masses remained consistently hostile. When Cromwell expelled all Catholics owning land in Ireland, priests and people were welded together in the bond of common suffering. Everyone hated the Protestant government, and longed for a Stuart restoration, the return of the old religion and the native Catholic aristocracy. (James II might have achieved this, had he won the Battle of the Boyne in 1690.)

As one of the most devout members of the Catholic family of nations, Ireland has always contributed generously to the Papal coffers. Gregorovius reported that such was its devotion to the Holy See when he was in Rome in 1860, that 'The single diocese of Dublin alone, *in that starving island*, has in three months contributed 400,000 francs to Peters' Pence – twice the amount collected in New York City.'[3] Ireland has always been represented prominently in Rome. At the time of the Italian seizure in 1870, there were no less than a dozen different Irish religious communities in the city. In addition to the Irish College for training priests, and the Irish churches of St Patrick and St Isidore, there were the houses of the Irish Dominicans, the Irish Franciscans and the Irish Christian Brothers. The Carmelites and Redemptionists also had Irishmen at their head. Among their denunciations of the Italian seizure of Rome was that of Dr Kirby, the head of the Irish student college, who announced publicly, 'The Italian Government has behaved in a manner which has excited the horror and indignation of the whole world. They have acted with hypocrisy, perfidy, conspiracy, and finally with open violence, despoiling His Holiness of His sacred Principality. Against this most execrable violence, we Catholics of Ireland raise our voice in solemn protest.'[4] Another Irish prelate, Bishop Vaughan, preached a sermon on St Patrick's Day, referring to 'the organized band of robbers and bandits which is the Italian government'.[5]

These outbursts caused considerable embarrassment to Sir Augustus Paget, the British Ambassador to the Italian State, since

Ireland was then a part of the United Kingdom. In his despatch of 8 January 1871, he stated:

> I ask myself whether it is tolerable, whether it is commonly decent, that the Superior of a British establishment in the capital of the Kingdom of Italy, living under its laws, claiming as they do at every minute the aid and support of Her Majesty's Minister accredited to the King of Italy, should make a parade of their sentiments of virulent hostility to that Sovereign and his Government, using towards them in an address delivered on a solemn occasion and intended for publicity, offensive, libellous and seditious language.[6]

What embarrassed Sir Augustus Paget even more was that these Irish Catholics in Rome were using their friendly relations with the Vatican as a platform for anti-English propaganda. They had succeeded, he said, in persuading the Vatican and its mouthpiece, the *Osservatore Romano*, of the rightness of their cause, and he quoted that journal as congratulating 'the movement of the Irish clergy in favour of Home Rule, which takes on every day a more favourable development'.[7] Sir Augustus came to the conclusion that the Vatican sided with the Irish Home Rulers, adding, 'Her Majesty's Government may take into consideration whether it is desirable and expedient to continue even unofficial diplomatic relations with a Power [the Vatican] which through its agents is openly and avowedly advocating and promoting schemes for the dismemberment of the British Empire.'

This was not true. Sir Augustus's sympathies – it has been seen before – if not openly anti-Papal, lay with the Italian Government. He had always disapproved of the intransigence of Pius IX, and he did not like him personally. From this it was only a step to seeing the Pope as a supporter of anti-Protestant, and therefore anti-British, measures. In fact, as one of Sir Augustus's predecessors in Rome, Odo Russell, had said when the Fenian Brotherhood was beginning its campaign of violence in Ireland, neither the Pope nor the Catholic episcopacy supported Irish Home Rule. 'It is,' Mr Russell reported, 'the *lower* Irish clergy who support the Fenians. They even denounce their own bishops.'[8] Pius IX himself, with his natural dislike of revolutionaries, undoubtedly disapproved of the Fenians; to Mr Russell he described them as 'The Garibaldians of

England'. His successor, Leo XIII, went even further. In a Pontifical letter to the Irish clergy, he enjoined them '. . . to do nothing contrary to the obedience due to the legitimate authority . . . Ireland,' he said, 'can obtain all she wants if she remains within the limitations of the law.'[9]

An indication of where Papal sympathies lay is given by a document in the Vatican Archives, assessing the Irish situation in 1888: 'From our point of view, it would be preferable not to have a native Irish Parliament [i.e. Home Rule] because, judging from the example of other Catholic countries since 1870, it would almost certainly be anti-clerical, and would elaborate the view expressed in some Irish papers that the Pope should keep out of Irish politics. On the other hand, the English Parliament which at present governs Ireland takes no part in either clericalism or anti-clericalism.'[10]

Yet the Irish were continually pressing the Vatican to make an open statement condemning 'the British atrocities in Ireland'. Of these 'atrocities', one Irish priest, Father Cauly, referred in *The Irish World* to:

. . . a remote district called Finney, where you will find a ruined and roofless chapel – with the poor people kneeling outside when the Holy Mysteries are offered up. And who reduced this chapel to its present state? They will tell you – Lord Leitrim! The tribute which this English landlord, and those like him, demand in the form of rents is exorbitant. The little of the soil of their forefathers which remains to the Irish people is now rack-rented by these English land-holders to a pitch which has reduced them to perennial paupery. Their cattle, pigs, fowls, eggs, milk and butter, instead of nourishing their half-starved families, are sold to pay the rent. Their very clothes are pawned.

Another Catholic priest, Father Conway, used stronger language during Mass at Headford. He said that the English landlords should be 'hung by the heels and not by the neck; the latter punishment would come in time.'[11] Such sentiments were expressed even more violently at meetings of Charles Parnell's Irish National Land League, commonly called the 'Agrarians' and proscribed by the British.

Exaggerated as much of this language was, there was some truth in it. Even the British Government recognized that legislation to control the high rents must be introduced; and it was engaged in doing so. But what it would not tolerate were the acts of violence which accompanied the Agrarians' demands. Their grievances were soon seen as a convenient pretext for the violent men, the Fenians, the Moonlighters and other desperadoes, to spread anarchy throughout the island, and expel the English altogether. The British Government had become convinced that the Irish Catholic clergy were encouraging, if not playing an active part in, this subversion. It was at this point, with assassination becoming a daily occurrence, that the British Government appealed to Rome – in the form of a letter from Lord Stanley to Cardinal Nina of the Rota, who was known to be close to the Pope.

'The Agrarian agitation,' he wrote, 'would be of minor importance, were it not accompanied by that perpetual scourge in Ireland – the denunciation of individuals who pay their rent to the landlords, followed by their assassination. Here we are convinced that the Catholic clergy is playing an active part against tenants who pay their rent. It is scandalous that priests should denounce people on the very steps of the church, after they have come out of Mass. . . .' He went on to pay a remarkable, if unconscious, tribute, to the political power of the Pope. 'Any measures, however energetic, which the English Government may take to put an end to these outrages can have only a temporary effect. Only action by the Holy See can influence the Irish clergy to cease supporting these murderers.'[12]

It was after these complaints by the British Government that Leo XIII decided to send a Papal Legate to discover the truth, and to report on the role played by the Catholic priests in the Home Rule agitation. For this he selected Mgr Ignazio Persico, a Neapolitan educated by the Jesuits, one of the ablest men in the Vatican diplomatic service, and in his early sixties. Leo XIII's written instructions for Mgr Persico were 'to clarify what part is played by the Irish clergy in the Agrarian agitation' and 'to exhort the Irish bishops to moderate as far as possible any political action by that clergy'. A more personal instruction was 'to avoid as far as possible accepting private invitations to stay, and to prefer hotels'. Nor should the Papal Legate frequent public meetings.

Mgr Persico knew something about Ireland, and he did not relish the task. But he was a man of faith and determination. As he wrote at one point during his six months in Ireland, 'All the violence of the

Irish press campaign against me will not deter me – preoccupied as I am with the prestige of His Holiness, and the mission with which he has entrusted me.' The material quoted here is drawn largely from his report, which is now in the Vatican Secret Archives for the year 1888. [13]

Mgr Persico arrived in Dublin on 7 July 1887. In his first despatch to Rome, he stated that he was finding it hard to follow the instructions about not accepting invitations. He had intended staying at the Gresham Hotel, but the Archbishop of Dublin, Mgr Walsh, who had given a lavish reception for him, insisted on his staying in the bishop's palace. 'Mgr Walsh said that if I did not stay with him,' reported Mgr Persico, 'it would not only diminish his own standing, but make an extremely bad impression on the public.'

His first week in Dublin was the most agreeable part of his Irish stay; he was warmly welcomed and everyone, whatever their politics, appeared anxious to help him. He was visited by all classes of the population, and received a large and enthusiastic correspondence. He reported that 'A dozen land-owning Lords have invited me to stay, some of them having come over specially from England for the purpose.' Hospitality was also offered by the Irish Nationalist politicians, the Home Rulers. In every part of the population, he was aware of 'the great love of this people for the Holy Father', and he realized how deeply religious the Irish were.

During his week in Dublin, Mgr Persico was able to form some impression of the most important Prelate in Ireland, Mgr Walsh. 'A most knowledgeable man,' he wrote, 'with a nimble wit, and a great worker.' But he added, with the first touch of the critical perception which marks his whole report, 'The public meets the Archbishop daily – not in person, but in the newspapers, either in the form of letters to the editor, or in articles. The latter deal mostly with political matters, rarely with religion.'

Mgr Persico then travelled south to Rochestown, County Cork, where he became aware of the pressures which would be put on him – in this case from the British Government side, in the person of a certain Captain Ross, whose attentions were most pressing. 'Captain Ross,' he wrote, 'is one of the most ardent supporters of the English landlords in their contention with the Irish people. . . . I have reason to believe he is a secret agent of the English

Government. He has insisted on imposing himself on me as much as possible since my arrival, and has sorely tried my patience.'

He stayed five days in Rochestown where, in reaction no doubt to Captain Ross's attentions, his inclination was to sympathize with the Irish Home Rulers. To Rome he reported on 10 December 1887, 'I must tell you that the state of this country is getting worse, owing to the increasingly repressive measures introduced by the English Government. And the numerous arrests of perfectly respectable Irish persons made on the most preposterous grounds. It would seem that the English Government wishes to provoke the Irish people into acts of rebellion.' Here he was referring to the Coercion Act which the British Government had just passed. In its name, arrests could be made on the simple testimony of a policeman; and condemnation pronounced with no more authority.[14]

Nevertheless, Mgr Persico was determined to be objective, aware that the rights and wrongs of the Agrarian situation did not concern him, but only the part the Catholic clergy were playing in it. From Cork a few days later, he reported sombrely on this: 'I fear that the Irish clergy, instead of trying to calm the political passions, are intent on stirring them up. The violence of language employed by some of the priests exceeds even that of the Nationalists. Nor have I heard any condemnation of their language by their bishops.'

After staying in a number of towns – Longford, Sligo, Queenstown, Londonderry – Mgr Persico began to form an opinion of the Agrarian League and its Plan of Campaign. This title sounds innocuous enough but, as he said:

The so-called Plan of Campaign is nothing less than a *military* campaign, and its principal weapon is the *boycott*. This is a kind of civil excommunication, which isolates the denounced person who has agreed to pay his rent to the English landlord, so that no one will have anything to do with him. No shopkeeper will serve him, no artisan, carpenter, plumber or peasant will render him service. What is particularly scandalous is that in some cases the denounced tenant is deprived of his place in church, and his children are refused religious instruction by the priest! Equally scandalous – to see a number of Catholic priests in the audience at the Plan of Campaign meetings! Moreover, these meetings generally take place on Sundays, immediately after Mass, so that the priest goes directly from the altar to the hustings. I will refrain from quoting the language used by some of the priests on these platforms, particularly the younger ones. They degrade their sacred Ministry, and set the worst example to the population.

Of the young priests in the College of Maynooth, the principal seminary of Ireland, Mgr Persico wrote, 'They are full of the spirit of revolt. Instead of acting as Ministers of Peace, they sow further discord. They oppose civil authority, and refuse to pray for the Queen. Some of these young priests even give lessons in socialism.' He referred to three of these priests on a platform at a political meeting applauding when the speaker said, 'If Jesus Christ himself came down on this platform and dared to oppose the Agrarian League, he would be whistled out of the room.'

Mgr Persico then gave some examples of boycotting in which priests were involved. He reported that a certain '. . . Mr Fitzjames, a Roman Catholic gentleman residing about three miles from Six Mile bridge, County Clare, is being savagely boycotted. This is encouraged and sanctioned by the priests in the diocese of Killaloe, and has culminated in his being fired on, and seriously wounded, on the public highway.'

Mgr Persico's next stop was the diocese of Kerry, the home of the 'Moonlighters':

The state of this diocese is one of langour, not to say apathy. The clergy here display few commendable virtues, and appear terrified of the Moonlighters. These ruffians, who claim to be part of the Agrarian League, are in reality nothing more than common highwaymen. The country lends itself to their activities, because it is mountainous, and a large part is wooded and inaccessible. The Moonlighters specialize in hold-ups and murder. The Bishop of the diocese, Mgr Andrew Higgins, is an indecisive man who says he has withdrawn completely from politics. This is of course a matter for congratulation, but it appears that it derives more from fear of the Moonlighters than anything else.

Mgr Persico was equally critical of the Bishop of the neighbouring diocese, Waterford and Lismore, Mgr Piers Power, whom he described as 'neither young in body nor nimble in spirit, and dedicated, I fear, to spiritous liquors'.

Mgr Persico spent five months in this way, visiting most of the Irish dioceses, in a tour of such thoroughness that some of the Irish bishops became apprehensive. They would have been even more apprehensive had they known what he reported to Leo XIII. Of the Bishop of Dromore he wrote, 'The Bishop here, Mgr Leahy, has governed the diocese for thirty-five years. Not only is he advanced in years, but he has for some time been paralysed, and is not always in his right mind. Last year he was given a coadjutor to help him, Mgr McGivern. But would you believe it – the old Bishop insists on keeping all control of the diocese in his own hands, leaving to Mgr McGivern only the benedictions and sanctifications.' It was much the same in the diocese of Killaloe, which was also ruled by elderly men: 'The Bishop here is Mgr Michael Flannery, who has been in charge for thirty years. Decrepit and a permanent invalid, he has been absent from the diocese for several years, and is at present resident in Paris.' Of the diocese of Cloyne he reported, 'The Bishop here is afflicted with almost total deafness. Consequently the clergy are not supervised as they should be, they are left very much to their own devices.' In the diocese of Clonfert, he described the Bishop, Mgr Patrick Duggan, as '. . . advanced in years, and evincing signs of mental aberration. I would say he is virtually insane, and should be removed.'

Mgr Persico criticized many of these bishops on account of their age and decrepitude which, he admits, was not their fault. But he found some of the younger bishops, alert and active men, reprehensible on other grounds. He had already referred to Archbishop Walsh of Dublin, who had entertained him on his arrival in Ireland, as a man who wrote too often to the papers. He now commented:

The Archbishop of Dublin is an openly avowed Nationalist and Home Ruler, closely linked with Parnell and the Plan of Campaign. His forceful character has imposed him on most of the Irish clergy, who are terrified of him. Woe to any Bishop who does not think as the Archbishop of Dublin does! He loves to breathe the aura of popular acclaim, and to be the idol of the people. He claims to defend the rights of the Irish common man; but in this defence he goes too far, with frequent letters to the press, couched in a language unsuitable for a high ecclesiastical dignitary. He could do great things as an Archbishop, but his mania for politics and publicity outweighs his good qualities.

Mgr Persico dealt with some thirty dioceses and, in contrast to his criticism of the Irish bishops and clergy, he wrote most favourably of the Irish people:

In its heart of hearts, this people is Catholic and sound. If it errs, it is not due to lack of Catholic feelings, but to the force of circumstances, and to the ardent and impetuous Irish temperament. I would say more – that because this people is so religious, the future of Ireland lies in the hands of the priests; and that if the people have gone astray, it is the fault of the priests, because the Irish people instinctively follow their religious leaders. Their attitude is, 'If the priest does not condemn what I do, then my conscience is clear, and I can do it.' The bane of this country today is that political agitators have acquired almost complete power over the population. The Fenian agitation, based originally on a just cause, its object being certain legitimate rent reforms, has taken quite a different course. It is now simply an excuse for acts of violence and murder. In spite of this, a large proportion of the Irish clergy support them, as much by example as by words.

He was much struck, he said, by the fact that when reciting the Lord's Prayer, Irish priests omitted the passage '. . . as we forgive them that trespass against us. . . .'

It was on the basis of this report that Leo XIII now published his 'Decree on Ireland', an unequivocal condemnation of the Fenians, the Plan of Campaign and boycotting. He supported it with the Encyclical *Saepe Nos* of August 1888, severely condemning the murder of opponents, and including a wealth of detail which could only have come from an exceptionally well-informed source, that is, Mgr Persico.

After this Mgr Persico wrote:

The Papal Decree has been received very badly here. It is attributed to me, and I am now under constant attack. The same Bishops who gave me such a welcome six months ago have changed completely. They are now cold and hostile. My post is full of threatening letters couched in the coarsest terms. Every vituperation is levelled at me, including the threat of lapidation. I will refrain from quoting the language they use.

Indeed, the Irish Nationalists were furious; for the Papal condemnation was followed by Gladstone's suppression of the Land League by putting Messrs Parnell, Dillon and Sexton in prison. To the Catholic Nationalists, it seemed that their Pope had betrayed them. Nevertheless, Leo XIII's exercise in Papal diplomacy, the despatch of a Legate, had been justified. As a result of his Decree, the violence abated, and the number of Irish priests openly supporting the agitators decreased.

What can be learned from this visit? First, it would appear that the Pope's authority among a religious people like the Irish, and with it his invisible influence over politics, was considerable. The jubilation in England, and the dismay in Ireland, with which the Pope's Decree was greeted confirm this. Secondly, in a completely different field, Mgr Persico's mission revealed the diplomatic disadvantages for Britain of having no official relations with the Holy See. Had these existed, a Concordat would have been reached by which the British Government would have had a considerable say in the nomination of Irish bishops. Not having the advantage of the advice of Ireland's rulers (the British Government) in the matter, the Vatican had no alternative but to accept the advice of the Irish episcopate in creating new bishops, an episcopate itself in a degenerate condition. The Irish bishops naturally advised promotion for priests who shared their political views, which were generally openly hostile to England.

During the decades leading up to the First World War, the situation remained unchanged. In spite of the Papal condemnation, in Rome itself the Irish groups continued their anti-English propaganda. During the war, the Irish Catholic College became, in the words of the British Minister, Count de Salis, 'a hotbed of conspiracy against England'.[15] Irish Catholic circles, he said, openly sympathized with the Central Powers. This was a source of considerable embarrassment to the Vatican, which wished to remain strictly neutral during the war.

The Vatican was further embarrassed by a number of Irishmen

who appeared in Rome during the war, claiming to represent 'The Irish Republic' – which of course at this time did not yet exist – and all of whom, it appeared, were called Kelly. Prominent among them was a certain John Kelly, styling himself 'Ambassador of the Irish Republic'. He had limitless funds and gave rowdy dinners at the Grand Hotel, to which he invited the Irish priests resident in Rome. Then there was a Count Kelly, who set up as an intermediary between the Vatican and 'The Delegation of the Irish Republic at the Coming Peace Conference'. At first, the Vatican took him seriously; but when it was discovered that he was not a Count at all, but a member of the Third International, they dropped him. Of the same name was the Sinn Fein propagandist Thomas Kelly, a native of New York, who mysteriously became appointed Supernumerary Chamberlain at the Vatican.

Another Irishman styling himself 'The Marquis McSweeney' also obtained a high post at the Vatican during the war. It was subsequently discovered that he too was not a nobleman, but an Irish butcher's son who had married the Brazilian heiress Cavaleranti de Albuquerque. He became suspect to the British Embassy because, having divorced the Brazilian lady, he married Her Highness Countess Anna von Schlitz, a relative of the German Kaiser. The English diplomats in Rome became convinced that this 'Marquis McSweeney' was working for the German Secret Service, while protected by his official status at the Vatican.

An Irishman who proved an even greater embarrassment to the Vatican during the war, owing to his eminence, was Dr Daniel Mannix, the Principal of Maynooth College, the chief Catholic seminary in Ireland. In 1917, he toured the United States making inflammatory speeches against England. On one occasion in New York, he addressed an audience of some fifteen thousand Irish-Americans in Madison Square Gardens, from a platform crammed with Irish priests. England, he told them, was America's greatest enemy, and he hoped that immediately Germany had been defeated, America would declare war on England and liberate Ireland. He described America as 'The knight errant of the little nations'. 'America,' he said, 'will never fail her dark Irish Rosaleen . . . the dark Rosaleen whom you love, and I love, will soon stand a nation again among nations. . . .'

In England, questions were asked in Parliament about Dr Mannix, and Lord Curzon, the Foreign Secretary, instructed

Count de Salis to make a protest. 'Only the Vatican,' he said, 'can prevent the pernicious utterances and activities of this turbulent priest.' After seeing the Cardinal Secretary of State, Count de Salis was able to report to London, 'The Holy See fully supports His Majesty's Government in deploring the behaviour of this Irish priest.' When Dr Mannix came to Rome for the regular *ad limina* ('home') visit he was, on the Pope's instructions, officially reprimanded for his anti–British activities. After that, no more was heard of him.

Count de Salis later reports that after the war, when Irish Home Rule agitation was rife again, Lord Balfour came to Rome for an audience with Pope Benedict XV, and tried to make a bargain with him. He suggested that in return for the Pope's using his conciliatory influence on the Irish in Rome, Britain would support the Holy See's candidature for the League of Nations. He also tried to play on Papal fears of Communism by indicating that the Sinn Fein was Communist-inspired, and would in the long run present a danger to the Irish clergy and Church. De Salis reports that Benedict XV appeared singularly unimpressed by this, and said that he had no desire to join the League of Nations anyway. However, he agreed to use his influence with the Irish clergy in Rome.[16]

At the beginning of this account of Vatican–Irish relations, we observed that the Vatican has generally tried to avoid too close an involvement with Ireland. On balance, the events described here between 1870 and 1922 would seem to confirm the wisdom of this policy.

11

The English Anomaly

The events in Ireland in the closing decades of the nineteenth century necessarily brought Britain into unofficial contact with the Papacy. More than three centuries before, on the excommunication of Queen Elizabeth I in 1571, England's Embassy at the Vatican had been withdrawn. For those three centuries, with the exception of a brief interlude in 1687 when James II sent Lord Castlemaine to Rome, Britain had no official relations with the Holy See. It would seem that after such a drastic measure as the excommunication of an English monarch, all contacts with the Papacy must irremediably be lost. Add to this in 1588 the Spanish Armada, which had been actively supported by Sixtus V; and the very word 'Papacy' became anathema in England. The official attitude was, in the words Shakespeare puts into the mouth of King John,

> . . . henceforth, that no Italian priest
> shall tithe and toll in our domains. . . .[1]

Yet during these three centuries both sides found it expedient on a number of occasions to establish unofficial contacts, for purely pragmatic reasons, strategical, commercial, even personal.

The first instance of this was in 1618, concerning the marriage of the Protestant Prince of Wales (later Charles I) to the Catholic Infanta of Spain. At this time a mysterious figure, the Capuchin monk Alessandro Montferrato, shuttled back and forth between London and the Vatican bearing revised drafts of the marriage contract, whose political implications could be crucial for both countries. In the event, the marriage never took place. Again when, after Austerlitz in 1806, Britain found herself with only one ally on the continent, Pope Pius VII – who had also refused to submit to Napoleon – diplomatic contact with Rome was essential; and a certain Mr Erskine was sent there for that purpose. Although entirely without official status at the Vatican, he negotiated the conditions by which the English fleet was allowed to use the strategically important Tyrrhenian ports of the Papal States. After Napoleon's defeat, the British Government wished to show its appreciation of this boon; in 1819 the Prince Regent sent Sir Thomas Lawrence to paint Pope Pius VII's portrait for the royal collection. As a further token of British esteem, a complete set of casts of the Elgin Marbles was presented to His Holiness.

During the nineteenth century, the Catholic population of the expanding British Empire was greatly increasing, and the British Government found it advantageous – if only for the maintenance of law and order in those parts – to solicit the good offices of the Vatican on a number of occasions. This was done by an exchange of unofficial letters between the Cardinal Secretary of State Consalvi and the British Foreign Secretaries Castlereagh and Canning, dealing with such refractory questions as the province of Quebec which, although under British rule, was populated almost exclusively by French Catholics; or of Malta, which was also under British rule, but whose native population was devoutly Catholic. In both these situations when friction arose, as it frequently did, the Vatican played a conciliatory role.

In 1831, the British Government went further, and posted a permanent, but still unofficial, representative to Rome, Sir Brook Taylor. Although he was a career diplomat, Sir Brook had no official status at the Vatican; and he was given strict instructions that his communications with the Foreign Secretary, Lord Palmerston, were to be in the form of private letters, not the normal official despatches. His written instructions were: 'You shall hold such spoken and written communication with the Papal Government as you may deem necessary, always preferring the former to the latter, and taking care not to give official form to either.' In 1840, Lord Lansdowne, in a famous passage, explained to Britain's Protestant Parliament why the Vatican should not be ignored. 'The condition of the Pope's sovereignty,' he said, 'is quite peculiar. As a temporal sovereign, he is only of the fourth or fifth order. But as a spiritual sovereign, he is not only of the first order but he possesses, whether you like it or not, immense power over men's minds.'[2]

Sir Brook Taylor was followed in 1832 by Mr Aubin, and by Mr Petre in 1844; both were stationed in Rome, but still only as unofficial agents. That this was again of value to the British Government was proved shortly after Mr Petre's arrival – in connection with the protest by a number of Irish Catholic bishops against an Act of the British Parliament concerning charitable requests and donations. Trivial as this may sound, it could have led to bitter recriminations, even conflict, between England and the Irish bishops, whose power was considerable. The British Government was most anxious to avoid this, and it instructed Mr Petre to enlist the aid of the Vatican in influencing the Irish bishops. As a result of his petition the Vatican intervened, and the bishops desisted from their opposition. The British Government expressed its appreciation to the Vatican in an unofficial letter drawn up by Mr Petre: 'H.M.'s Government is fully aware that the satisfactory decision by the Irish prelates is due in great measure to the wise and conciliatory counsel addressed to them by His Holiness the Pope.' On a number of other occasions in the late nineteenth and early twentieth century, as we have seen, the Vatican used its good offices in Ireland.

Mr Petre was followed in 1853 by Mr Lyons, and in 1858 by Odo Russell. Both these missions were still shrouded at least in semi-secrecy. It would seem that this last posting was not a happy one; for Mr Russell, a member of the great Whig family of the Reform Bill, was a convinced Liberal, and he informed the Pope in person that it was high time he introduced liberal reforms into his Papal States. These were the days of Britain's greatest power, when she felt it her duty to export her liberal ideas all over the world. To Mr Russell's representations, Pius IX replied mildly, but unequivocally that the 'turbulent and intriguing' Italian mind was unsuited to such things. (His exact words are given in Chapter 4, p. 72.)

Britain had in fact actively contributed to the undermining of the Pope's temporal rule by giving asylum to those enmies of the Church, Mazzini and Garibaldi, who had openly proclaimed their intention of overthrowing the Papal State and incorporating it into Greater Italy. When Garibaldi came to England in 1865, he was treated like a conquering hero. Gladstone spoke of 'the seductive simplicity of Garibaldi's demeanour – a union of the most profound and tender humanity with fiery valour'. Garibaldi was flattered when thirty English towns and municipalities gave him an official reception. All this adulation of the man who was generally regarded as the greatest 'Hammer of the Church' since Luther, who had referred to the Vatican and its denizens as, 'that nest of vipers living in idleness and sloth on the right bank of the Tiber, whom we shall exterminate', and who craved 'a new revelation which will supersede effete Christianity', was hardly likely to further the cause of Anglo–Vatican reconciliation.

The other main impediment to the restoration of official relations was the powerful Nonconformist lobby in Britain, which the Government dared not ignore. Homage to the Pope by any British delegation visiting Rome brought down the wrath of these Protestant extremists. One of them, the Dunfermline Protestant Defence Association, objected vehemently when a party of some four hundred British bluejackets from a naval squadron in the roads off Civitavecchia visited the Pope in 1904. In its complaint to Parliament, the Dunfermline Association wrote, 'We solemnly protest at the unpatriotic action of the British Admiralty in sanctioning this visit. The British officers and sailors commenced their degrading and humiliating exercise by superstitiously kneeling at the so-called Tomb of the Apostle, and afterwards attending a blasphemous and idolatrous Mass! Each man prostrated himself at the feet of the Anti-Christ, and slavishly kissed his hand.'[3]

A further, more unlikely, impediment to the re-establishment of official relations was the conduct of English Catholics themselves, when they came to Rome to pay homage to the Head of their Faith. Like all minority groups, they tended to be intemperate in manner and language. As already recounted, a delegation of English Catholics headed by the Duke of Norfolk presented an address to the Pope which was gravely insulting to the King of Italy, and which led the Ambassador to declare that he was ashamed of his countrymen. 'The Duke's language,' he reported, 'surpassed in vehemence and insult to the King of Italy and his Government anything which has hitherto been uttered in Italy by the clerical extremists, if such a thing is possible.'[4] The words he referred to in the Duke's address were '. . . the unhappy condition today of this poor country, Italy . . .' and 'We all hope and pray that the coming century may witness the restoration of the Roman Pontiff to his position of temporal independence [this implied the eviction of the Italian Government from Rome] which Your Holiness has declared necessary for the effective fulfilment of the duties of Your worldwide charge. We pray that it may witness the cessation of the evils which afflict our Church, particularly in professedly Catholic countries [i.e. Italy].' The Duke anticipated that 'In God's good time, England will return to the ancient Faith, to the barque of St Peter and her well-beloved pilot.' The howl of indignation in Protestant England which went up at this can be imagined; it was equalled only by the anger of the Italian press.

The British Ambassador also criticized the behaviour of another great English Catholic family, the Noels, when they came to Rome. The head of this family, the Earl of Gainsborough, was accompanied by his wife, son and daughter, and they stayed at the Albergo d'Inghilterra near the Spanish Steps. The proprietor of this hotel had in a spirit of patriotic zeal hoisted the Italian tricolour on the flagpole above the main entrance. The Gainsboroughs had central rooms on the first floor, and from their window the Italian flag could be seen only a few feet away. According to the British Ambassador, the Gainsboroughs must have spoken disparagingly of the flag in front of their children, '. . . for their Papal sympathies are well known'. When they went out for a walk leaving the children behind, their son Edward, aged sixteen, climbed out of the window on to a ledge, detached the flag, and dropped it into the street below. Soon an angry crowd collected outside the hotel. At this point the daughter, Lady Constance Noel, not to be outdone by her brother, went to the window and shouted down at the crowd '*Evviva Papa Pio Nono!*' ('Long live Pope Pius the Ninth!') to which the crowd shrieked back '*Evviva Vittorio Emmanuele!*' The young Edward followed his sister to the window where, in the words of the Roman newspaper *Don Pirlone Figlio* the next day, '. . . the English youth applied to the name of our King that barrack-room term with which Chambron replied to the enemy demanding his surrender at Waterloo'. At this the crowd became hysterical, and had not the proprietor managed to bar the front door, they would have invaded the hotel shrieking, 'To the Tiber with them!' With great presence of mind, the proprietor ran up to the bedroom and escorted the young couple down the back stairs and out of the building to the Minerva hotel on the other side of the Corso. The Roman press gave full publicity the next day; it asked what would happen in London, if an Italian insulted the Union Jack in this way.[5]

If these incidents were impediments to the resumption of Anglo-Vatican relations, the British treatment of Catholics throughout her Empire was not. Paradoxical as it may seem, Great Britain – this very Protestant nation – was far less anti-clerical than the traditionally Catholic lands. In the words of the Vatican newspaper *Osservatore Romano* in September 1893, 'While so many Catholic countries are attacking the Catholic Church, England, true to her principles of liberty, has accorded that same gift to her Roman Catholic minority – in a way which must make many continental Catholics envy the lot of their co-religionists in England. In that land, the State does not interfere with the liberty of conscience, nor with the social action of the Catholic Church.' In the Vatican Secret Archives is a note: 'Grateful acknowledgement by Pope Leo XIII for the justice and protection which the Catholic Church has enjoyed during the reign of Queen Victoria throughout the vast extent of her realm.'

Whether due in part to this or not, it is a fact that in the second half of the nineteenth century, while Catholicism regressed in the traditional Latin lands, it advanced in England and other heretical countries. In both the Anglo-Saxon and Teutonic worlds, many new Catholic churches were built each year. After Newman's conversion in 1845, a host of others followed; by 1870 it was estimated that some two hundred Anglican clergymen had followed his example. According to the sociologist Gorman in his study *Converts to Rome*, by the end of the century this figure had increased to 556, together with 'an impressive number of members of the nobility', some four hundred, with a hundred generals and admirals, and 256 lawyers and physicians. 'And,' he says, 'with this gilded band went ordinary men and women to the tune of about ten thousand a year.'

The Englishman who had the closest relationship with a Vatican and with Pius IX personally was Henry Manning. (For the dominating role he played in the Dogma of the Infallibility see Chapter 1, p.17). He was elevated to the Purple in 1875, the first English Cardinal since Reginald Pole in the time of Mary Tudor.

There was one aspect of Manning, however, with which it appears from British diplomatic sources in Rome (Sir Augustus Paget and Mr Herries) that the Pope and his Secretary of State were less pleased. It seems paradoxical that Manning, the most Ultramontane of prelates, was also a believer in democracy, contending that Catholicism would be re-established in England not by the upper classes, but through democracy. Pius IX abominated democracy, describing 'universal suffrage' as 'universal lying'; so that it seems extraordinary that Manning should have obtained such an influence over him. Moreover, the Pope and his Secretary of State Antonelli were far from enthusiastic about Manning's avowed intention to extirpate Protestantism from England; in the present situation, they much preferred Protestantism to atheism. That they thought Manning too extreme is revealed in Sir Augustus Paget's despatch: 'Manning received something of a reprimand at the Vatican this morning I understand, for the violent and aggressive manner in which he conducts his Archiepiscopal duties in England.'[6]

The French Ambassador to the Vatican, M. de Corcelle, appears to confirm this:

Manning's opinions are his, and his alone – frequently in sharp contrast to those of the rest of the Curia. He is regarded here as one of the staunchest supporters of the Papal authority as defined at the 1870 Vatican Council; but at the same time as a Utopian individualist, who takes too great a part in politics. Manning's eloquent advocacy of a *modus vivendi* between Vatican and State obtains, as can be imagined, little support here. He also proclaims that the Italian capital should move back to Florence – or on to Naples! I have had several conversations with him on English policy, and he recommends that his country, France and Austria should all join in a pact with the Holy See against the pretentions of Prussianized Germany. This is indeed Utopian.'[7]

Sir Augustus Paget's expectation that Manning would for this reason fail to obtain a Cardinal's hat was, however, confounded. Whereupon Paget wrote, 'I am told that Manning said it was a much greater satisfaction to him to be raised to the Purple now in the time of the Pope's affliction, than it would have been under more prosperous circumstances – which happy days however he is convinced will return to the Catholic Church, with all her lost possessions and the temporal power of the Pope.' Gregorovius has a revealing description of Manning in 1870, in his *Roman Journals*: 'Sat near Manning at the Arnims last evening and closely observed this English fanatic, a little grey man looking as if encompassed with cobwebs . . . he extended his hand to be kissed by new arrivals in the manner of an elderly courtesan accustomed to such acts of homage.'[9]

On the death of Pius IX and the accession of Leo XIII in 1878, Manning's influence at the Vatican waned. It seems that Leo XIII was by no means as enthusiastic about him as his predecessor had been. So in the last fifteen years of his life in England, Manning turned his attention to social questions, with which his name is now firmly associated. He sat on two Royal Commissions, one for Housing the Working Classes (1884), the other on Primary Education (1886); and he did much for the Irish poor who formed a large part of his flock. He took a leading part on behalf of the dockers in settling their strike of 1889, when he was denounced as a socialist. He always denied this, but said he favoured some of the socialists' methods for relieving poverty. In later years, his strenuous advocacy of the claims of the working classes, his declaration that 'Every man has a right to bread and work', attracted Leo XIII's attention, when the Pope was issuing his famous social Encyclical *Rerum Novarum*. But this remarkable English convert never again enjoyed the great power he had wielded in Rome under Pius IX, in that heyday of his career, the time of the First Vatican Council and the Proclamation of Infallibility.

Relations between the British Government and the Vatican continued to improve in spite of setbacks from time to time due to the 'Irish Question'. In the Vatican Archives for 1883 is this comment on the 'English Anomaly':

It seems anomalous that the most determined enemies of an official English representative at the Vatican – and a Papal representative in England – are the Irish bishops. The explanation is that they know that a direct representative of the Pope resident in England will deprive them of the absolute authority they have exercised for so long [since the English break with Rome in the sixteenth century] in Catholic ecclesiastical affairs, and especially in the appointment of Colonial bishops in the British Empire, in whose selection the English Crown might wield a beneficial and legitimate influence. Today, most of the Colonial bishops, being Irish, are nominees of the Primate of Ireland.[10]

The Irish Catholic M.P.s sitting in Westminster presented a further anomaly. They were jealous of potential English influence at the Vatican, which the establishment of official relations would have encouraged, and they continuously opposed any move in that direction.

The only other setback to Anglo-Papal relations was caused by the Boer War. Here the Vatican sympathies lay with the Boers (at least as expressed in the Vatican press, particularly the *Voce della Verità*). M. Amisard, the French representative at the Vatican, pointed out in 1900: 'Cardinal Rampolla, the Secretary of State, has always expressed sentiments unfavourable to the Anglo-Saxon races, whose progress appears to him to constitute a growing peril for the nations of Latin origin and culture. He is following the English setbacks in the Boer War with the closest attention, so close that it is clear where his sympathies lie.'[11]

Catholic opinion in England was offended by these articles in the Vatican press, and the English annual pilgrimages to Rome were discontinued during the Boer War, including the one of the Papal jubilee. Cardinal Vaughan on a visit to Rome ostentatiously walked out of a meeting of the *Propaganda Fide* (the committee on missionary activities) when a young Dutchman addressed it in his native tongue. When Cardinal Rampolla was asked by the French Ambassador how authentic were the articles in the *Osservatore Romano* and the *Voce della Verità*, he replied disingenuously that neither of them were official or unofficial organs of the Holy See. The latter was therefore not responsible for the views expressed therein (except for the official news column in the *Osservatore Romano*, 'Nostre Informazioni').

It was not until the World War of 1914 that it was possible to re-establish official relations with the Holy See, and then for an entirely pragmatic reason. During the first months of the war, the British became aware that, because the Entente had no relations with the Holy See,[12] the Central Powers enjoyed a great advantage, thanks to their well-staffed Embassies at the Vatican. There is much to be learned at this sounding-board of the world; political as well as ecclesiastical information of all kinds pours into the Vatican through its nuncios, bishops, priests, and missionaries from all over the world. Moreover, whereas the diplomat of the lay states comes into contact with only a limited section of the population of the land he is accredited to – the upper and official classes – the Catholic priests and missionaries move among all classes, and can report to their bishops every shade of public opinion. A later German Ambassador to the Holy See, Herr von Weizsäcker, referred to 'that incomparable centre of information called the *Propaganda Fide* with its polyglot printing press for all the languages of the world, even reaching out to Tibetan, Armenian, and Lapp'. [13]

Sir Rennell Rodd, the British Ambassador to the Quirinale, described the situation in 1914:

> A consideration for us in dealing with clerical influence here lies in the fact that, practically, only one side in the war is represented at the Vatican – the Central Powers. There is, it is true, a Belgian Minister, but he is very old and is seldom seen anywhere. There is also a Russian Minister, but Russia is always distrusted in Roman ecclesiastical circles, and the representative's influence may be regarded as nil. With France, diplomatic relations were of course broken off years ago. On the other hand, the Central Powers are strongly represented. The Austro-Hungarian Ambassador, Prince Schönberg, is a conspicuous figure with high prestige. The Prussian Minister, Herr von Mühlberg, eminently competent and by his long experience at the Wilhelmstrasse [equivalent to Downing Street] closely connected with the administrative machine, is active in promoting the interests of his Government. The Bavarian representative, Baron de Ritter, carries weight with the clericals by his reputation for devoutness. All these three diplomats are constantly engaged in offering hospitality to the ecclesiastical hierarchy and to the priesthood, who are not a little swayed in their sympathies by these attentions. . . . A great deal of the pernicious literature poured out from German printing presses is disseminated through these channels. . . . [14]

Even the most anti-Papal groups in England had to admit that in time of war, the Vatican was too valuable a centre of information to be ignored. Britain accordingly established a Mission there in December 1914, under Sir Henry Howard. In the Italian State Archives a further reason is given for this. England, it says, hopes Italy will soon enter the war on the Entente side, and is most displeased with the Pope for instructing his clergy to encourage Italy's neutrality. If an English Mission were to be opened at the

Holy See, says the Italian memo, it would be able to bring pressure on the Pope to desist from this pacifist advice.[15]

Although a Catholic, Sir Henry Howard did not prove a very satisfactory choice – for that very reason. A Foreign Office Memorandum in 1917 advises:

> In future it would be better to send a man who is not a Catholic. The English Minister should naturally be someone of importance, but he should not be filled with an unreasoning awe of the Pope; this precludes anything like friendly intercourse, still more argument with His Holiness. Moreover, by sending a Protestant, we shall emphasize to the Vatican that our Mission is purely political, having nothing to do with religion – as political as a Mission to the Dalai Lama might be. Secondly, although the Vatican professes to be flattered by the courtesy of H.M.'s Government in sending a Catholic, they really don't care a fig. It is a matter of complete indifference to the Vatican if we are represented by a Mohammedan or a Buddhist. Prussia, for instance, is represented at present by Herr Mühlberg who is more of a Jew than a Lutheran.[16]

The cynical nature of these counsels explains why after the war, attempts were made in the British Parliament to withdraw the Mission, and break off diplomatic relations again. The war was won. Britain had got what she wanted. Moreover, during the Mission's existence at the Vatican, the British Parliament had been bombarded with petitions from bodies ranging from the Presbyterian Church of Scotland and the Home Counties Baptist Association to the Londonderry Apprentice Boys and the Mens' Bible Class in Liverpool, all deploring, often in violent terms, 'the English Government's connivance with Popery'. Typical was the objection of the first of these bodies:

> We enter our earnest protest against the suicidal [sic] policy pursued by the British Government in pandering to the nefarious intrigues of the Papacy. . . . Every step taken to satisfy the claims of this foreign power, with its aim of overthrowing the constitutional government of Great Britain and setting up the temporal power of the Pope again, has led our nation into deeper water. . . . The present deplorable condition of Ireland follows

from the intrigues of the Papacy. Is it not time that an effective stop was put to dallying with the Man of Sin's claims and his intrigues against this Protestant nation?[17]

The ghost of Titus Oates walked again. In less intemperate language, their general objection was that a British Legation to the Holy See was contrary to the Act of Settlement of 1701, and at variance with the King's Coronation oath.

The arguments for and against the Mission continued until 1922. Sir Alexander Cadogan of the Foreign Office thought that in the short term Britain ought to retain it, because it might be of value in the difficult Irish and Irish-American relations; but that *in the long term* she should withdraw because, as he minuted, 'The influence of the Vatican in world politics must be antagonistic to our country, both on account of our historical championship of Protestantism, and because we are normally in the van of liberal progress in thought and policy.' This was repeated by Mr Harold Nicolson, then a junior clerk at the Foreign Office, who minuted: 'The Mission has done no positive good since its institution. The only argument for retention is a negative one – that offence would be given to the Holy See if it were withdrawn.'[18]

Against these objections, however, was ranged more powerful opinion, notably Mr Vansittart and the Foreign Secretary himself, Lord Curzon. The former pointed out that while there were only two million Catholics in Britain, there were thirty million in the Empire, and the number was increasing. It was important, said Vansittart, to be able to influence the Holy See in ecclesiastical appointments in the colonies and India. It was also noted that although the scope of the Mission was in the first instance connected exclusively with the war, it had soon proved of value in other fields where friction with Catholics was liable to arise, notably: the troubles in French-speaking Canada in connection with the language question in schools; questions connected with the Holy Places, under British mandate since 1918, and the claims of France there to a religious Protectorate; Ireland, and the right claimed by the British Crown of presentation of certain bishoprics in Bombay.

In all these matters, Mr Vansittart was supported by Lord Curzon who, in answer to a Parliamentary Question in November 1923, replied, 'His Majesty's Government have decided after full and careful consideration that it is desirable in the public interest to continue the diplomatic representation of Great Britain at the Vatican, which has been in existence since the first year of the war, and which has been attended with beneficial results.'[19] However, to appease the powerful Protestant and Nonconformist lobby, the Government had to adopt the compromise solution of not appointing a British *Ambassador* to the Holy See, as did all other countries – but only a Minister, and a Protestant one at that.[20]

12

The Achievement of Leo XIII

The achievement of Leo XIII is symbolized by the changed circumstances outside St Peter's at his Coronation in 1878, and at his death twenty-five years later in 1903. The conduct of the Italian Government on both occasions is significant. For the first, his Coronation on 3 March 1878, all the arrangements had been made for it to take place in St Peter's; but two days before this, the *Camerlengo* Cardinal countermanded them and transferred the ceremony to the Sistine Chapel. This change was explained by the British Ambassador to the Italian State, Sir Augustus Paget.[1] He says that the Camerlengo in charge of the Coronation ceremony had conveyed to the Italian Government a request that, in view of the many untoward incidents which had occurred with the Turbolenti in public places, the Government should provide police and troops in sufficient numbers outside St Peter's to maintain order while the three-hour ceremony unfolded. To this the Government replied curtly that as the election of the new Pope had not been announced *officially* by the Vatican to the King of Italy, the Italian Government had no knowledge of the existence, let alone the accession, of Leo XIII. In these circumstances, they regretted that they could not provide protection for a non-existent ceremony.

Contrast this with a similar request at the time of Leo XIII's death, twenty-five years later. Although during his reign relations with the Italian State had improved, he had never renounced the temporal claims of the Papacy – which meant that official relations between Church and State still did not exist. At his death there could therefore be no *official* notification of it to the State authorities. Nevertheless, on this occasion perfect understanding appears to have existed between the Vatican and the State. The approaches to St Peter's were occupied by police and troops, who were discreetly drawn up out of sight behind Bernini's colonnade. The flags on the municipal buildings on the Capitol were at half-mast. The bands which usually played in the public squares were silenced. The theatres were closed for two days. The shops put up their shutters. When, some days later, the election of the new Pope, Pius X, was announced from the exterior loggia of St Peter's, the Italian troops drawn up in the Piazza presented arms. All this would have been impossible when Leo XIII came to the Papal Throne twenty-five years before.

Leo XIII's achievement is summed up in the Malachy sobriquet for him, *Lumen in coelo* ('Light in the heavens').[2] During his reign, the situation of the Papacy had greatly improved, and his 'light' was everywhere apparent. In those twenty-five years, the Catholic Church, far from becoming progressively weakened as its adversaries had forecast, had gathered strength and believers. Leo XIII had made himself acceptable, even congenial, to the ministers of foreign powers with whom Pius IX had refused to have dealings. In Ireland, Germany, France, Poland, he had succeeded in promoting between Catholics and the governments of those very different countries an atmosphere of mutual understanding and compromise. The British Ambassador, Sir Rennell Rodd, wrote of Leo XIII after his death:

. . . appreciated for his lofty character and aspirations, and the phenomenal activity of his mind. Unlike his predecessor, he always understood and employed a measured language . . . as parsimonious with his benedictions and maledictions as his predecessor was prodigal. He personally announced his accession to those States with which Pius IX had no relations, indicating his desire to resume friendly relations. . . . The diminution of the "prisoner in the Vatican" mentality is due to his frequent appearances in later years on festive occasions in St Peter's.[3]

Leo XIII has been aptly compared with an earlier Pope who had also inherited a crucial situation from his predecessors, and who employed his diplomatic skills to redress it: Pius IV, the famous Pope of the Council of Trent in 1545. At that time the Reformation had just opened the most serious schism in Christian Europe since the time of the rival Pope at Avignon. Pius IV was successful in his dealings with the European powers, not as a religious zealot, but as a scrupulous jurist; not by masterful authority, but by pliant diplomacy; not by forcing, but by following, the current of events. In the same way Leo XIII, three hundred and fifty years later, was always prepared, if he could not obtain the whole, to be satisfied with the part; if need be, to compromise religion for the sake of expediency; who used the Papacy – in the words of Sir Rennell Rodd – 'as an international political agency'. By adroit comprom-ise, Leo XIII succeeded in arresting the encroachments of the State on ecclesiastical administration in France and Italy. In a diplomatic battle with Germany lasting six years he successfully contained, and finally thwarted, the most powerful statesman in Europe, Prince Otto von Bismarck (see Chapter 6).

In 1870, wherever the Church had looked, she had seen new liberal governments threatening to eradicate clerical influence from their lands. Yet during the next twenty years, these governments had learned to their cost that they were, by the very nature of liberalism, at the mercy of constantly shifting Parliamentary majorities, and that if they were to keep in power, they required all the support they could find; and this included that of practising Catholics in their lands.

Leo XIII was quick to appreciate this, and to take advantage of it. His method for dealing with the secular powers, retreating in one field only to advance in another, revealed a statesmanship unknown in any Pope since his namesake, Leo XII. Yet in whatever field Leo XIII moved, he never departed from the religious principles on which his behaviour was based. He would have contended that this was nothing new, because the Church had been saying it since the fifth century, when Pope Gelasius I announced: 'Mankind is governed by two powers – the Supreme Pontiff and the Caesars. Since the Church's aims are transcendental, it is the greater of the two – just as the spirit is greater than the flesh. The Church cannot be subjected to Caesarean authority.' All this Leo XIII included in his Encyclical of 1885 on relations between Church and State, *Immortale Dei* ('To Immortal God . . .'), in which he asserted that the Vicar of Christ, by virtue of an authority transcending that of lay governments, has the right to advise governments and act as their guide.

In the Italian State Archives for 1898 is a memorandum summing up Leo XIII's diplomatic skills – and the danger they presented to Italy. The writer, a senior Italian diplomat, gave an example of Leo XIII's 'Machiavellianism'. He instanced the desire of two countries, France and Germany, to obtain special facilities from the Pope for the Protectorate of Catholics in the Orient (for these could promote national, as well as religious, interests). The ambassadors of the two countries, M. Poubelle and Herr von Bülow, are most assiduous, he says, at the Vatican to obtain this valuable concession. 'For some months', he writes, 'Leo XIII has played a most artful game of cat and mouse with them both. He would indeed belie his Machiavellian reputation, if he did not nicely hold the balance between these two ambitious rivals, being careful not to discourage either of them. Both M. Poubelle and Herr von Bülow come away from their regular visits to the Vatican smiling, apparently satisfied. But later they find that they have achieved precisely nothing.'[4]

Pius IX would have no dealings with the Italian State, refusing even the help of an intermediary. Leo XIII did not depart from this official line; but he was prepared to communicate with the State through any suitable person – on one occasion a most unusual one. The use of Frenchmen, Germans or Europeans would have implied partiality, so he employed a Turk, Galliani, the Turkish Consul in Rome. In the Italian State Archives is a comment on this Turk: 'Signor Galliani is a Catholic of Greek origin, who contrives simultaneously to be pro-Catholic, pro-Greek, and pro-Mahomet. Such a man is a boon to this Pope. Although he is accredited to our Government, this does not prevent the Turk from having continuous relations with, and being on the best of terms with, the Vatican. On a number of occasions, we have employed him on secret missions to the Pope, who readily receives him.'[5]

These 'secret missions' are understandable for, towards the end of Leo XIII's reign, the Italian Government was becoming most curious about what was happening at the Vatican, and in particular about the Pope's state of health. Although coming to the Papal Throne in frail health and at the age of sixty-seven, Leo XIII had proved far removed from the 'stopgap' Pope everyone had expected. He was now entering on his ninety-second year. As his reign proceeded, the Italian Government had become aware that the Vatican, far from losing every vestige of temporal power, was again becoming a European centre of considerable importance.

Would this continue after Leo XIII's death? In the later years of his Pontificate, the Italian Government became so interested in his health that it opened a special department in the Palazzo Braschi, the Ministry of the Interior, concerned exclusively with the subject.

Intelligence of these inquisitorial activities occasionally percolated into the Vatican, where they were a source of some amusement to Leo XIII. His personal physician, Dr Lapponi, was followed everywhere, and an observer was placed outside his house, to watch him discreetly on his daily visits to the Pope. If he stayed only half an hour in the Vatican, it was assumed that the Pope was in good health. But sometimes the visits were prolonged, providing the government gossips with wild surmise. On one occasion, Dr Lapponi arrived at 4 p.m. and did not leave until 11 p.m. The Roman papers came out the next morning with the headline that the Pope was seriously ill. In fact, the Pope had been having his afternoon nap when the doctor arrived; the latter did not wish to disturb him and had waited. When the Pope awoke, he was in the best of humours and invited Dr Lapponi to sup with him that night and tell him the city gossip. On being later shown a copy of the *Popolo Romano*, which paper carried an article announcing his approaching death, the Pope laughed and quoted the Italian proverb, '*Morte desiderata vita allungata*' ('A longed-for death prolongs life').[6]

The recovery of Papal fortunes during the reign of Leo XIII undoubtedly owed much to the Pope himself; but there were also certain circumstances outside his control which played an important part. The new Italian State, which in 1870 had presented itself to the Italian people as in a sense an alternative to the Papacy, had not flourished as expected; many Italians were disillusioned, in particular the middle and commercial classes, who had regarded the unification of Italy as a certain source of financial gain. That this had not materialized was due principally to the high cost of becoming a great power and joining the Triple Alliance; to the huge military and naval establishments required for it, the mammoth cannon and leviathan battleships, and the resulting burden of taxation.[7] Italy aspired to empire, to imitate the British, to expand overseas and become a great Mediterranean power again. Her gaze was turned on Africa, Tripolitania and Libya, to the past glories of the great Scipio Africanus:

Figlia di Roma l'Italia si desta
Del elmo di Scipio si cinge la testa
'The daughter of Rome, Italy awakes
and sets Scipio's helmet on her head.'

The youth of Italy was accordingly exhorted to join up, to learn
to wield the musket and the bayonet, to become inured to hardship
and inspired with the love of danger. But all these efforts to instil
Romans and Neapolitans with the old martial virtues were in vain.
The nation proved incapable of returning to the glorious days of
Scipio.

Moreover, if geographical unity of the peninsula had been
achieved, ethnic unity had not. The elements composing the new
Italian nation were too disparate. Italy had been a land of
independent city states for too long. The industrious Florentine
looked down with contempt on the lazy, poor but proud Roman.
The Venetians regarded the Milanese as barbarians. The Genoese
nourished a century-old hatred of the Venetians. And all of these
considered themselves superior to what they saw as the indolent,
dirty, and untrustworthy Neapolitan. This disillusion with the new
Italian State is summed up by the Cardinal Secretary of State
Rampolla in a circular:

> Italy is not doing well. She is beginning to question the stability
> of the building she has erected from so many component parts.
> The Italian State founded on revolution, penetrated with secret
> societies [he is referring to the Camorra and its numerous
> Mazzinian offshoots], with no conservative counterbalance as
> long as Catholics abstain from the Parliamentary urns, is
> beginning to feel the need for surer foundations. Those who have
> repudiated the lesson of history and all paternal tradition,
> believed they could erect a many-faced edifice on the ruins of the
> monolithic Papacy. They could not imagine that this new
> edifice, spurning the natural centre of gravity [the Papacy], must
> sooner or later collapse.[8]

Leo XIII's lot was cast in quieter times than those of his
predecessor, and he was freer to indulge his literary tastes and
projects. One of his most memorable achievements was the
opening of the Vatican Secret Archives in 1880 to scholars of all

nations and religious faiths. Until then, they had remained under Sixtus V's sixteenth-century interdiction that no lay researcher might work in them. In contrast to this, Leo XIII proudly announced that the Church had nothing to fear from laymen discovering the truth. A Dante-lover, he also encouraged young clerics to read the *Divine Comedy*, which had been proscribed on account of its advocacy of Italian unity, and for depicting a number of Popes in Hell.[9]

Where he differed from Pius IX was that he did not isolate himself, nor withdraw into the Vatican. Leo XIII believed that the Pope must take a visible part in the affairs of men, preach the eternal values to these 'moderns' who believed that by inventing the motor car and other mechanical gadgets they had transformed themselves into gods. He did not take his predecessor's view that with such misguided mortals there could be no dealing. Leo XIII would not ignore them; he would save them from themselves. On the other hand, he realized that science had a part to play in the modern world, and he encouraged Catholic scientific congresses. Whereas his predecessor's pronouncements on these and similar subjects had aroused hostility towards the Church among the statesmen of Europe, Leo XIII's aroused sympathy. In the words of the French Catholic journal *Le Monde*, 'Where Pius IX opened an abyss, Leo XIII traversed it with a bridge.'[10]

13

Pius X –
Signs of Conciliation

In our own times we have become so accustomed to having the common man as ruler – Hitler, Stalin, Mussolini, Tito, etc – that we often forget that, until the twentieth century, these leaders were the exception rather than the rule. It was the same with the Papacy. Until Pius X in 1903, there had not been a peasant Pope since Sixtus V in 1588. All the intervening Popes came from the upper or educated classes. But Giuseppe Sarto, who ascended the Papal throne in 1903 as Pius X, was the sixth son of a Veneto postman.

Certain historians have pointed to a Papal phenomenon – that a new Pope is often the direct opposite of his predecessor. Certainly, the personalities of Pius IX and Leo XIII had contrasted, the political intransigence of the former, the diplomatic address of the latter. This contrast was now repeated between Leo XIII and his successor Pius X. Leo XIII was the finished scholar, the skilled diplomat and man of the world. Pius X had never been out of his native Veneto, where he had risen owing to his patent qualities of simplicity and sheer goodness to become Patriarch of Venice. The Veneto is a region of formal Catholicism and restricted intellectual curiosity; and Giuseppe Sarto's limited experience of the modern world was responsible for his native distrust of politicians and intellectuals. The German writer Dr A. Hoch says that when, at a Papal audience, he referred to certain political questions of the day, Pius X replied, 'I understand nothing about politics. I am not a diplomat. My policy is there——' He turned and pointed to a crucifix hanging on the wall.

When Delcassé, the French Foreign Minister, was informed that the new Pope was very 'spiritual' and unworldly, he observed that this could be dangerous. He said that for a Church such as the

179

Catholic, worldwide in its responsibilities and the scope of its activities, *all* acts of its leader are political acts. A purely 'spiritual' Pope, he said, acting only according to the dictates of his conscience as a priest, without considering their possible political effect, might be acting very dangerously both for the Church and the world. Cardinal Manning said much the same, if in a different way, when he was asked why the Holy Father should touch on politics at all: '. . . because politics are a part of morals. What the moral law of the Ten Commandments is to the individual, politics are to society. Politics are nothing more than the morals of society.'[1]

The election of Giuseppe Sarto to the Throne of St Peter came about in an exceptional way. It had generally been assumed before the Conclave of 1903 that Leo XIII's Secretary of State, Cardinal Rampolla, would receive the greatest number of votes. To many of the Curia Cardinals, he was the man best suited to follow in the steps of Leo XIII. Cardinal Matthieu summed up this attitude: 'We have just lost a Pope who has restored the prestige of the Papacy. What better than to elect as his successor the man who was his closest adviser and the sharer of his thoughts? The devoted collaborator in all his great designs? Where can we find such experience in world affairs?' Yet Rampolla was defeated in an unexpected way, by the Emperor of Austria's use of the *Veto*.

It is worth recalling at this point that the year was 1903, when the great powers were already taking up their dispositions, lining up for the struggle ahead. Both the emerging adversaries, the Triple Alliance and the Entente, were canvassing potential support; and that included the Papacy.

The *Veto* (Latin: 'I forbid') was a historical right shared by the four great Catholic powers, France, Austria, Spain and Portugal, of excluding any candidate for the Papacy whom one of them objected to. In those days, the Papal States were a political power to be reckoned with, and a new Pope could be a powerful ally or adversary. The last occasion when the *Veto* had been used was in 1846, by Spain to defeat the candidature of the ex-Nuncio in Madrid, Cardinal Giustiani.[2] In 1903, thirty years after the loss of the temporal power, everyone regarded the *Veto* as an antidiluvian weapon which would never be used again. However, the Archbishop of Cracow, Cardinal Puznya, was instructed by his master, Emperor Franz Josef of Austria, to invoke it, if Cardinal Rampolla appeared to be obtaining the requisite number of votes.

During his long period as Leo XIII's Secretary of State, Cardinal Rampolla had been consistently hostile to Austria and the Triple Alliance, and friendly to its enemy, France.

The Conclave opened on 5 August 1903, when Rampolla as *Camerlengo* announced the ballot results. He read out the first ballot without displaying the slightest emotion – that Cardinal Rampolla was leading with twenty-four votes, followed by Cardinal Gotti with seventeen. On the next ballot, Rampolla had advanced to twenty-nine, while Gotti had fallen to fifteen. (Cardinal Sarto had at this time only ten.) Rampolla now seemed assured of the requisite two-thirds majority. Then came the thunderclap. The Archbishop of Cracow communicated officially to the Conclave his Emperor's *Veto* to the candidature of Cardinal Rampolla. The ensuing scene was described in the British Ambassador, Sir Rennell Rodd's, despatch: 'It appears that Cardinal Rampolla was flabbergasted, and that in his capacity as *Camerlengo*, he spoke up sharply to the Archbishop of Cracow, "Tell your Emperor in Vienna that the Conclave will tolerate no outside interference with its freedom of election!" '[2] Nevertheless, this intervention had the desired effect; Cardinal Rampolla received only one more vote that afternoon. It soon became clear that because he had a number of opponents among the Italians, he now had as many votes as he was likely to secure. The opposition of the Austrian and German cardinals, following the lead of the Archbishop of Cracow, meant that he could never obtain the two-thirds of the sixty-two available votes. The next day a number of his supporters, realizing that his chances were fading, transferred their allegiance to Cardinal Sarto, preferring him to Cardinal Gotti. The result, concluded the British Ambassador, 'means the rejection by the Sacred College of Rampolla's pro-French policy, and a triumph for the partisans of the Triple Alliance'.[3] The use of the *Veto* on this occasion was also an indication that, although the Papacy had lost its temporal power, it still exercized a political force in the world. Otherwise, the Emperor of Austria would not have taken such a drastic step.

No one appears to have been more surprised than the Patriarch of Venice himself. When, a week before the Conclave, he had left Venice by train for Rome, he had bought a return ticket; and on his arrival in Rome, he had laughed at his friend Dr Ernesto's suggestion that he might have a chance. 'I do not think,' he said, 'that the Holy Ghost would commit such a folly.' When it became clear in the Conclave that he was likely to win, he remonstrated with his supporters. Josef Schmidlin, the German Papal historian, reports that his eyes filled with tears while, pale and trembling, he entreated them to disregard him: 'I am unworthy! Forget me! My election would be the ruin of the Church.'[4]

In the opinion of the American Cardinal Gibbons who was present, this very self-depreciation made him, in the eyes of the Sacred College, all the more *papabile* ('fit to be Pope'). To his repeated assertions of his unworthiness and poor health, Gibbons and his supporters reminded him – somewhat ineptly, it would seem – of the saying of Caiaphas, 'It was expedient that one man die for the people than that the whole world perish'.[5] If he returned to Venice, they said, his conscience would torment him for ever. Confused and near to fainting, he entreated them, 'Let this cup pass from me!' But when the final figures were announced, he agreed meekly, 'So be it! It is God's will.' He took the name Pius in admiration, he said, of the three Piuses of the nineteenth century, who had borne their sufferings so bravely – Pius VI and Pius VII under Napoleon, and Pius IX under the new Italy.

The new Pope was corpulent, moon-faced, with a cheery smile, kindly of heart, and entirely without pride. He spoke the dialect of the Veneto, and when he was informed that he would in future have to employ the first person plural in referring to himself, he replied that it would be time enough to think about that after his Coronation. He knew Church Latin but no foreign languages, and was the first Pope in modern times unable to speak French. In an earlier Consistory when, as Patriarch of Venice, he had been summoned to Rome, he had found himself sitting beside the French Cardinal Lecot. The Frenchman was amazed that this eminent Italian Cardinal could not speak French. Such a man could surely never become Pope. According to Pius X's biographer Marchesan, the conversation was as follows:

'*Votre Éminence est sans doute Archévêque en Italie. Dans quelle diocèse?*'

'*Non parlo francese,*' replied Cardinal Sarto.

Whereupon the French prelate put the question in Latin: '*In quaquam diocese es archiepiscopus?*'

'*Sum patriarcha Venetiae.*'

'*Non loqueris gallice?*'

'*No.*'

'Ergo non es papabilis siquidem papa debet gallice loqui.'
'Verum est Eminentissime Domine! Non sum papabilis. Deo gratias!'[6]
Cardinal Lecot had to admit some years later at the Coronation of Pius X that this conversation had happily not been a prophecy.

The Coronation took place in St Peter's, and it was clear at the outset of his reign that Pius X intended to be 'the people's Pope'. The British Ambassador, Sir Rennell Rodd, who was present at the ceremony, reported:

It was his express wish that the special enclosure reserved for distinguished personages, diplomats and officials, should be restricted to the smallest possible dimensions; and that St Peter's should be open on the day to all classes without distinction. Although admission to such ceremonies is normally restricted by ticket, no limit was put on the number issued to parish priests all over Italy for distribution. To all intents and purposes, it was a ceremony with open doors. I estimate that there were upwards of fifty thousand people going in and out of St Peter's that morning.[7]

The British Ambassador described the ceremony, also making some pertinent observations on the personality of the new Pope:

At ceremonies of this nature in Rome, little restraint has in the past been imposed upon, or shown by, the public, who are accustomed to express their feelings by clapping or acclaiming in a manner little consistent with the dignity of a sacred edifice. As Pius X appeared, seated on the *Sedia Gestatoria*, preceded by the traditional seven candles, there was an outburst of applause. But it was immediately silenced by an eloquent gesture of disapproval from His Holiness. The silver trumpet then sounded, and the procession advanced into the body of the church. . . . The new Pope seemed at once to acquire a dominant influence over the dense mass of people, whose gaze was concentrated on him. Again and again throughout the ceremony, he repressed by a stern glance or gesture their enthusiasm, which repeatedly attempted to express itself in jubilation. . . . At last, after the interminable ritual, the Adoration of the Sacrament, the Rosary, the Advance to the Throne, the Cardinals' Act of Obedience, and the strange symbolism of the transitory nature of human greatness conveyed by the burning of a piece of tow steeped in wine held up to his face, *sic transit gloria mundi* ['thus the world's glory passes'], the mitre was removed and the Tiara with the Triple Cross was placed on his brow by Cardinal Macchi. Tumultuous applause broke out – to be again silenced by the Pope with a stern regard, and by pronouncing the Benediction in a most impressive manner. . . .

Thus, in his first moments as Head of the Catholic Church, Giuseppe Sarto made his personality felt, in humbleness not in pride; for as he said afterwards, 'It is not good that the servant of the Lord should be applauded in the house of his Master.'

The immediate problem facing Pius X was that of selecting a Secretary of State. The filling of the post was of some urgency, for the new Pope had little or no experience of foreign affairs. The choice he made appears to have been a good one, exceptional in that it was not an Italian, and that never before in the annals of the Church had such a young Secretary of State been appointed. Mgr Merry del Val was only thirty-eight. He was exceptional, too, in his cosmopolitan ancestry. In his veins flowed the blood of Spain, Ireland, England, Scotland and Holland – an accomplished linguist, a diplomat and a man of the world. Pius X explained his choice: '. . . because he speaks six languages, and knows the problems of all the countries'.[8]

The immediate problem facing the new Secretary of State was that of relations with Italy. Under Leo XIII, as we have seen, these had been steadily improving. But one of the first events of the new reign set them back – the assembling in Rome, after the Pope had only been on the throne a month, of an International Congress of Freethinkers. On being apprised of this, Cardinal Merry del Val immediately registered a strong protest to the Italian Government, at permitting an openly atheistic body to congregate in the Eternal City. But the anti-clerical element in Parliament had recently increased; not only was the protest ignored but, adding insult to injury, the Collegio Romano was selected as the venue for the freethinkers' congress – the ancient Jesuit College founded by Gregory XIII in 1579, where Father Bellarmine had lectured on the Trinity! Moreover, the authorities granted a sixty per cent reduction in railway fares throughout Italy for those freethinkers attending. Had it not been for the King's personal objection and intervention, one of his senior government ministers, for Education, would have opened the Congress officially. As it was, the Mayor of Rome, the atheist Nathan, made the inaugural speech. 'Rome,' he said, 'is a fitting arena for the noble struggle of the human intellect against superstition on which you are all engaged.' He organized a procession of eight hundred freethinkers who, preceded by bands and banners, marched to the breach at the Porta Pia, the Italian 'shrine' where, thirty-four years before, the Popes had been dispossessed of their patrimony. In face of this, there was little that Pius X and his Secretary of State could do except continue to protest, to close the Vatican during the week of the freethinkers' congress, and to order expiatory services to be held in all the churches of Rome.

This Mayor of Rome, Nathan, proved to be one of the sharpest thorns in the side of the Vatican since Garibaldi. The Vatican had originally objected to his mayoral election, as 'a provocation and an insult that a Jew who has been educated in England, and has been a Master of the Grand Orient [that is, a Freemason] should be appointed to the highest magistrature of the first Catholic city in the world'. Nathan founded an anti-clerical association with the provocative name of 'Giordano Bruno'. Its headquarters were situated in the Via della Porta Angelica, just beneath the Pope's private apartments. From his window, His Holiness could look out and see the red flag waving outside.

The 'Nathan incident', as it came to be called, was in itself of no great importance, but its international repercussions were. On 20 September 1910, the anniversary of the Italian occupation of Rome, Nathan made a speech at the Porta Pia, which contained not only sarcastic references to the Pope's Infallibility, but a number of obscene remarks about the Virgin Mary. If the indignation among religious people had been confined to Rome, or even Italy, the incident might soon have been forgotten. But the international press reported it widely. In Austria and Germany, it caused a veritable furore. Meetings of Catholics took place up and down the land to protest against these 'unheard-of insults to our Blessed Virgin by the Jewish Freemason Mayor of Rome'. The Mayor of Vienna, Herr Porzer, called on the Italian Ambassador in the Austrian capital, and warned him that 'The Pope's protection against insults of this nature is *no longer a purely Italian affair* but affects the whole Catholic world.' 'He was insolent enough to tell me,' reported the Italian Ambassador, 'that if we Italians cannot keep order in our own house, someone else will have to do it for us.'[9] The Catholic Ladies of Vienna then entered the fray. The Italian Ambassador reports that a huge *Frauenversammlung* (women's assembly) took place in the Vienna Rathaus, where the ladies passed a resolution that 'The base contumely and outrageous insults to the Virgin Mary pronounced by the Italian Jewish Freemason Nathan in Rome on 20 September have aroused the contempt and revulsion of the entire civilized world.' Further embarrassment was caused by the Bishop of Cologne, Cardinal Fischer, who travelled specially to Rome to present to His Holiness a protest signed by several thousand German Catholics at 'the Nathan insults to the Virgin Mary and the supine inability of the Italian Government to discipline him'.

The prospects for reconciliation seemed bleak, and Pius X's first pronouncement appeared to indicate, to the dismay of the moderates in the Vatican, that he was returning to the policy of Pius IX. The fact that he had taken the same name also pointed to this. 'We can take no other course,' he said, 'than that laid down by our predecessors – to restore all things in Christ, and repair the indignity which has been done to our Church.'

Nevertheless, on 14 June 1904, some ten months after his accession, the *Osservatore Romano* published a remarkable article which, to those accustomed to the periphrastic language of this Vatican mouthpiece, could mean only one thing: that the Holy See was revising its claims to the temporal power. The paper stated that the 'liberty' of the Church had its origin in the abandonment of Rome by the Eastern Emperors after Constantine; and then followed this most sibylline pronouncement:

The Church cannot divest herself of that guarantee until other ways of protecting her rights *better adapted to that end, or on parallel lines have been found* [italics author's]. . . . The only question at issue is whether it is lawful for the Church to accept a new juridical existence, in order to return gradually to the condition of the pre-Constantine era, to which it is evidently the desire of the returning Paganism to relegate her [this apparently a reference to the present Italian State]. . . . The civil principality she has claimed not as an end, but as a means of guaranteeing the liberty and independence offered by Providence, which the Church could not renounce until Providence had made it clear to her that a *better means could be found for ensuring these indispensable conditions* [italics author's].

Involuted this language may be, but it was clear enough to the Ultramontanes in the Vatican, who were most alarmed.

In reading the documents of the period, the first signs of this more conciliatory attitude towards the State are found in the despatches of M. Nissard, the French Ambassador to the Holy See. On 1 May 1903, he described the laying of the foundation stone for the rebuilt Campanile in St Mark's Square, Venice, by the Savoyard Count of Turin. Present at the ceremony was the Patriarch of Venice, Cardinal Sarto (he was not yet Pope). The French diplomat commented, 'This is the first time since 1870 that a Prince of the Church has appeared at a ceremony conducted under the auspices of the House of Savoy.'[10]

It was manifest that Giuseppe Sarto would be less hostile to that House than were his predecessors. Unlike them, he had never been a citizen of the Papal States, having been born and bred in the Veneto, where he had spent all his life, a greater part of it under Austrian rule. In those days, members of the Savoyard Royal Family frequently visited the City of the Lagoons for diversion; and after its incorporation into the new Italian State in 1867, the flagship of the Savoyard navy under the flag of the King's brother-in-law, the Duke of Genoa, was often anchored there. On several occasions, the Patriarch of Venice met members of the Royal Family in the city, and in 1897 he had a friendly conversation with the Crown Prince. When Cardinal Sarto arrived in Rome in 1903, and was elected Pope, he had of course to ignore the Savoyard Royal Family officially; but he already knew several of its members personally.

That the situation in Rome itself was changing is revealed in another despatch from the French Ambassador, a year later. 'Certain Cardinals of the Curia,' noted M. Nissard, 'appear to be establishing relations with the "White" aristocracy of Rome. It is not unusual now to come upon a member of the Sacred College seated at the dinner table beside a lady of that aristocracy, or even a Lady-in-Waiting to the Queen of Italy.'[11] He also referred to the

187

'allurements' which attract these ladies to take the road to the Vatican; of which the most significant example is described by the Papal Chamberlain, F. A. MacNutt. He related that one evening not long after Pius X's accession, a stately female figure, heavily veiled, was seen to descend from a simple carriage in the Cortile del Pappagallo. She was immediately ushered by a waiting footman up a small back staircase to the Sala dei Paramenti, where the Pope was pacing up and down, reading his breviary. The mysterious figure remained nearly an hour in his company, and then departed as she had come. She was Queen Margherita.[12]

On another occasion, the Duke and Duchess of Genoa were received unofficially and clandestinely by the Pope. 'The first time,' noted the French Ambassador, 'for over half a century that a Prince of the House of Savoy has set foot inside the Bronze Doors. What is certain,' he deduced, 'is that Pius X is adopting a completely different attitude towards Papal audiences. Regarding himself as "Father of All Catholics", he feels he cannot refuse an audience to anyone with respectable credentials, even if they are Italian State officials.'[13]

A further indication of conciliation was the presence of the Bishop of La Spezia at the launching of an Italian warship, the *Reina Margherita*, in 1904. He celebrated Mass on board and consecrated the Italian national flag. Then, in the presence of the Queen, he made a patriotic speech invoking the blessing of Heaven on the House of Savoy and its sovereign. On this, the British Ambassador to the Quirinale commented, 'It appears that the Bishop's speech had previously been submitted to, and approved of, by the Pope.'[14]

This year 1904 may be regarded as the turning-point in Italo–Vatican relations.[15] Henceforth, Papal and civic dignitaries were to be seen together on official occasions. Members of Parliament, Deputies as well as Senators, with their wives and families, visited the Vatican and walked in its gardens. The new French Ambassador, M. de Courcel, reported on 27 May 1904 that the Pope had just received two Deputies; one, Signor Galli, an ex-member of the Cabinet of the notorious anti-clerical Francesco Crispi; the other, Signor Santini, Deputy for one of the Roman *rioni* (wards).[16] In Rome, the Cardinal Vicar Respighi paid a visit to the army hospital, where he was received by the commanding officer with military honours.

The next year 1905 was marked by the official visit of the King of

Italy to Bologna, once the second city of the Papal States Its Bishop, Cardinal Svampa, took part in his reception and the attendant festivities. The French Ambassador reports that the Cardinal presented his homage to the King and accepted the royal invitation to dinner. That evening, having been received with the honours due to a Prince of the Blood, he sat at the right hand of the monarch.[17] Further royal visits were made that year to the cities of Cremona and Brescia, where the local bishops again paid their respects to His Majesty.

Another sign of conciliation was the tacit support given by a large number of eminent prelates to the Italian invasion and annexation of Turkish Tripolitania. The Church could hardly repudiate a policy which promised a wider extension of the field for its missionary activity. Moreover, as Sir Rennell Rodd somewhat cynically pointed out, 'It is well known that the Catholic bank, the Banco di Roma, has large commitments in Tripoli. It regards the Italian annexation as indispensable to safeguard its capital invested there.'[18]

A more important indication of improved relations came from the Pope himself, over the *Non Expedit*. This prohibition on Catholics voting in Italian Parliamentary elections had been faithfully observed by the devout since it was announced by Pius IX in 1871. '*Ne eletti ne elettori!*' he had said ('neither elected ones nor electors'). In 1906, Pius X informed the Italian episcopate that henceforth he would leave it to their individual discretion in the matter of Parliamentary elections. If they considered that a Parliamentary candidate who stood for order and propriety seemed in danger of defeat by a Socialist or Liberal, the *Non Expedit* need not be enforced: Catholics could in that case vote for the former candidate.

Principally as a result of this, in the 1909 Parliamentary elections, twenty-four candidates who were practising Catholics were elected, a cause for great rejoicing in moderate Vatican circles. But Pius X would not allow them to form a Catholic *political* party. This may seem strange, in view of the support given to the Church in Germany during the *Kulturkampf* by the Zentrum political party. But a disinclination to share responsibility for political disaster explains why the Church discourages political leadership by priests. Its view is that, broadly speaking, all politicians are, by the very nature of their calling, venal and corrupt. The Church does not wish to be closely associated with such a body of men, when the inevitable scandal comes to light. The Church therefore prefers to have Deputies in Parliament who are Catholics – as many as possible – but who remain isolated individually, exercising their beneficial influence on their own, not in concert with others. The corruption, when it comes to light, will, therefore, be confined to isolated members and not to a body enjoying the patronage of the Pope. In the words of Hergenrother, 'Pius X does not want Catholic Deputies. He wants Deputies who happen to be Catholics.'[19] In any case, a Catholic Party in Italy would have been too small numerically to achieve much; it was best in the circumstances to throw the weight of clerical support on the side of reasonable and moderate politicians.

A revealing side-light is thrown on the attitude of the Socialists towards the Papal relaxation of the *Non Expedit*. About this time, a petition was mooted in Parliament that the suffrage should be extended to illiterates. The Liberals and Socialists were of course normally in favour of such measures, as a very proper piece of 'democratic progress'. But on this occasion, they opposed it violently. The reason was that extension of the franchise to illiterates would increase the voting power of the Catholics, the peasantry being all 'under the thumb of the priests'.

The Italian Socialists were naturally displeased at these signs of reconciliation between Church and State, and they did what they could to restore the tension. One way was to uncover some clerical scandal, or supposed scandal – such as the affair of the Nuns of Milan. The Socialist press reported the discovery of a series of revolting sexual crimes committed on children in a Milanese religious house, by some nuns who were using their religious seclusion to conceal the extent of their immorality. They claimed that the Archbishop of Milan had given the institution his blessing, and they published sensational revelations, including the diary of a boy called Besson, who described the orgies. An outcry arose all over Italy at this supposed nunnish turpitude. But it finally transpired that the child was subject to hallucinations, and had invented the whole story himself.

The only other scandal of note which the Socialists uncovered, and for which the Vatican was held responsible, concerned the Nicaraguan Ambassador to the Holy See. In 1906 this diplomat, who bore the high-sounding name of Count Cralo di Matzenauer, was found to be supplementing his salary by selling Nicaraguan consular posts all over Europe to the highest bidders – rich tradesmen who wished to secure a social position as unpaid 'Pro-Consuls'. He was able to do this – the Socialists claimed – from the protection of his diplomatic immunity in the Vatican. He was recalled by the President of Nicaragua and dismissed the service. But the anti-clericals made much of this 'nest of corruption concealed behind the walls of the Vatican'.[20]

It was fortunate both for Italy and the Vatican at this time that the eleven-year rule of Pius X coincided almost exactly with that of Giovanni Giolitti, the President of the Italian Council of Ministers, a man who believed above all in moderation. The most outstanding politician between Cavour and Mussolini, Giolitti was at the head of affairs in Italy almost continuously from 1903 to 1914. His merit lay in his ability to compromise – or as his enemies put it, 'to be Mr Facing-Both-Ways'. He possessed the almost incredible faculty of being conservative and 'progressive' at once. He knew how to face opposition resolutely when he was sure of success, as well as to give way and resign when he was not – and to wait patiently for the opportune moment to return. In this way, he managed to keep on reasonable terms with the Vatican without alienating the Socialists, whose votes were essential for his legislation.

An instance of this: in 1908, the Socialist Deputies, headed by the ferocious anti-clerical Bissolati, introduced legislation to suppress religious education altogether in schools. Giolitti dared not openly oppose this, because the Socialists formed a powerful body in the Chamber. Equally, the Vatican was adamantly opposed to such a proposal. As head of the Government, Giolitti achieved the seemingly impossible. He proposed that while religious instruction should form part of the normal curriculum in primary schools, it could be eliminated in localities where a majority of the municipal councillors so desired. In the latter case, however, the school buildings were to be open for religious instruction *which would be given out of school hours* to those children whose parents wished it. So well did Giolitti present his case that his proposals were passed and both sides apparently satisfied.

Giolitti's origins and upbringing were responsible for this most unusual brand of Italian politician. By birth a Piedmontese, Giolitti had the character of that unemotional people. Educated as a lawyer, he had remained until the age of forty a civil servant in the Ministry of Finance, where he had become adept in all the complications of its subtle machinery. In 1901, he became a Parliamentary Deputy and then Minister of the Interior, in which capacity all the Prefects of Italy were under him; and on the Prefects depended the management of the electorate. He knew precisely the needs and aims of every Deputy and every constituency in the country, and what concessions to make to secure their support. He was not an orator, and his speeches never exceeded a quarter of an hour, and were totally devoid of those flowers of rhetoric with which Italian politicians invite applause. On being once accused of speaking too briefly in a debate, he replied, 'I regret that it is impossible for me, when I have finished what I have to say, to go on speaking.' Nor had he any great intellectual resources: he never originated anything. But after listening to the views of others, he adopted the most opportune of the counsels submitted.

Personally, Giolitti was a modest man of regular habits who avoided society, disapproved of luxury, and remained all his life comparatively poor. He was said to have refused the distinction of a title, preferring to remain in the unostentatious condition of the middle class from which he sprang. His only passion was love of power; his relaxation, like that of the legendary Roman hero Cincinnatus, to work in his garden. Such a man, while always upholding the interests of his country, was unlikely to cause the Papacy the embarrassment and tribulations it had known at the end of the nineteenth century. With such a man the Pope could co-operate.

14

The Power of the Pope

In the three decades which followed the Italian seizure of Rome, the principal enemies of the Catholic Church were, we have seen, the various atheist groups in a number of guises; anarchists, nihilists, positivists, freethinkers, socialists, the Turbolenti. These men may have differed about the means they advocated, but all agreed on the end: the elimination of the Catholic Church's hold over the mind of man, and ultimately the elimination of the Catholic Church.

Most of them openly proclaimed this, so that the Church knew exactly where it stood with them, and could take the necessary defensive measures. But in the first years of the Pontificate of Pius X, a more insidious enemy appeared, more dangerous as he saw it, because it came from within the body of the Church itself. A group of prelates who were deeply religious men demanded that the Church, instead of condemning the materialism of the modern world, should come to terms with it. For this reason, their movement assumed the somewhat graceless title of 'Modernism', by which was meant broadly the adaptation of the Catholic Faith to modern discoveries, scientific and historical. The Modernists called on the Pontiff to reconcile the Church with 'progress, liberalism and modern society'. They did not demand that the great truths of the Catholic religion should be altered, but that they should be considered afresh in the light of modern knowledge. In the words of one of their leading exponents, the French priest Alfred Loisy, they wished 'to adapt the Catholic religion to the intellectual, moral and social needs of the times'. 'Christian dogma,' said Loisy, in his book 'L'Évangile et l'Église', 'must be expressed in terms of contemporary knowledge, and it is always liable to modification, in relation to the progress of that knowledge. Dogmas are not truths fallen from Heaven and preserved in the precise form in which they appeared. They are living, not dead tenets.'

193

Loisy and his fellows contended that modern historical research had rendered many of the accepted interpretations of the Bible untenable – the Mosaic authorship of the Pentateuch, the Deluge, the Ark, the miraculous experiences of Joshua and Jonah, and so on. These events were symbolic, not factual. For instance, the world had not been created by God in six days, as described in the Book of Genesis; this meant 'six periods of years'. They contended that the traditional dogma promulgated by the Council of Trent in 1545, that all the books of the Bible had been written under the Divine inspiration of the Holy Ghost, were no longer defensible. From this attack on the historicity of the Old Testament, they turned to the Gospels, questioning St John's authorship of the fourth, as well as that of the Acts of the Apostles, the Book of Revelations, and the Epistles of St Paul. Modernism was essentially humanitarian, its goal a perfected Christian society on earth.

The most important Italian accession to its ranks was the writer Fogazzaro (1841–1911), a devout Catholic whose best known book was *Il Santo* ('The Saint'). In this work he described some young men addressing the Saint in these terms: 'Today, the Catholic Church, which proclaims herself the channel of life, fetters and stifles all that is youthful within her. She seeks to support all that is old and dilapidated. To us, these things mean death, distant but inevitable death.'

The Modernist movement was even more active outside Italy, in France and Austria, and among devout Catholics in the Protestant countries, England and Germany. In Austria, the Professor of Canonical Law at the University of Innsbruck, Professor Ehrmund, shocked the traditionalists with his set of lectures entitled '*Katholische Weltanschauung und freie Wissenschaft*' ('The Catholic View of the World and Free Science'). In these he questioned, on scientific grounds, miracles, the cult of relics, the Dogma of the Immaculate Conception, the Holy Trinity, even the divinity of Christ. In France, Marc Sangier founded a Catholic movement called *Le Sillon* which, in spite of its religious basis, was an attenuated form of Marxism. It advocated the deliverance of 'the people' from all authority not emanating directly from themselves, and it denied the principle of government by any elite, let alone a Catholic one.

In England, the Modernist standard-bearer was another priest, the ex-Jesuit Father George Tyrrell. In his book *Christianity at the*

Crossroads he wrote, 'My task is to hammer away at the great unwieldly carcass of the Roman Communion, and wake it from its mediaeval sleep. . . . We do not travel today by coach, or wear jerkins, or speak the language of Chaucer. . . .'

We may note here that the word 'Modernism', as denoting something new, is a misnomer. Six centuries before this, the famous 'Friar of Oxford', Roger Bacon (*c*.1214–94) had outlined his own brand of 'Modernism'. Like Tyrrell and his friends, he was a sincere Catholic, but he also considered that the Church must take more account of scientific phenomena. His principal treatise *Opus Majus* deals with an astonishing number of scientific subjects for those days, from possible methods of circumnavigating the globe, mechanically propelled boats and flying machines, to optics and the importance of mathematics in natural science. He was the first to describe the magnifying glass and spectacles. Yet at the same time, his religious conviction was demonstrated in the famous remark: 'A little knowledge inclineth a man to Atheism; but depth of knowledge bringeth man's mind back to Religion.' Pope Clement IV, suspecting Bacon of heresy, asked him to give an account of his views. Bacon wrote the *Opus Majus* and sent it to the Pope who, after he had read it, ordered Bacon's arrest and imprisonment. Bacon remained in prison ten years.

The impression may have been given until now that Pius X was a mild man, and that his outstanding quality was goodness of heart. This was broadly true; but in his case, gentleness did not mean weakness, nor compassion compromise. In the words of one of his biographers, Carlo Falconi, 'Pius X was a mixture of *curé de campagne* [country priest] and angel with a flaming sword.'[1] It frequently happens that when such men, after a series of insults and reverses, retaliate, their adversaries are disagreeably surprised. This happened now; for Pius X possessed all the instincts of the fighter, not for himself but for his belief, which far transcended any human or personal considerations. His abomination of those whom he called 'the spreaders of errors' brought forth an unexpected power of invective.

He said of the Modernists:

These people expect to be treated with oil, soap and embraces. But what they need – and what they will get – is a good fist. In a duel, you don't measure the blows you give – you just go on

195

giving them. War is not made with charity. It is a struggle, a duel. Our Lord scourged the Philistine traders with a whip. The error these men are spreading is much more deadly than those of Luther, because they are aimed not only at the Catholic Church, but at Christianity itself. They are trying to bring the Church to the world, not the world to the Church – reducing sacred things to a natural level, depriving religion of the supernatural.[2]

He instinctively feared that if the Church followed the Modernists, Catholicism would become a species of Humanist doctrine, not far removed from Protestantism itself. Then, like the latter, it would gradually degenerate into a number of sects, each with its own hierarchy.

In 1907, he condemned the Modernists unhesitatingly in the Decree *Lamentabile* and the Encyclicals *Pascendi*, and *Saepe Dei*, the strongest Papal anathemas since those of Pius IX thirty years before. *Pascendi* prescribed the purging of all recalcitrant personnel in Catholic university faculties and seminaries; the nomination of a Censor for every Catholic publication; the installation of a 'Vigilance Committee' in every diocese; and the submission every three months of a report to Rome by all bishops on their subordinates. In *Lamentabile*, he enumerated in sixty-seven clauses the 'errors' of the Modernists, most of them extracted from the writings of Loisy and Tyrrell. In suitably Biblical language, he ordered the bishops to 'trample underfoot all fleshly imprudence and, heedless of the outcry of the wicked, to proscribe and tear from the hands of the faithful all bad books and writings'. He commanded all priests to sign an 'anti-Modernist' oath.

In this he was supported in the Vatican by a powerful body of traditionalists, or 'Integralists' as they now called themselves who, under the leadership of the fanatical Cardinal De Lai, founded a *Sodalitium Planum* ('Association of Regularity'), a kind of secret society for combating 'Modernism' anywhere in the world. It attacked unreservedly all suspects, be they bishops, prelates, eminent Catholic laymen or perfectly respectable lay institutions. It founded anti-Modernist journals in all the European capitals. Many priests were, at its recommendation and on a mere suspicion of guilt, removed from clerical office and relegated to a monastery. Often an anonymous denunciation was sufficient to condemn a priest. In Sicily the Bishop of Piazza Armerina suffered in this way when he was denounced to the *Sodalitium Planum* by a group of local ladies for his 'Modernism'. Many of the accused defended themselves in pastoral letters, but this did not save them. Whoever they were, if they did not meet the exacting requirements of the *Sodalitium*, they were removed from office. When the Würzburg Professor Hermann Schell's book *The Church and Progress* was placed on the Index, its devout author was so overcome with grief that he expired. Of this incident the British Minister in Munich, Mr Fairfax-Cartwright, commented, 'The Schell affair has caused strong resentment to Papal interference in German affairs. Ultramontane influence at the Vatican has crushed the memory of a German Professor of exemplary life and devout belief.'[3] The same treatment was meted out to the French Academician, Mgr Duchesne, whose *Histoire de l'Église ancienne* ('History of the Ancient Church') had been a classic for twenty-five years, and whose author had been congratulated on it by Leo XIII.

The German Papal historian Josef Schmidlin, who is generally well disposed towards the Papacy, said about the *Sodalitium Planum:* '. . . an evil secret society which has had disastrous effects not only in the political but in the cultural field. If Pius X cannot be accused of being the instigator of this worldwide plot [sic], which has denigrated and destroyed so many fine and noble Catholics, he must at least be censured for having protected it.'[4]

In fact, it seems that on a number of occasions it was less the Pope himself than the Integralists such as Cardinal De Lai who were responsible for these Draconian measures. The incident of Don Sturzo exemplifies this. In Sicily, the socialworker priest, Don Luigi Sturzo, had in 1905 become mayor of his town, Cattagnioni. It is unusual for a priest to be mayor, but he hoped thereby to improve the lot of the peasantry. He was informed from Rome that 'the office of mayor is not compatible with the cassock', and that a special Apostolic Visitor would come and examine him to determine if he were a Modernist. When he learned that the Visitor had been sent by Cardinal De Lai, he feared the worst. This seemed confirmed when he was summoned to Rome for an audience with the Pope. He relates that as he knelt before the Pope, he was trembling. But Pius X smiled and said, 'Well Father Mayor, so they haven't excommunicated you yet?'

'But Your Holiness,' replied Don Sturzo, surprised, 'surely it is Your Holiness who does that?'

'I – no!' laughed the Pope. 'But be on your guard against *them!*'

Don Sturzo says that the Pope then 'blessed me and my social work with paternal affection'. The incident is a comment on the power of 'them' to whom the Pope referred, the Integralists who surrounded him.[5]

The spectacle of a Pope calling upon the intellectual leaders of the twentieth century to stand still, and reverse the direction of their thought, has in it a touch of both the sublime and the ridiculous. The Italian Liberal papers were quick to compare Pius X's decrees with the methods of the Holy Office in the Middle Ages. Indeed, the general feeling was that the condemnation of Galileo was being repeated. The British Ambassador in Rome, Sir Edward Egerton, deplored '. . . the recent severe measures taken by the Pope against the Modernists, which are scarcely likely to bring about a peaceful settlement of the problem. An increased feeling exists among the clergy that they should be allowed a greater measure of independence in regard to political and social matters. All the younger priests are tired of seeing the Church as a refuge for those who are afraid – afraid of science, afraid of liberal thought, afraid of democracy.'[6]

Nevertheless, such was the prestige of the Papacy that Pius X's decrees were almost everywhere respected and obeyed. As good Catholics, the leading Modernists dutifully resigned their university teaching posts; while ninety per cent of the clergy took the anti-Modernist oath.

The effect of the Papal Encyclical *Saepe Dei* was felt most severely in Germany, where one of its phrases, equating the Modernists with the Protestant reformers of the sixteenth century, and condemning them as 'anti-Christian, rebellious, and materialistic', outraged the Protestants. Meetings of protest took place all over the country, and questions were asked in the Reichstag about 'the unheard-of insults of the Pope against the Protestant faith in Germany'. It seemed that the hostilities of the *Kulturkampf* would be renewed. The Socialists took advantage of the situation to ask in Parliament what measures the Prussian Government intended to take 'to prevent similar perturbations by the Pope of the confessional peace in Germany'.

At this time, the Conservative Government under Bethmann-Hollweg had been able to maintain its position in the Reichstag in the face of strong Socialist opposition only by an alliance with the Catholic Zentrum Party. But now the Encyclical *Saepe Dei*, with its open attack on the Protestant religion, endangered the alliance. In the words of the Government journal *Neue Deutsche Allgemeine Zeitung* (14 June 1897), 'While the Encyclical which is responsible for all this turmoil ought soon to be forgotten, it will suit Bethmann-Hollweg's Socialist adversaries to keep it constantly before the public. The Socialists and Radicals will take advantage of it to cause a rift in the Conservative-Zentrum alliance.' If this collapsed, the Socialist-Radical group would become the new Government. Thus, the Government of the most powerful nation in Europe was directly affected by a Papal Encyclical.

Bethmann-Hollweg naturally wished to keep on good terms with the Zentrum Party, but he had to satisfy the demands of his own Protestants, by condemning the Encyclical and its attack on their Church. He did so in as anodyne a form as possible, stating publicly that the Encyclical had deeply wounded the Protestant population of Germany; and that he had instructed the German Ambassador at the Vatican to make the strongest possible protest to the Cardinal Secretary of State. 'By this Encyclical,' he said, 'the Roman Curia [he did not say "the Pope"] has thrown stones into the garden of the Prussian state.'[7] He also announced that in future no teacher would be allowed to continue his work if he had taken the Pope's anti-Modernist oath.

In Holland a similar situation developed. The country had been effectively governed for the past five years, as in Germany, by a coalition of the two big denominational parties, the Catholic and the Protestant, who had become associated politically in order to oppose the Socialists. The Italian Ambassador at The Hague reported that the latter naturally took advantage of the Encyclical's attack on the Protestant Church to sow discord among the two parties which formed the Parliamentary majority. He reported the Socialist Deputy van Doorn as saying that, as the House of Orange was an institution deriving entirely from the Protestant Reformation, the Pope in his Encyclical *Saepe Dei* had insulted the royal house. Van Doorn demanded an apology, and that strong measures should be taken against the Dutch Catholics who thus 'recognize a foreign Head of State, and not their own'. The anti-Modernist Encyclicals were greeted all over the world in much the same way, with satisfaction by socialists and enemies of the Church; and with dismay and embarrassment by devout Catholics.

It was left to Pius X's successor, Benedict XV, to reverse the process after 1915, and withdraw Papal support from the Integralists and Cardinal De Lai. A paper in the Quai d'Orsay Archives describes this reversal of policy. It was written in Rome by M. Henri Gonse, who stated:

From the first days of Benedict XV's reign, he let it be known that he wanted to hear no more of Integralism. Indeed in his first Encyclical *Ad Beatissima* [November 1914], he expressly forbade the use of that word, saying that it tended to place Catholics in different categories – in particular the terms 'an integral Catholic'. He has recalled a number of Modernist priests like Father Samaria, whom Pius X had exiled from Italy. And he has attempted to muzzle Cardinal De Lai, by giving him the honorific role of Chancellor of the Roman Church. Benedict XV has also stated that during his Pontificate no serious work of scholarship, whatever attitude it adopts, shall be placed on the Index. . . . But the new Pope soon became so involved in international affairs, owing to the war, that he has had little time for these questions, which he has had to leave to the free play of the bureaux, that is at the mercy of Cardinal De Lai and his friends.[8]

15

French Atheism and the Rupture with France

The French Socialists and Radicals who dominated their governments in the last years of the nineteenth century had no sympathy with Leo XIII's policy of *Ralliement*, of the Church adapting itself to the republican form of government. They would have preferred an Ultramontane Pope like Pius IX, preferably a monarchist, whom they could stigmatize as the enemy of modern France. This would be the pretext for attaining their long-term goal, complete rupture with Rome. But as long as Leo XIII lived this proved difficult; he would not allow himself to be goaded into precipitate and unconsidered reaction to their insults and provocations. But with his death in 1903 and his replacement by a more intransigent Pope, the Socialists felt that the time was ripe for fresh anti-clerical action.

They had been arguing among themselves for some time as to which was the greater evil, capitalism or the Catholic Church, whom they regarded as working in harness.[1] In the words of one of their Marxists, Guesde, 'The spiritual servitude which is Catholicism prepares the material servitude which is Capitalism.' They intended to destroy both; the only question was, which to strike first? Guesde considered that a great deal of energy had been wasted in Ferry's day, in the 1880s, by attacking the Church, and that they should direct their efforts first against capitalism. When that was destroyed, the Catholic Church in France would collapse on its own. But his faction was defeated in 1902, and the new Socialist leaders, Waldeck-Rousseau and Combes, decided that the attack on the Church must come first. They believed that the Catholic Church was creeping back into its old pre-1789 position. The Socialist Deputy Zavaès said in the Chambre in March 1901;

Is not the glorious Revolution of our ancestors ever present in the memory of us all today? And when I speak of Revolution, I am not thinking of that Convention which drove out the traitors within, and repulsed the traitors without, and which in the most difficult and tragic hour for France replied to the coalition of feudal Europe by throwing at its feet the head of the traitor, Louis Capet. . . . No, it is not to the Convention that I refer . . . it is to that phase of the Revolution called the Constituent Assembly, which stated on 12 February 1790, 'The religious Orders are incompatible with the social order and the public weal. They must be exterminated!' Citizens, we ask you at this dawn of the twentieth century to return to the example of our forefathers in 1790.[2]

The President of the Council, Émile Combes, addressed the Chambre in the same terms: 'Once again, the Catholic Church in France has organized itself into a despotic hierarchy, leading the people to an ideal totally opposed to modern society, plotting the destruction of the political and social edifice erected by the glorious French Revolution. In the last ten years, the religious congregations have multiplied tenfold. Citizens, we have to undo in a very short time the clerical reaction of a century.' He also pointed out that at the beginning of the Second Empire in 1852, the property belonging to the religious congregations was valued at fifty million francs; but that today (1902) it was a thousand million! (Here it must be admitted that, even if these figures were exaggerated, there can be no doubt that the congregations had increased greatly in the second half of the nineteenth century, both financially and numerically. Moreover, most of their property was held in mortmain, a form of tenure which made it extremely difficult to tax or alienate.)

Émile Combes was the son of a tailor, and in his youth he had been a seminarist. Now, like so many apostates, he vehemently repudiated his early beliefs. The Draconian anti-clerical legislation which he presented to Parliament on 10 November 1903 went far beyond anything Ferry had envisaged in 1879. It included the dissolution of some twelve thousand Catholic schools, and the exclusion of all priests from teaching posts. One of his principal aims was to prevent the teaching Orders, in particular the Jesuits, from preparing the sons of the upper classes for the military academy of Saint-Cyr and the Naval and Polytechnical Colleges. He was convinced that the officers of the army and navy were not only on the side of the Church (*'le sabre et le goupillon'* again), but were still royalist at heart. But this was not enough. Combes wanted a total break with Rome, and he saw that now was the moment to accomplish it.

Pius X, who had only just acceded was, we have seen, unfamiliar with European diplomacy. He and his Secretary of State, Merry del Val, were considering what should be the Church's reaction to the new French anti-clerical laws, when Combes and his Radical Government played their trump card. They contrived a State visit by the President, M. Loubet, to King Victor Emmanuel II in Rome. This would be the first time that France had officially recognized the Italian occupation of Rome. Because previous French governments had always assured the Vatican that they would never insult His Holiness in such a way, this was bound to provoke a reaction in such a man as Pius X. Combes seems to have foreseen this. He hoped thereby to goad the Pope into some intemperate action which he could present to the French nation as 'Vatican interference in French affairs'.

The Pope himself described his predicament to a French journalist. He said he would not receive the French President, because he could not depart from the attitude which was his last means of making a protest against the act of spoliation perpetrated by the House of Savoy in 1870. He insisted, however, that by not receiving the President he was not being discourteous, because he fully understood the reason why the French President must come to Rome. He would not have taken offence if the President had been received in any other city than Rome – in Florence or Turin. Indeed, he would have welcomed it. But in Rome – what would the French say if any foreign Head of State made an official visit at this time to Alsace-Lorraine (still under German occupation)?[3]

This expressed a more reasonable attitude than is generally attributed to Pius X; and it is difficult to condemn him, in view of the evident intention of the Italian authorities to humiliate him by the French visit as much as possible. First, they arranged for the reception of the French President by the King of Italy in the Quirinale. This was a gratuitous insult to the Pope, because it was his Apostolic Palace, which had been sequestered by the Italian State in 1870. Also planned was a visit by the French President to the Porta Pia, where the historic breach made in the walls on 20 September 1870 was the symbol of the Papal capitulation to Italy. After this, as a final humiliation, the King of Italy would accompany the French President in his phaeton on a drive round the Leonine walls of the Vatican. Add to this that when the French President arrived the Italian socialists, not to be outdone, ostentatiously laid a wreath on the statue of Giordano Bruno next to the Farnese Palace, the French Embassy where M. Loubet would stay.

We cannot tell how Leo XIII would have reacted to these insults; but Pius X acted very much as Pius IX would have. The Vatican had stated earlier that no Catholic Head of State could cross the threshold of the Quirinale 'without giving grave offence to His Holiness', and that the Pope would not receive any Head of State who did so.[4] When the French Government made a formal application for a Papal audience, the Pope fell into the trap. He refused it publicly, and at the same time addressed a strong letter of protest against the President's visit to all countries with which the Vatican had diplomatic relations. In this letter he referred to France as 'once the eldest daughter of the Church, but now her ungrateful and rebellious daughter', a statement which received wide publicity in the world press. It was now the French Government's turn to say that it had been insulted, that an affair which concerned exclusively itself and the Vatican had been publicly mooted by the Pope in the capitals of the world. In the French Chambre on 27 May 1904 M. Delcassé, the Foreign Minister, announced that it was this communication to foreign Governments which France considered inadmissible. Jean Jaurès referred in *L'Humanité* (17 March 1904) to '. . . this attempt by Pius X to sow dissension between two great peoples on the occasion of their reconciliation. After this episode,' he said, 'what is required now is complete emancipation of France from political interference by Rome. Separation has become a national necessity.'

Combes had got what he wanted: evidence of 'Vatican interference in French affairs'. His Government accordingly drew up the Separation Law, which was passed in the Chambre by a large majority. The century-old Concordat of 1801 was abrogated. The Separation Law expressed the State's complete indifference to religion, for it or against it. In this way, Combes laid the foundations for a neutral or lay French State. Article 2 of the Law stated: 'The Republic neither recognizes or supports any one particular religious cult.' Provided the various Churches, Catholic, Lutheran, Calvinist, Methodist, or the Jewish and Muslim religious establishments, did not infringe civil law, they could henceforth exist like any corporate body, the Association of Pastry-Bakers or the League of Fishermen. The privileged position of the ancient Catholic *Ecclesia Gallicana* was repudiated; it was declared a private company, its standing no greater and no less than that of the Baptists or Jehovah's Witnesses.

By skilful compromise, Leo XIII had succeeded in arresting and minimizing the encroachments of the French Republic on Church prerogatives and property. Within a few months of his death, Pius X had undone all this, and he was confronted with the very situation which Leo XIII had evaded. In the Italian State Archives is a comment by the Italian Ambassador in Paris: 'In the matter of separation of Church and State, a majority in the Chambre were originally against it. But after the Pope's *colossal blunder* [italics author's] in protesting to the world against President Loubet's visit to the King of Italy, they have swung the other way. They now support Combes.'[5]

How 'colossal' was the Pope's blunder? In the Quai d'Orsay Archives is a report by the French Ambassador to the Quirinale, M. Barrère, of a conversation he had with Cardinal Agliardi on the subject. Agliardi, said the French Ambassador, was generally regarded as the most knowledgeable in foreign affairs of the Curia Cardinals:

Cardinal Agliardi told me that the Secretary of State, Merry del Val, is responsible for this disastrous rupture with France. He says Merry del Val is too young and inexperienced at the age of thirty-five but that the Pope has a blind confidence in him. Agliardi says it is a veritable infatuation, because the Pope, who speaks only Italian — and that in its Venetian form — and who comes from the humblest origins, has an immense admiration for this polyglot young Secretary of State, with his aristocratic manners. Any foreign policy he promotes, the Pope agrees with unhesitatingly. Cardinal Agliardi is also vehement in his crisicism of the Pope. The Pope's naïveté, he says, is revealed in his attitude to the rupture with France. This disaster to the Church, which Leo XIII strove to avoid at all costs, the present

Pope seems to regard as of the smallest consequence: 'In a month's time,' the Pope says, 'it will be forgotten.' Devoid of all culture, ignorant of the essential conditions for the prestige and reputation of the Church, this Pope is totally oblivious of the effect of his words and actions – at least that is what Cardinal Agliardi says. The Pope has no idea, he says, what is a diplomatic Note, nor what the interruption of relations with a great European power entails. Foreign countries are unknown to him, and he imagines that the denunciation of the Concordat by France, the separation of Church and State, signify simply more liberty of action for the Church in France, more independence for the clergy.[6]

There was one notable difference between the new Socialist leaders of the French Third Republic and their Jacobin ancestors of 1793 in their approach to the Catholic Church. The new leaders realized that to ignore the existence of the Church altogether – as the Jacobins had – would be premature and utopian; people would still want to go to church. So, by the law of 1905, the *Associations Cultuelles* were established for the respective cults, Catholics, Calvinists, Lutherans, Methodists, Jews, Muslims, etc., based on the unit of the parish.[7] These were bodies of churchgoing laymen who were to hold and administer religious property, and to provide from it funds for maintaining Church buildings and holding services; they would also pay the stipends of the clergy.

The minority faiths, Calvinist, Methodist, Jewish, etc., accepted this system, even seeing in it certain advantages. Their stipends would be paid and their buildings maintained. They could select their own hierarchy, pastors, parsons, rabbis, mullahs, etc., without reference to the State. But the Catholic Church refused to recognize the *Associations Cultuelles*, on the ground that it would thereby become merely a branch of the public service, its bishops higher-grade, its priests lower-grade civil servants. For the committees which ran the *Associations Cultuelles* were to be composed of laymen so that, in the words of the Italian Catholic paper *La Tribuna*, 'Catholic bishops in France will henceforth have to take their orders from the local chemist or land-surveyor.' The French Socialists had assumed that the Catholics, like the other denominations, would accept the *Associations Cultuelles*, on account of the public funds provided. They did not realize that to a system as hierarchical as the Catholic Church, a democratically constituted body like the *Associations Cultuelles* was inconceivable. In his Encyclicals *Vehementer* and *Gravissimo* ('Vehemently' and 'Most Grave') of 1906, Pius X condemned the *Associations Cultuelles*, and forbade Catholics to join them.

Everything now depended on the French Catholics themselves. The Cardinal Secretary of State, Merry del Val, told the Papal Chamberlain F.A. MacNutt[8] that unless the Catholics in France now defended their religion, no one else could do it for them. The French Government's determination to break with the Vatican and inaugurate a period of active persecution of the Church was now patent, and no concessions on the part of the Pope could have any effect. 'Let the French Catholics,' said Merry del Val, 'follow the example of the persecuted Catholics in Bismarck's Germany. By uniting in their own defence those German Catholics defeated the *Kulturkampf*.'[9]

Both Catholic clergy and their flocks in France obeyed these instructions, making all the sacrifices that they entailed. By refusing to join the *Associations Cultuelles*, the Catholic clergy forfeited some thirty million francs annually, in stipends and funds for the upkeep of their churches. Like the German clergy during Bismarck's *Kulturkampf*, they now had to live a hand-to-mouth existence, obtaining their stipends from charitable and private sources, collecting funds at marriages, baptisms, funerals, etc.

The monastic Orders also followed the Papal ruling, remaining in their monasteries and convents until forcibly evicted. The worst instance of this took place at the famous Grande Chartreuse in Savoy, where the French army officer entrusted with the task gave the order for eviction to his troops – and then resigned his commission. The troops arrived to find fires burning on the hillsides, and the bells tolling. Hundreds of peasants armed with sticks, and barricades of carts, trees, and rocks blocked the way. The soldiers had to break down the barriers and doors of the monasteries, where they found the monks inside at their devotions. They had to remove them bodily, while the crowd outside sang the *Parce Domine*.[10]

Within a year of these forcible seizures, the Government declared that the condition of certain Catholic churches was too bad for repair (which was not surprising, because they had no funds for upkeep). As a safety precaution, the Government therefore closed them. In his book *La Grande Pitié des Églises de France* ('The Great Misery of the Churches of France'), Maurice Barrès describes how in December 1909 the priest of Grisy-Suines was informed by the mayor that he must provide funds from the church treasury for repairs to his church. The mayor knew quite well that he had none, so he announced an auction of church property, 'on behalf of the repairs'. Barrès describes the auction in the church: 'In the streets outside I met youths who had just bought the choirboys' vestments for fancy dress, wearing soutanes and little skullcaps. They were dancing, gesticulating and singing. In the church, some fifty people were standing around an auctioneer who was doing his trade on the steps of the altar.'

Within two years of the Separation Law, most of the ten thousand Catholic parishes in France were without a priest. In the rural dioceses, the priest had four or five parishes to administer, covering an area of several hundreds of square miles; so that Mass could be celebrated in each not more than once a month. Unless the priest lived among rich parishioners, he generally had to practise a side profession – the favourite being beekeeping. But an unexpected form of support came from abroad. In the French archives is a report by a certain Mgr Guthlin, who had been sent to Rome by Delcassé when relations were broken off, as a semi-diplomat to keep an eye on Vatican affairs:

> Groups of Catholics in various countries are showing their sympathy with the Catholic Church's predicament in France. . . . The movement is active in the Anglo-Saxon countries, and meetings of Catholics deploring 'the spoliation of the French Church' have taken place in London, Liverpool, Dublin, Limerick, Boston, Chicago, Cincinnati, etc. They are organizing a system for boycotting French goods and imports. Moreover, they show their support in a practical way, with subscriptions *'pour le clergé et le culte en France'* ['for the clergy and worship in France'].[11]

Not only did the French clergy resist the temptation to accept the stipends from the *Associations Cultuelles*; many of them retaliated forcefully, in word and deed. In a speech in Colbert the Abbé Bergey announced, 'Each time they, the Freemasons, empty one of our churches, we will empty one of their Lodges.' The

Government took this threat, and similar pugnacious statements by priests, so seriously that when persons in clerical garb were seen in the neighbourhood of a Masonic Lodge, a police guard was placed on it.[12]

The French episcopate instructed the faithful on how to oppose the anti-clerical laws. Catholics were to bombard the Deputies in Parliament, as well as persons eminent in banking, industry and finance, with petititions presenting their grievances. 'Let us,' advised the French bishops, 'take a leaf out of the communists and socialists' book. When they go on strike, they go in a mass procession to the doors of the ministries, prefectures and town halls (mairies) with protestations and ultimatums. We will do the same.'

A few French bishops submitted to the new law, and followed the Government's instructions. Pius X was ruthless with them. In the Quai d'Orsay Archives for July 1904 is a document stating that the Pope is simply deposing them. In it, the French Ambassador in Rome reported on the case of the Bishop of Laval:

The town of Laval possesses a community of Jesuits. Although the new Law dissolved them, they ignored it, and continued their indefatigable teaching. Whereupon the Bishop of Laval, *out of respect for the new Law*, instructed them to desist from this, and disperse. This was his undoing. For the Zelanti in Rome, who had been kept in abeyance during the reign of Leo XIII, have appeared in force again, and taken advantage of the simplicity of his successor Pius X – of the pious and innocent soul of this Venetian gondolier. As a result of their insistence, the Bishop of Laval and a handful of French prelates like him have been summoned to Rome and relieved of their posts.[13]

But these were exceptions. For the French clergy's courage and firmness in face of this persecution, Pius X congratulated them in his jubilee speech of 19 November 1908. Although until now, he said, he had only been able to sing a *Miserere* for them, he felt he could henceforth replace it with a *Te Deum*.

The result of this persecution was, paradoxically, in some ways advantageous to the Church. One fact was that the French Government no longer possessed any say in episcopal appointments (as stipulated in the old Concordat). The Holy See was now free to choose its own bishops, and it soon built up a strong and independent French episcopate. A member of Parliament, M. Méline, had warned Combes of this. 'A side effect of your Separation Law,' he said, 'will be to make Catholics more Catholic. It will also increase the authority of the Pope over the French clergy.' The French Senator L. Jenouvrier said much the same:

> The extraordinary Governments we have had in the opening decade of this century, have been over-confident, too cock-sure. . . . They claim to be creating a new society in their own image, according to their own whims, passions, likes and dislikes. One fine day they say, 'The Pope is a hindrance to our plans. *Ergo* we will have no more Pope!' The French Ambassador to the Pope is recalled, relations with the Holy See are broken off. They think they have rid themselves of the Pope for good. Poor fellows! Never has the Pope's presence in France been more deeply felt than today. Never has his authority been more respected – since they ignored it. Never has the religious question been more alive and vital in France – since they stated that it did not exist.[14]

M. Jenouvrier then made this prophecy:

> A century-old tradition, to which the Popes have always subscribed, holds that in the Levant all Catholics, whatever their nationality, are protected by France. This dates from the time of François I, when of all European nations we French were pre-eminent there. The French missionaries were responsible for this, so that the Levant has always constituted a kind of second France – overseas. But you will see what will happen now. The French Government will no longer enjoy this ancient right of protecting Catholics whatever their nationality, *so valuable to the spread of French influence* [italics author's], when it ignores the existence of the Head of their Church.

This influence was of the greatest importance to France. In the great missionary period of the nineteenth century under Gregory XVI, France had placed at the service of Rome her missionaries, her money, her diplomacy, even her ships and soldiers. By 1875, of the 6,000 missionary priests throughout the world, 4,500 were French; and France was regarded by Rome as the protecting power for all

Catholics, of whatever nationality, in these lands. In Constantinople and Jerusalem (both then under the Ottoman Empire), France's diplomatic representative at Catholic ceremonies was granted special liturgical honours, which were withheld from those of other nations. At High Mass in Jerusalem, the French Consul was seated in a place of honour and specially censed by the thurifer (incense bearer). France had the right to appoint the Catholic bishop of Alexandria, and the Apostolic Visitor in Baghdad. All this was of considerable value for French prestige and influence throughout the Levant. A comment by a French Deputy in the Chambre, M. Gayrand, about the Sisters of Saint Vincent de Paul in Jerusalem sums it up: 'The best part of our influence is due to these Sisters, their schools and institutions which care for the lepers. They do more for France and our language than do a hundred thousand French bayonets.'[15]

The importance to France of the missions in the Far East is also confirmed by an Englishman, a Member of Parliament, Mr Walton, who sailed up the Yangtse in 1901. He stated in the House of Commons, 'I went up the river for 1,500 miles, and found the country swarming with French Catholic missions. They transmit back to their country much useful information about the mineral wealth and commercial openings. Thanks to her missionaries, France is gradually acquiring a monopoly over the exploitation of all the mineral fields. Thanks to the topographical work, too, of the French Jesuits, I had a well charted map of the river, without which I could not have travelled.'[16] As late as 1928 a British diplomat, Sir John Tulley, described how, on a trip in China, he became aware of the influence wielded by these missions. 'In the eyes of the Chinese,' he wrote, 'the Catholic Church is simply the French Church. Any good it does is attributed to France.'[17]

The gravest comment on the situation now developing to the detriment of France was expressed by the French Foreign Minister himself, M. Delcassé, in a memorandum to the President of the Council, Émile Combes. In this, he warns of:

. . . certain consequences of our 1904 Law suppressing the Catholic teaching congregations and their novitiates. . . . Your Excellency is not unaware, I think, of the considerable role played abroad by these congregations in the diffusion of the French language and culture. In the Levant, the Orient and Latin

America, the number of youths and girls at present receiving education in the French language is in the neighbourhood of 200,000 – and this thanks entirely to our Catholic teaching congregations. . . . Without entering into the reasons for the suppression of these congregations in France, I cannot refrain from pointing out to Your Excellency that this will entail, in a relatively short time, the almost complete extinction of a French education for this numerous foreign youth.[18]

His warning proved justified. By 1913, the French Ambassador in Constantinople, M. Bompard, was complaining that '. . . as a result of the closing of the novitiates in metropolitan France, the Catholic Orders here are being increasingly recruited from other countries. Even a congregation as essentially French as the *Frères de la Doctrine Chrétienne* ['Brothers of Christian Doctrine'] now numbers twenty-five per cent Italians. At this rate, in fifteen or twenty years' time, most of the French mission establishments in the Ottoman Empire, teaching or nursing, will have fallen into the hands of the Italians.'[19]

In this first decade of the twentieth century, Italy was still feared militarily as a great power. Unjustified as this later proved to be, she had just defeated the Turks in North Africa and annexed Tripolitania from them, and had her gaze fixed upon further conquests in the Near East. The French Ambassador at the Quirinale, M. Barrère, endorsed the fear of his colleague in Constantinople:

Until our Separation Law of 1904, we had the right of protecting in the Ottoman Empire not only the French foundations but all Catholic establishments, of whatever nationality. Since 1904 the Holy See, while not inaugurating an active policy against us, has adopted the line of *laissez-faire*. Since then, foreign missions, in particular the Italian, *encouraged in every way by the Italian Government*, have begun an insidious attack on our missions, and on the principle itself of the French Protectorate. . . . In 1906 and 1907 the Dominicans and Franciscans, in 1911 the Carmelites, ingeniously purged of their French elements, passed under the Italian flag. In this way, we have lost dozens of schools, convents and churches, all withdrawn from our influence. In Constantinople itself, we have lost Saint-Pierre, 'the second parish of the Nation'. And this without counting the hundreds of village schools maintained once by our missions, and which served our cause admirably.[20]

This was true. After the rupture of relations in 1905, the Vatican had withdrawn these privileges from France. The Apostolic Delegate in Constantinople informed the French Ambassador that he would no longer be granted liturgical honours, and that in future an Italian would be installed as Apostolic Visitor. In Egypt, where French influence had been especially strong, a new Franciscan college for native priests, which was almost entirely Italian in character, was opened. In Palestine, the French religious teaching Orders were replaced by Italians, Belgians, Germans, and Americans.

The French Ambassador to the Quirinale then made some suggestions:

Only the Vatican can halt this process, but in the present circumstances we can hardly expect the Vatican to do much for us. I therefore suggest that, in the absence of an official French representative to the Holy See, the first urgent measure which our Government must take if it wishes to preserve our position, even much diminished, in the Levant, is to assure immediately in metropolitan France the reopening of the Catholic novitiates. All our agents in the Ottoman Empire, our Consuls at Smyrna, Beirut, Jerusalem, Damascus, Aleppo, etc., are unanimous about this.[21]

His advice was heeded at the Quai d'Orsay, as the recommendation of its *Directeur des Affaires Politiques* reveals: 'We must start from the premise that no attempted solution has the slightest chance of success as long as we have no agreement with the Holy See. Everything concerning the Catholic missions – their foundation, their functioning, their recruitment even, depends upon Vatican support. It is to the Vatican that we must turn to save what we can of our prerogatives in the Levant. It is therefore essential without delay to find a reason, a pretext, for engaging again in conversation with the Vatican.'[22] (These recommendations were made in 1913, but it was not until 1925 that they were implemented by the French Government.)

The next setback to France as a result of the Separation Law came with the declaration of war in August 1914. Again, Combes and his Socialists had not foreseen the importance to France during the European war of having a representative at the Vatican. Connected by bishops and nuncios with all parts of the world, the Vatican was exceptionally well informed on the progress of the war, and where the sympathies of the neutral nations lay. Other countries which had not been represented at the Vatican before 1914 quickly became aware of this and established legations. Britain did so as early as December 1914, to be followed by Japan, Holland, Finland, Poland and Peru. But France, hoist with her own petard, remained outside. 'Why,' complained the French Deputy, Robert David, bitterly, 'have we ostracized ourselves from this marvellous observatory?'[23]

Another aspect of the war which favoured the Church – and militated against the French anti-clericals – was the patriotic conduct of the French priests at this time. Before 1914, the Socialists could rely in their anti-clerical campaign on the support of a large part of the population. '*Sus à la calotte*' ('Down with skullcap') and even '*Bouffer du curé*' ('Eat up the priest') were popular cries. But during the war, thanks to the valour of the priests in the front line, where many of them were conscripted as ordinary soldiers, the public attitude changed. Of the 80,000 priests from all countries who fought in the war, 45,000 were French; and of these 5,800 were killed, mostly in the trenches.[24] This was the famous *Union Sacrée*, of layman and priest, forged by their comradeship at the front. By 1918 the old anti-clerical slogans were being uttered only by a handful of fanatics.

'What France does today, Europe does tomorrow.' It was almost inevitable that when Combes introduced his Separation Law, it would not be long before other Latin countries followed suit. It took only four years for the French anti-clerical storm to cross the Pyrenees.

The Portuguese Revolution against Crown and Altar began in 1910, when King Carlos I and his eldest son were murdered in the centre of Lisbon, and the Republic was declared under a Freemason, Alfonso Costa. He immediately introduced legislation on French Socialist lines repudiating Catholicism as the State religion. True to the Pombal tradition of the eighteenth century, he then attacked the Jesuits as 'an anomaly in modern society'. Their congregations were disbanded, their houses given over to civilian use. Church property and charitable institutions were secularized. Any form of religious ceremony was henceforth to be confined to the interior of the church, and all religious processions and gatherings in the open were prohibited. The Faculty of Theology at the Catholic University of Coimbra was closed. Civil marriage was made obligatory, and divorce permitted by mutual consent. Priests who could be persuaded to abandon the cloth were granted a pension, and preferment before other citizens in obtaining civil employment.[25] The Italian Ambassador in Lisbon reported that the Nuncio, Mgr Tosti, was 'threatened yesterday by a howling mob in his summer residence at Cintra' – adding gleefully, 'Only the prompt appearance of the *Republican* mayor saved his property from total destruction. He had to leave Portugal clandestinely, with his seat in the train booked under another name.'[26]

'Within two generations,' proclaimed the Prime Minister, Alfonso Costa, 'we shall have eradicated the Catholic religion entirely from our land.' But this prognostication proved to be another example – as in the case of Combes – of the inexpertness of these newcomers to statesmanship. Within three years of the implementation of these decrees, the Portuguese Government became aware – in the same way as the French Government before it – that the great Portuguese overseas Empire was being adversely affected. Without financial support from Lisbon, its Catholic missions were becoming dependent on foreign subsidies and personnel. And here, even more than France, Portugal among all European nations had been proudest of her overseas achievements, seeing herself as the oldest colonial power in the world, spreading the benefits of European civilization to the furthermost corners of the globe. These 'benefits of European civilization' had been disseminated almost entirely by Portuguese missionaries. Bestowing on Portugal in 1493 the grandiose title of *Padroado del Oriente* ('Patriarchate of the Orient') Pope Alexander VI had granted her 'jurisdiction over all the new-found possessions to the east of the twentieth line of longitude'.

A memorandum by the British Foreign Office on Portuguese achievements in India refers to:

. . . the great labours and splendid triumphs of Portuguese missionaries. Even today all the most important centres of

Catholics throughout India and Ceylon – important in quality and culture as well as in numbers – are descendants of converts made by the Portuguese missionaries. What Portugal has done in the Far East is attested by the numerous churches which still stand as silent monuments of religious fervour; the ruins of those destroyed by the Maharattas; the wayside symbols of the Cross found in many streets, lanes and villages – all these are a constant reminder of the influence of Portugal in this part of the world.[27]

Yet by 1913, as a result of Costa's Separation Law, most of the Portuguese missions were closed. In Angola, only a handful of the thirty parishes remained. Of the twenty-four missions in Espirito Santo, five were closed and the rest had a constantly diminishing personnel. In Mozambique, of the ten parochial missions, only four remained. It was the same in Guinea, São Tomé, Principe and Timor. The Portuguese Government excused itself, stating that it had 'drawn the legitimate deduction from the developments which have taken place since 1911' (that is, since the Separation Law); and it made the hypocritical suggestion that the Catholic missions *in the Portugese colonies*, but not in Portugal itself, would be recognized as juridical entities. The overseas missions were to be supported not only by financial subsidies but by grants of land, buildings for schools and training colleges. Having financially starved or actually suppressed the missions, the Government now decided to restore them and render them as efficient as possible; and it informed the Vatican of its intention.

For the full restoration of the Church's century-old position, Portugal had to wait until after the First World War and the government of Antonio Salazar. A practising Catholic, he negotiated a new Concordat with the Holy See by which the famous *Padroado del Oriente* was restored – not indeed on the grandiose lines of the sixteenth century, but confirming the Portugese patronage over the dioceses of Goa, Cochin, and Meliapor in India; and in the Far East over Macao, Timor, and Malacca. Once again, as in France, the missions had played a decisive political role.

16

The Achievement of
Pius X

Pius X is the only Pope since Pius V (1566–72) to have been canonized. He must therefore be rated – in the eyes of the Catholic Church at least – as one of the exemplary Popes of the last four hundred years, certainly the Pope whose life is to be so regarded. To the layman this may appear anomalous. In his eleven-year Pontificate, Pius X reversed most of the diplomatic achievements of his predecessor, and lowered the prestige of the Papacy in Europe. For, at Leo XIII's death in 1903, Catholicism had again become a political force which secular governments respected. Leo XIII had been careful never to allow questions with these governments to arise which he knew he could not solve. If he foresaw such a situation developing, he affected to ignore it, while at the same time taking measures to retard its development. An example of this was his attitude towards the restoration of the monarchy in France and to the Boulangists, as well as to French Republicanism.

Pius X, on the contrary, was temperamentally incapable of circuitous or calculated measures: if he saw a danger approaching, he met it head-on. Concentrating all his efforts on upholding the claims of religion and the spiritual authority of the Church, a man of God and a shepherd of souls, he remained strangely aloof from mundane considerations and practical consequences. His very election had been a diplomatic humiliation for the Vatican, the result of outside influences by the Austrian *Veto* of 1903. This was followed by the rupture of relations with France and Portugal.

In the domain of doctrine, Pius X's intransigent attitude towards scientific discovery, his Encyclical *Pascendi* condemning the Modernists as 'the blind leading the blind' (*caeci et duces caecorum*),

217

had earned the Papacy the scorn of all European intellectual circles. The Italian Ambassador in Berlin commented gleefully in 1911 on '. . . the clumsy way the Vatican is now handling relations with Germany . . . the blows of the Vatican follow one another regularly, interspersed with inept attempts at pacification.'[1] He listed three instances. 'The Pope has just humiliated the University Catholic Faculty here by promising its professors that if they renounce their Modernist views and recant publicly, they will not be penalized. Most of them accordingly did so. But it seems he broke his word, for he has since denounced them as "base and vile".' The Italian Ambassador then alluded to the Encyclical *Saepe Dei* which set the whole Lutheran Church ablaze in Germany and the Dutch Church in Holland. As the third example, he stated: 'His other gaffe in Germany has been to get the Catholic trade unions to come to some sort of terms with the Socialist trade unions. . . . This has alienated the big industrialists, who were on his side before.'

The English diplomat, Fairfax L. Cartwright, said of Pius X in 1907, 'Access to his presence is becoming increasingly difficult, as he dreads being given any definite advice on political questions. The Cardinals who have his ear are the Spaniards, Merry del Val and Vives y Tuto, prelates noted for their narrow and bigoted Catholicism. In political questions, they are more likely to be guided by purely theological views than by reason and practical wisdom.'[2]

Pius X's achievement was essentially spiritual and domestic, confined to the internal affairs of the Church, and to the Vatican itself. It was here that he made his mark, such as no other Pope had since Gregory XIII, and to which in part his posthumous canonization must be due. Leo XIII, absorbed in his great design abroad, had little time for the details of Vatican administration. Indeed, he had often closed his eyes to irregularities, even improbities, within the Vatican – a legacy left by Cardinal Antonelli. At Leo XIII's death in 1903, the finances of the Vatican were in a deplorable state. When Pius X acceded, he found a jungle of departments, often in conflict among themselves, a confused mass of government offices dating from before 1870, many of which no longer had any *raison d'etre*. One of the particular scandals was that of the *Spedizionieri*. These were agents or intermediaries between the Curia and anyone requesting an audience with the

Pope, for which they levied a commission. They were chosen from among a few dozen old Roman families, who enjoyed considerable profit from the monopoly. Leo XIII had known about it, but he realized that if the practice were suppressed, these powerful families might be alienated. But this did not deter Pius X. Immediately after his accession, he disbanded all the *Spedizionieri*.

He also made a detailed investigation of the other sinecures with high-sounding but meaningless names – the Abbreviator of Great and Small Residences, the Abbreviator of the Major and Minor Posts, and a number of sub-departments which had multiplied out of all proportion to the work involved. This was due primarily to the need after 1870 to find work, or make work, for the hundreds of Papal officials who had been expelled from their offices after the Italian seizure of the Papal States and Rome. Pius X reduced the Papal bureaucracy by half, the number of departments from thirty-seven to nineteen, the congregations from twenty to eleven. He also suppressed the *Scagnozzi*. Those were itinerant priests who had migrated to Rome from the provinces, generally clerics of low quality who had displeased their bishops in some way. Scores of these men led a haphazard existence in Rome, living off alms or collections in church when they managed to say a Mass, or from the patronage of a cardinal or senior prelate. They had become a disgrace to their cloth, and occasionally appeared in the law courts on charges of larceny. Unless they could now show that they had been accepted officially for work in a specified diocese, Pius X expelled them from the city.

To understand Pius X's achievement we must go back to his first unhappy experiences in Mantua, where he was appointed bishop in 1884. He had found the diocese in a lamentable condition, the priests idle and neglectful of their duties; a large part of the population estranged from the Church, the upper classes through Freemasonry and liberalism, the lower through Marxism and socialism. People no longer went to Mass, and civil marriage was increasing. This made a deep impression on Bishop Sarto, who for twenty years had been accustomed to the devout and even tenor of Veneto parish life. There was not a great deal he could do in the city of Mantua itself; but in one limited field where he considered licence in church had gone too far, he acted characteristically. This was the matter of church music.

Since the great days in the sixteenth century, when Palestrina's

Mass for Pope Marcellus had saved church music from being banned as licentious, it had again deteriorated to the point of becoming virtually secular. By 'deteriorated' we do not mean that the music was poor (who could say that of Mozart's *Laudate Dominum* or Pergolesi's *Stabat Mater?*), but that people went to church less to be elevated spiritually by the music, than to enjoy it. The plainsong dignity of the Gloria, the Credo, and the Kyrie was now adulterated with themes more suited to the opera house than the church, and the calm tones of the choir were supplanted by the dramatic delivery of individual singers. Solo tenors and sopranos sang in operatic style from the chancel to churches packed with audiences, who did everything but clap to show their approval. They were less interested in the elevation of the Host at the high altar, than in waiting for their favourite singer to appear in a *cavatina* or a duet.

Bishop Sarto was well versed in musical liturgy. As Bishop of Mantua, and later as Patriarch of Venice, he had been the first eminent Italian prelate since the time of Pope Marcellus to expel profane music from the church. One of his first decrees, the *Moto Proprio* ('In Fitting Style'), enacted that the model for church music was henceforth to be the Gregorian chant. When he became Pope, he did not forbid serious modern music, but it must not be of a theatrical nature, or suggestive of profane themes. He prohibited the use of the vernacular, which had crept in over the centuries, and prescribed that the liturgical text was to be sung in ritual Latin. Women singers were excluded and replaced by boys. The piano was forbidden in church, as 'a noisy instrument', and replaced by the organ. Pius X instituted an Episcopal Commission to enforce these rules, and he set up a *Schola Cantorum* to teach a correct singing style. These reforms were far from popular. The hymns *O Felix Roma* and *Adeste Fideles*, which had long been favourites of all classes in Rome, were now suppressed as non-Gregorian, which was much resented.

Pius X also restored the *Italianità* ('Italian-ness') of the Sacred College, in which foreigners had secured a majority under Leo XIII. In Pius X's four Consistories, his seventeen cardinal creations were all Italians; and of the cardinals residing in Rome, the Curia, henceforth only two were non-Italian. Thus the cosmopolitan outlook of Leo XIII was replaced by the 'Latin' one of Pius X. It was hardly surprising therefore that the Vatican became less well-informed about countries whose mentalities differed from that of the Latin races.

Pius X was the only Pope in modern times – and one of the few in the history of the Papacy – to possess thaumaturgical powers. This gift, the *Talitha Cumi* of his Saviour ('Damsel, I say unto thee, arise'), also contributed to his subsequent canonization. There are a score of cases of paralysed persons being cured at his touch. His biographer, F. Segmuller, lists a series of his miracles, among them two nuns who were cured of tuberculosis, and two Spanish children paralysed from birth who walked again after being touched by Pius X.[3]

He also had the gift of foresight. When, during the Tripoli War of 1910, the Secretary of State came to him with the figures of Italian casualties he declared, much moved, 'But this is nothing – nothing compared with those in the *guerrone* to come.' (*Guerra* is the Italian for 'war', and the suffix – *one* means 'huge'.) When informed in 1912 by Merry del Val about the second Balkan conflict, he said that that too was nothing, because in a short time, the *guerrone* would be on them all. When he was walking in the Vatican gardens in the early summer of 1914 with the Brazilian Minister, Signor Bressau, who had presented his departure credentials, Pius X said, 'You are lucky indeed, my friend, to be leaving Europe at this moment. You will thus avoid the greatest war of all times, which is just about to break over us all.' The man who knew so little of international politics predicted this before the shots were fired at Sarajevo.

He also explained the coming *guerrone* in more practical terms. It had been rendered inevitable, he said, by the behaviour of the European governments since 1870, and the base attacks on the Catholic Church in their countries – Bismarck in Germany, Combes in France, Costa in Portugal, Cavour and Crispi in Italy. Their punishment was merited, and their peoples were about to atone for the sins of these men by a *guerrone* such as had never been known in human history.

Pius X's Pontificate may be considered under three heads: international affairs; religion; and Italy. If in the first of these he failed, in the second he succeeded, and in the third he obtained a measure of success. During his Pontificate, the Vatican and the Quirinale gradually established a *modus vivendi*, and when he died in 1914, the Italian Government issued an official eulogy. In the latter part of his Pontificate, after France had lost most of her Protectorate of the Orient, Italy replaced her, and worked amicably in harness with the Vatican's *Propaganda Fide* which directed the Italian missions overseas.

Even the enemies of the Papacy recognized Pius X's qualities: the tenacity of his views, his burning zeal for the faith, and yet the kindliness of his heart, his cheerful disposition and unaffected manner. The celebrated mediaeval prophecy by Malachy about the Popes dubbed Pius X with the soubriquet *Ignens Ardens* ('Kindling and Burning'); and the title was apt, for he could on occasion blaze forth with fulminations worthy of Pius IX. But the rigour of his condemnation was always tempered by the expression on his face and in his eloquent eyes, of sorrowful pity and tenderness towards the subject of his anathema.

People respected the simple life he led, sleeping on an iron bed in a bare room, rising at 4 a.m., writing all his letters in his own hand. Of all Popes he must have been the least nepotist. Leo XIII had granted position and titles to members of his family, the Peccis; but Pius X would have none of that. When he came to Rome as Pope he was accompanied by his only relatives, three sisters; they were quickly besieged by every place-seeker and intriguer in the Vatican. But it availed these people nothing. Twice a week the sisters would take a glass of wine with the Pope, and they would all then recite the Rosary together. When a flatterer told one of the sisters that her brother was 'a Saint', she replied, 'No, he is not a Saint. He has been a good priest and a good Bishop, and I pray he may be a good Pope. But Saint he never was.'[4] She was wrong. Ten years after his death he was canonized.

17

The 1914 Dilemma – Benedict XV

It would certainly have mortified Pius X had he known that one of his last acts – which appeared ostensibly to be concerned only with the welfare of his Catholic subjects – would be in part responsible for the bloodiest war which has ever been fought. This act was the Serbian Concordat of 1914, dealing with the 'Protectorate' of Catholics in the Balkans. The faculty of 'protecting' Catholics in various distant parts of the world has, as already seen in the case of France, always been coveted by the European Catholic powers. France was most jealous of it in the Orient, where she used it over the centuries most effectively to promote her own interests, commercial and strategic, until her self-inflicted rupture with the Vatican in 1905. Italy attempted to obtain it in Egypt in 1910 from the British mandatory power. At various times and in various places Germany, Austria, Spain, Belgium and Canada have all claimed it.

Until the Balkan Wars of 1912–13, Austria-Hungary had the right granted by the Pope of protecting the interests of Catholic minorities in the Balkan lands ruled by Turkey – Serbia, Albania, Macedonia, the Epirus – with the accompanying advantage of having access to them whenever she liked. This gave her considerable prestige and influence in the Balkans. The insignificant number of Catholics in Serbia did not warrant an individual Concordat for that country, nor for its neighbours; and Austrian protection was deemed sufficient for these people. But after the defeat and eviction of the Turks in the first Balkan War of 1912, Serbia became a greatly enlarged state, comprising Macedonia, the Epirus, and a part of northern Albania. Her Catholic population now increased by some forty thousand souls, so that she was in a

223

position to ask the Holy See for direct representation, in the form of a Concordat. It is a Papal principle never to refuse a request for a Concordat. Pius X accordingly sent an emissary, Mgr Eugenio Pacelli, to undertake the negotiations in Belgrade.[1]

Austria was naturally aggrieved at losing her Protectorate and its influence in the Balkans, particularly as Serbia, after her victories in the Balkan Wars – over Turkey in 1912, and over her neighbours in 1913 – had become insolent and overbearing. In the Italian State Archives is a despatch from the Duke of Averna, the Italian Ambassador in Vienna, reporting that Serbia had insisted at the Vatican that there should be no 'third party' (a reference to Austria) to the Concordat negotiations, which are being 'ingeniously conducted by the wily Serbian diplomat Veskic'.[2] In another despatch, the Italian Ambassador in Belgrade reported that Austria had officially informed the Vatican of her strong objection to the Concordat being concluded between Serbia and the Holy See.

The Concordat negotiations lasted four months, and were completed just before the Sarajevo assassinations. The Italian Ambassador reported again from Vienna, that the Austrian Government had come under strong criticism at home for not taking more energetic steps to prevent the Serbian Concordat, as this would give 'an enormous fillip to Slavonic irredentism throughout the entire Danubian Empire'. 'The Austrian press and people,' he wrote, 'consider the Serbian Concordat a major diplomatic defeat for their Government.'[3] Under the heading, 'Yet another defeat for us,' the Viennese paper, *Die Zeit* (25 June 1914) wrote:

> This Concordat is the work not only of Serbian diplomacy, but behind it one discerns the directing hand of Russia, which has used all its influence through its Ambassador at the Holy See to bring it about. Now Serbian prestige will be inflated, and its bishops and priests will become an important factor in pan-Slav agitation. This will doubtless stimulate Albania into asking for a Concordat too, in order to release it from the Austrian Protectorate. . . . Why in Heaven's name should Austria have made such a vast financial outlay in these Balkan lands on behalf of our Protectorate, *which is not so much religious as political* [italics author's], only to throw it away in a matter of weeks, and without a struggle?

The *Arbeiterzeitung* went even further in its patriotic fervour: 'So – it has been possible to induce the Vatican to follow a policy contrary to the interests of Austria – the only power which protects the Vatican! After this humiliation, will the voice of Austria ever be listened to again?'

Then, at this crucial moment in June 1914, with the Austrian Government being accused by its own people of a supine and incompetent policy in the Balkans, came the Sarajevo pistol shots. It is hardly surprising that the Austrian Government, to reassert itself in the face of such criticism from its own people, delivered the fatal ultimatum to Serbia. The Serbian Concordat undoubtedly contributed to the uncompromising terms in which it was drawn up, and which made war inevitable.

The Serbian Concordat negotiations were conducted in the last days of the Pontificate of Pius X; though that apolitical and pacifist Pope could never have appreciated what their full consequences would be. As it was, the outbreak of the First World War, the *guerrone* which he had foreseen, plunged him into a state of gloom and despondency from which he never recovered. He died a month later, at the end of August 1914, utterly broken; and it was left to his successor, Benedict XV, to lead the Catholic Church during the greatest and bloodiest war in human history.

The Conclave of 31 August 1914 was necessarily hurried. A new Pope had to be elected, who must persuade the warring powers to come to the conference table. So hurriedly was it convened, that the American cardinals did not arrive in time. It is generally supposed that, had they been present, they would have opted for the 'liberal' candidate, Cardinal Maffi. As it was, in times of crisis the usual tendency to favour a conservative asserted itself. Early on the second day, Cardinal Giacomo Della Chiesa, the Archbishop of Bologna and an aristocrat, was elected as Benedict XV with relatively little opposition. Owing to the war, the ceremonies connected with his Coronation were reduced; it took place not in St Peter's, but in the semi-privacy of the Sistine Chapel, on 6 September 1914.

The Della Chiesa family had been prominent in the Golden Book of Genoese Nobility since the sixteenth century, having contributed three Senators to that once mighty Republic. By the nineteenth century their fortunes had somewhat declined, and

Giacomo was born in 1854 in a rented apartment in the Palazzo Magliavecchi, which was described by his biographer Vistalli as 'a five-storey bourgeois building'. His father, the Marchese Giuseppe Della Chiesa, was a lawyer who, although deeply religious, insisted when the young Giacomo expressed a desire to enter the Church, that he should first take a civil law degree. Although of modest means, he was able to pay for his son's education – also for his other son Valerio to enter the navy, from which, in the best Genoese tradition, he was to retire as an admiral.

After leaving university with his law degree, Giacomo Della Chiesa studied at the Archbishop's seminary in Genoa, and then entered the College for Noble Ecclesiastics in Rome, which trains Papal diplomats. It was soon clear where his talents lay; and his first post took him to Spain as secretary to Cardinal Rampolla, when that distinguished diplomatist was Nuncio in Madrid. The young Della Chiesa was present at the funeral in 1885 of King Alfonso XII, and during the regency of his widow, Maria Christina of Austria. He took part in the Papal mediation between Spain and Germany over the Caroline Islands. Back in Rome, he worked almost exclusively in the Congregation for Extraordinary Affairs, until he became Archbishop of Bologna in 1907. It seems that Pius X was suspicious of the influence Cardinal Rampolla exercised over him,[4] because he was not advanced to the Purple till 25 May 1914, barely two months before the outbreak of the First World War.

All his experience being diplomatic, such a man would be admirably qualified for the task which lay ahead in August 1914. He seems to have been aware of this for, unlike his immediate predecessors, who had both pleaded their inadequacy when the Papacy was conferred upon them, he said he felt 'serene and confident', and he immediately began issuing orders, as a man accustomed to command. Although he had undergone such an intensive diplomatic training, he was not an intellectual; rather a conscientious bureaucrat with a store of carefully sorted, precise and accurate information. An unfavourable comment on this quality is provided by the Frenchman M. Henri Gonse who, in the absence of an official French representative at the Vatican, had been instructed to report unofficially from Rome on Vatican affairs: 'The new Pope Benedict XV is a born bureaucrat, preferring his colleagues to be like himself, meticulous about detail . . . he distrusts strong personalities. This is why among his new Curia creations, not one can be described as eminent either in character, intelligence, or culture. The new *Monsignori* of the Curia are so many well-schooled clerks, terrified of not acting through official channels.'[5]

A small, frail-looking man, Benedict XV had pinched features with an ascetic mouth, but enlivened by quick, darting black eyes. The Papal Chamberlain MacNutt described him: 'Of a sallow, bilious complexion with an impenetrable mat of thick, coarse, black hair . . . everything about him is crooked, nose, mouth, eyes, shoulders. Despite these blemishes, his bearing is dignified and he can never be mistaken for anything other than what he is – a gentleman.'[6] The Romans called him *Il Piccoletto* ('The Midget'), and their gossip related that he had such an inferiority complex about his diminutive figure that he had a habit of standing in front of a mirror drawing himself up. Count de Salis, the British Minister to the Holy See during the second half of the war, described him: 'He gives the impression that some defect in his growth at an early age has hindered the proper development of his heart and lungs.'[7] Nevertheless, this puny figure was to display, under all the stresses of the next five years, undismayed by his many fruitless attempts at peacemaking, an astonishing power of resistance. For if he was conscious of his unprepossessing appearance, he was equally aware of who he was: a member of a distinguished family, in a supreme post.

From the outset, he seems to have made up his mind about his foreign policy, to which he steadfastly adhered until the day of his death. Two days after his Coronation, he published an exhortation prescribing to the faithful prayers for the termination of the war, and urging the rulers of the belligerent powers to lay down their arms, and solve their differences by diplomatic means. The most impressive sentence in his plea called on them 'to reflect that this mortal life is already attended with enough misery and suffering as it is'. But the leaders of warring states pay heed to such lofty sentiments only when they feel that victory may elude them. In the autumn of 1914, all of them were far from that view, the French crying '*À Berlin!*', and the Germans '*Nach Paris!*'; while the youth of England, imbued with the spirit of Agincourt, was straining to get to France as quickly as possible, in case the war finished early!

When war broke out, it was generally assumed in Europe that the sympathies of the Vatican would lie with Austria and her allies. For in 1914, the one part of the world where the Vatican wished to see no change was Central Europe. The Austro-Hungarian Empire was Catholic by definition, and the Dual Monarchy was united to the Holy See by century-old ties. The bond between Throne and Altar had enabled Catholicism to influence policy in Austria more effectively than in any other country – in return for which the religious Orders, particularly the Franciscans, contributed largely to spreading and maintaining Austrian influence in the Balkans. M. Gonse, the French unofficial representative for Vatican affairs, commented, 'The Pope and the Austrian Emperor must now inevitably support one another – they are the only true conservatives in a Europe riddled with the democratic yeast.'

Austria's ally, the German Empire, although ruled by a Protestant, had a population of thirty million Catholics, some of them the most devout in the world. In the past thirty years, since the end of the *Kulturkampf*, Vatican relations with Germany had been steadily improving. Many devout Catholics throughout Europe regarded William II as the instrument chosen by Divine Providence for bringing down vengeance on France, the renegade 'eldest daughter of the Church'. Moreover, from East Prussia to the Carpathians, the Catholics of the Central Empires presented a solid, almost continuous, barrier to the expansion of Orthodox Russia.

On the other side, the Entente powers were all at variance with the Vatican. They included anti-clerical France, which had passed the Separation Law of 1905; Protestant Britain, which had had no official relations with Rome for four centuries; and Orthodox Russia, the Vatican's *bête noire*. In the latter's immense domains, persecution of the Catholic population, particularly in Poland, had been endemic for over a century. The Czarist Government did not allow any communication between the Pope and his scattered bishops there, except through the State administration. Even Catholic missals sent to Russia were censored. Mr Gregory, the British Chargé d'Affaires in Rome during the war, reported of his audiences with the Pope, 'Benedict XV has one obsession – Russia. In all the conversations I have had with him, he can never keep off the subject. Even the fear of another *Kulturkampf*, if Germany wins the war, pales in his eyes before the spectre of a Russian victory, and Russian troops on the Bosphorus.'[8]

Here Benedict XV was only voicing standard Vatican policy

towards Russia and the Orthodox Church. The Vatican had always preferred the Turk to the Slav in Constantinople, on account of the tolerance, indeed indifference, with which the former regarded the Christian faith. In Vatican eyes, Muslim indifference was preferable to Orthodox fanaticism; it preferred the Crescent on the cupola of Santa Sophia to the Greek Cross. As Britain and Russia were now allies (and later the British attacked Turkey in the Dardanelles), the Vatican firmly believed that the British Empire intended to evict the Turk from Stamboul, and replace him by the Slav. Sir Henry Howard, the British Minister at the Vatican, wrote on this subject to the Foreign Secretary, Sir Edward Grey, 'The Vatican is filled with alarm and foreboding by the agreement made between H.M.'s Government and Russia, giving Russia possession of Santa Sophia, with an extraterritorial zone to which the Holy Synod may be transferred – the erection of a rival establishment, as it were, to the Vatican on the shores of the Bosphorus. This can later lead, the Vatican believes, to the Orthodox Church extending its sway to the shores of the Adriatic.'[9]

This was confirmed from French sources. M. Gonse reported from Rome in November 1915:

All the information I have persuades me that the major preoccupation [sic] of the Vatican in the war is to form a front against the detestable Slav religion. . . . I am convinced that the Vatican . . . is in close touch with the German Government, with a view to combining all the Catholic forces of the West against the schismatic and miscreant East. The Pope hopes to enter the Levant in the wake of William II of Prussia. He entertains grandiose notions of becoming another Pius V, and playing a great role at the Peace Conference when the war is over. . . . He cannot rid his mind of the idea that Germany is bound to win the war.[10]

A month later, M. Gonse reported in the same vein:

The Pope continues his daydreams, his gaze turned tenderly towards Germany. That country always represents for him the advance sentinel of the West, guarding Europe against the hideous, schismatic East. . . . Germany, for her part, is well aware of the value of this *entente* with the Vatican. . . . The Pope has no agent more active on his behalf than the German Catholic bishops. Wherever they are, in the convent at Einsiedeln, in Cairo, Bucharest, everywhere, the German Catholics under the direction of their spiritual leaders are working indefatigably for Germany and the Pope – as if Germany and the Pope were one and the same thing.[11]

The Central Powers were certainly well aware of Vatican sympathies, and they made good use of them, particularly after Italy entered the war against them in 1915. To attract Catholics in neutral countries to their cause, rumours were circulated in the German and Austrian press that when the Central Powers had won the war, they would re-establish the Pope's temporal power, and expel the Savoyards from Rome.

Further evidence of Vatican sympathies for the Central Powers is revealed in a curious correspondence in the Italian State Archives for the year 1920. It consists of a series of documents published by President Masaryk, who had become head of the new Czechoslovak State after the war, and comprises the despatches to Vienna from Prince von Schönberg, the Austrian Ambassador to the Holy See during the war.[12] How Masaryk managed to get hold of these despatches is a mystery; for Austrian diplomatic documents are normally subject to the 'fifty year rule', and would not have been available until 1970.

In his despatch dated 2 March 1915, Prince von Schönberg reported:

Pope Benedict XV told me at the audience yesterday that he sympathizes with Austria-Hungary, not only because we are the first great Catholic power in the world, now that France has gone, but because the Vatican's political interest and ours coincide. He said he was now on friendly terms with the Italian Queen Mother Margherita and that, although she normally takes no part in politics, she has agreed to use her influence with her son, the King, to keep Italy from coming into the war on the side of the Entente. The Pope has certainly supported our efforts to maintain Italian neutrality. Here, he has brought his influence to bear not only on the Queen Mother, but on broader, Savoyard circles.

The Austrian Ambassador's conversations with the Secretary of State, Cardinal Gasparri, led him to the same conclusion: 'Cardinal Gasparri told me that if, despite all our efforts to prevent it, Italy declared war on Austria, it would be a most shameful act of treachery to an ally. His words were, "No robber could behave in a more cowardly way".'

This all sounds logical enough; but the suspicion that these despatches were apocryphal is aroused by certain remarks alleged to have been made by Benedict XV to the Austrian Ambassador. In one of the despatches, von Schönberg reported: 'The Pope made two observations to me which show how little Italian he is. He said that even though the Central Powers were now at war with so many countries, they would have little difficulty in conquering Italy. Secondly, after a number of observations about Austria's generosity – contrasting it with Italy's lack of it – he said to me in French, "*Je ne m'honore pas du fait d'être né dans ce pays.*" ("I rate it as no honour to have been born in this country.")' Such unpatriotic language seems unlikely; and the last remark, coming from an Italian aristocrat, highly improbable. A further ground for questioning the authenticity of these documents is that Masaryk was notoriously anti-clerical, and a freethinker.

Whether these documents 'discovered' by Masaryk alleging Papal sympathies for the Central Powers are authentic or not, one unfortunate incident, in which the Pope was involved when Italy came into the war in 1915, was cited by the Western Allies as indisputable proof of his pro-German leanings.

When Benedict XV was still Archbishop of Bologna, he had made the acquaintance of a certain Bavarian ex-Army officer, Captain von Gerlach, who had some years before exchanged his military uniform for the soutane. Von Gerlach had passed through the diplomatic College for Noble Ecclesiastics in Rome, to which he had obtained entry by his claim to kinship with the noble family of von Gerlach (subsequently proved to be spurious). The Pope, himself an ex-pupil of the College, was most sympathetic to priests educated there, and he took the young man into his service. Von Gerlach soon attained the privileged position of Chamberlain in regular attendance iin the Papal ante-chamber. The Pope made him a Monsignore, and he was entrusted with the care of the Papal wardrobe – the hats and insignia conferred on cardinals and other high dignitaries. In the words of Sir Henry Howard, the British

Minister at the Vatican, 'In spite of the doubtful and amatory [sic] past of Mgr von Gerlach, he evidently has a great hold over Benedict XV, who appointed him to his household only a few days after being elected Pope.'[13]

Before the Italian entry into the war, suspicion against this ex-military German priest had been aroused in Italian circles by his regular frequentation of eminent German ministers and politicians visiting Rome. Then one day in late 1916, the Pope received an urgent request from the Italian Government to send Mgr von Gerlach back to Germany. They said he was an 'undesirable enemy national', and that if he remained in Rome, they could not guarantee his safety. The surprised Pope rather reluctantly agreed; and von Gerlach was conducted to the Swiss frontier by Italian gendarmes. Scarcely had he crossed it, than he was indicted in Rome on a charge of high treason. A week later he was sentenced in his absence by an Italian military court to penal servitude for life. To the consternation of the Vatican, it appeared that von Gerlach had taken part in various acts of naval sabotage, including the dynamiting and destruction of the Italian battleship *Benedetto Brini*.

Nevertheless, the Government's case was far from convincing. The chief prosecution witness was an Italian naval architect, Bruno Tedeschi, who stated that he had had long conversations with von Gerlach about the Italian navy and its principal ships. He said that von Gerlach had offered him 100,000 lire to blow up the *Benedetto Brini*. The mystery deepened when Tedeschi was asked to identify von Gerlach from a group photograph of ecclesiastics; he chose the wrong priest. It seemed odd, too, that the Italian Government should have preferred to condemn him in his absence rather than try him in person. The assumption was that they had preferred to have him out of the country, because he might have been able to defend himself effectively in court.

If the Italian Government's intention was to present the Vatican in the worst possible light, as sympathetic to the Central Powers, they certainly succeeded; because the Italian and Entente press now condemned the Pope severely for employing Gerlach. This was followed by an outcry in Rome against all clerics or laymen of Germanic origin working in the Vatican. In the first category, came the Head of the Observantists, the German Jesuit Father Hagen; in the second, the German-speaking Swiss Guards, whose presence at the Vatican had been hallowed by centuries of service. Their

Commander Colonel Répond was reprobated for having a German wife. As for von Gerlach himself, he spent the rest of the war in Switzerland, where he threw his cassock into the nettles, and married a rich divorced lady.[14]

If the extent of Benedict XV's 'pro-German sympathy' is not proven, one thing is certain – he had every reason at the beginning of the war for distrusting the Entente powers. A month before the conversations he was alleged to have had with the Austrian Ambassador, von Schönberg, the Western powers had signed the secret Treaty of London (April 1915), granting Italy certain advantages if she would enter the war on their side. One of these, stated in Article 15 of the Treaty, was that 'France, Great Britain and Russia will support any opposition Italy may make after the war to the Holy See being represented at the Peace Conference.' The Vatican was aware of this, as revealed in the despatch of the British Ambassador to the Quirinale on 17 January 1916: 'It seems that the Vatican had learned about the Treaty from German sources . . . the latter are taking full advantage of it, informing the Vatican that after they have won the war, they will restore the city of Rome to the Holy See.'[15] The Quai d'Orsay confirmed this view. M. Henri Gonse, the French representative in Rome, reported in January 1916, 'It seems that the Vatican was informed of the Treaty during the recent stay in Rome of the Archbishop of Cologne, Cardinal Hartmann. It is said here that this German prelate offered Benedict XV *in the name of the Kaiser* the Presidency of the Peace Conference after Germany has won the war.'[16]

The German offers caused some embarrassment to the Vatican, because they made its proclamation of neutrality appear disingenuous. On 28 June 1915, the Vatican Secretary of State, Cardinal Gasparri, corrected that impression. He notified the Central Powers that the Vatican had no need of such help, that it intended to await God's good time for a solution of the 'Roman Question'. It did not require military aid, but would await the triumph of right which, the Church was convinced, the Italian people would in God's good time support. It was a forceful speech, in which he reiterated that the Vatican would not take sides, because it saw no difference between the Central and the Entente powers; both evinced the same overweening ambitions and 'avidity for conquest'. The only difference was that the Entente hypocritically hid their true aims under the mantle of fighting for 'liberal ideas' and 'liberty'. It was a fine word, 'liberty'; but, said Gasparri sarcastically, the conquests envisaged by the Treaty of London for Russia would deprive the Catholics of the Balkans of this liberty that the Western Allies were always boasting about.[17]

On this statement by Cardinal Gasparri, M. Gonse commented equally sarcastically:

Yes, the Vatican claims grandly to be above the common herd [au-dessus de la mêlée]. To the Pope this is just another war, a temporary political aberration, a senseless destruction of human lives and property – which he hopes will finish with neither victor nor vanquished. He does not understand that above and beyond the *political* aspect is the *moral* one. He should be the first to see this war as a Crusade. After the Hunnish atrocities in Flanders, Lille, Roubaix, Tourcoing, La Madeleine, the world is shocked that the new Attila should not be confronted by a new Leo the Great. The silence of Benedict XV has lowered the prestige of the Vatican throughout the world. As for France, the restoration of relations with the Vatican, which so many people advocate, now reverts to the Greek Kalends.[18]

Whatever its private sympathies, the Vatican's policy in wartime must publicly be one of strict neutrality. The truth of this was most effectively demonstrated as the war continued, by each side accusing the Pope of partiality towards the other. Clemenceau arraigned Benedict XV as '*le Pape Boche*'; while Ludendorff (the German second-in-command) called him '*der französischer Papst*' ('the French Pope'). After the war, Ludendorff published a number of articles on this theme.[19] He argued that the Vatican's aim had been that Germany should go to war with Russia, 'the German sword to destroy Russia'; and then, duly weakened, be defeated by the Western Allies. He also claimed that the Vatican had attempted, through the Austrian Empress Zita, to promote a separate peace between Austria and France, so that Germany could be isolated and destroyed.

How can this be reconciled with an almost identical accusation from the Entente side, by M. Herriot? He announced in the French Chambre that Benedict XV had attempted to sow distrust and discord among the Western Allies; and that the Pope had done all he could to dissuade the United States from supplying the Allies with weapons, munitions and food. The Italian Government went even further, attributing the Italian defeat at Caporetto to 'Vatican and Jesuit pacifist propaganda'. In England the Prime Minister, Lloyd George, accused the Vatican in 1917 of 'plotting a German peace'.

This hysterical behaviour by the leaders of both sides reveals how passions began to run out of control as the war continued. Even the episcopate of the belligerent nations was affected. The French Catholic bishops spoke of the war as a 'Crusade'; while the German Catholic bishops, in a pastoral letter protested, 'Germany is innocent of this war. It was imposed on her. We can testify that before God and man.' Both sides therefore expected the Pope, who was for this conjuncture conveniently regarded by everyone as 'the champion of the right', to pronounce publicly in their favour. As a prelate at the Vatican said to M. Loiseau, 'This century appears to be demanding of the Pope today what it condemned in the Pope yesterday. The nations want the Pope to throw himself into the mêlée with a thunderbolt in each hand, striking their enemies. But the Pope knows what this would lead to. When the war is over and everyone reconciled, the Pope would be at peace with no one.'[20] For much of the previous century the governments of Europe had done all they could to undermine the power of the Pope. Nothing that could humiliate him was spared. Now, they were appealing for his support.

A devout Catholic might well view the Pope in these circumstances as a Divinely constituted authority, of supreme moral power, who alone can judge, and if necessary condemn, the faults and crimes of nations and rulers. But no Pope, not even Gregory VII of Canossa fame, succeeded in establishing such a power – and that in a Europe which professed submission to the Church. He might humble individual monarchs, but he was never able to act as a supreme arbiter between lay States. We have seen that Leo XIII refused to act as arbiter over the Carolines dispute; he would only be a *mediator*. The Pope has always regarded it as his duty to teach and reprove, expressing his views in Encyclicals and pastoral letters to the faithful all over the world. He does not condemn institutions in any specific country – because the Church refuses to comment on, or be identified with, such transient human phenomena. As Benedict XV clearly put it, 'I cannot pronounce publicly upon disputed questions of fact, concerning which no evidence except *ex parte* statements is furnished to me.'

In the case of the invasion of Belgium, the Western Allies immediately demanded that the Pope should condemn Germany. This type of demand is fairly common: it was to be repeated several times during the Second World War. It is worth while examining how the Holy See replies to such a request. This was described in the Vatican newspaper *Osservatore Romano* in its issue of 30 January 1925. The Holy See, said the paper, in its determination to be neutral, would not mention any nation by name. But if reprehensible acts were committed, it would be the first to condemn them. Thus in the Great War, in connection with the invasion of Belgium, Benedict XV said in a consistorial audience on 4 December 1916, 'We see minority nations shamefully outraged, and many peaceable citizens taken from their homes and deported to distant regions'. The condemnation was clear, said the *Osservatore Romano*; but it could not be individual. We now know that the manner in which the Russians conducted the war in Poland was identical with that of the Germans in Belgium.[21] So the Western Allies would have to be condemned too. In short, Papal condemnation cannot descend to the particular, for the simple reason that the alleged cases of 'atrocities' cannot be confirmed during the war by the Holy See.[22]

Concerning Belgium, it is not generally known – certainly not in Allied circles – that at the beginning of the war, the German Government provided the Vatican and other neutrals with their explanation of why they had occupied Belgium. The relevant documents are in the Italian State Archives.[23] The Germans show that in August 1914 France had been about to invade Belgium, and that on purely military grounds for Germany's security, she had to be forestalled. The Germans cite the evidence of two Belgian witnesses, one of whom, an army officer, declared that on 26 July 1914 he had been present when a number of French and Belgian staff officers congregated in a house in the Boulevard Anspach in Brussels to discuss military collaboration in the event of France declaring war on Germany. The other witness, a certain Gustave Lochard of Rimogne, testified that on 28 and 29 July 1914, two regiments of French dragoons, the advance guard of the French army, crossed the Belgian frontier, and thereafter remained on Belgian soil. Having established a pretext for the *military* need to occupy Belgium, the German Government goes on to relate in its 'White Book'[24] the 'atrocities' committed against their troops by

the Belgian population. 'Wounded German soldiers have been
fearfully mutilated by the Belgian population . . . their eyes
gouged out, their ears, noses, fingers and sexual organs cut off,
their entrails opened. . . . In other places German soldiers have
been hung from trees, had boiling oil poured over them, in some
cases burned alive. . . .' At the end of August 1914, Don
Herwegan, the Abbé of the famous monastery of Maria-Lach near
Cologne, sent a telegram to the Belgian Archbishop of Malines
imploring him for the love of God to protect German soldiers from
the 'tortures' to which they were being subjected by the Belgian
population.[25]

What was Benedict XV to make of all this? He was receiving
similar stories from the Entente side of German 'atrocities'. He had
to weigh any statements he made with the greatest care; the
slightest word, or even question, from him could be interpreted in a
score of different ways all over the globe. He preferred in 1914 to
wait until something approaching the truth filtered through.

It was not until 22 January 1915 that the Pope made his definitive
pronouncement on Belgium – and then only because he could quote
the official admission, from the German Chancellor Bethmann-
Hollweg himself, that the German invasion of Belgium, although
necessary for German defence was, strictly, a violation of
international law. Here the Pope made a specific reference to
Belgium, and he besought 'the humanity of the enemy [he did not
say the Germans] who have crossed Belgium's frontiers, to lay
waste no more territory, nor to harm the Belgian population
further'.

Two weeks later, Benedict XV gave an audience to Herr
Erzberger, the leader of the German Zentrum Party, a practising
Catholic. In his memoirs, Herr Erzberger says that the Pope asked
him about 'the atrocities' committed in Belgium by the German
troops, principally Pommeranians and Mecklenbergers. 'The Holy
Father told me he had received reports that some hundred and fifty
nuns had been raped by German troops – in some cases in church,
during Communion! Would I go into the matter, and confirm that
this was not simply Allied propaganda?' Herr Erzberger expressed
surprise, but said that when he returned to Germany he would ask
Archbishop Mercier of Belgium, in the occupied zone, if this was
true. 'The Archbishop,' he later reported to the Vatican, 'was
unable to confirm that such atrocities had been committed.' The

incident reveals how careful the Pope has to be in wartime in accepting *ex parte* reports.

Seeing in the first year of the war that it was too early to repeat his plea for peace, Benedict XV addressed himself to the more modest task of alleviating the sufferings of the prisoners of war, as *Pastor Angelicus* ('Angelic Shepherd', in the sense of 'guardian angel'). In December 1914, he obtained an exchange of those prisoners made unfit by wounds for further military service. In May 1915, he obtained the transfer to Swiss hospitals of some thirty thousand sick and wounded prisoners from both sides, who were not in the category of the incapacitated. Through the Papal Office of Information, families were reassured about fathers and sons who had been taken prisoner.[26] The Pope's intervention on behalf of individual prisoners for exchange was not always successful; the British being hostile to the suggestion – although they benefited when the Hatfield brothers, who had been condemned to death by the Turks, were saved through the good offices of the Apostolic Delegate in Constantinople.

Less successful, too, was Benedict XV's other humane proposal – to resurrect an old Papal practice, the *Tregua Dei* ('God's Truce'), by which hostilities should cease on the days of certain religious festivals. He suggested that the belligerents should revive the custom for Christmas Day (and if a truce could be achieved for even one day, it might lead to further cessations of hostilities). Britain, Germany and Belgium agreed; but France objected, on the ground that the military operations in progress to expel the Germans from her soil could not be interrupted. A further obstacle was that neither Russia nor Serbia celebrated Christmas on the day which in the West was 25 December, since they still used the Julian calendar.

18

The Failure of Benedict XV's 1917 Peace Proposals

The Pope's earlier peace proposals had been largely ignored, and it required some determination on his part to make another attempt. But he felt by 1917 that, quite apart from the unparalleled slaughter at the fronts, the civilian population all over Europe was now suffering so acutely that, as Head of the Church, he would be guilty of dereliction of duty if he did nothing. He felt that after three years of such loss of life, the great powers might now be more prepared to consider a compromise peace. Moreover, with remarkable prescience he saw the greatest danger ahead. As early as 1916, he had said to Herr Erzberger, 'If this war continues much longer, we shall have such a social revolution in Europe as the world has not seen since 1789.' He was proved right by the Russian Revolution of 1917.

One negative factor for Vatican satisfaction at least emerged from the Pope's 1917 peace proposals: this was the flurry of excitement they caused in all the Chancelleries of Europe – an indication of the power, intangible but evidently ubiquitous, still wielded by the Pope. Had these proposals been made by some neutral lay state possessing considerably more material power, they would hardly have been noticed. As it was, the world telegraph cables hummed with their discussion, between London and Washington, St Petersburg and Paris, Vienna and Berlin. The press of all the belligerent powers devoted pages to them.

Benedict XV's 1917 peace proposals were made on two occasions – in February, and again, more importantly, in August. In February 1917, he limited himself to one aspect of the war – the plight of the civilian population. He suggested that the belligerents should stop trying to starve one another to death; the Germans with their

U-boat campaign against merchant vessels; and the British with their naval blockade preventing food from reaching the Central Powers. To this, the Germans replied that the submarine campaign had been forced on them by the British blockade; as long as it lasted, so would the torpedoing of merchant ships. The British reply was conveyed to the Vatican by our Minister, Count de Salis. 'The two activities referred to by His Holiness,' it stated, 'are of a totally different nature. A naval blockade of one belligerent by another has always been regarded as legitimate in time of war. But the indiscriminate destruction of civilians by the submarine is a new crime in the history of naval warfare. There can be no possible comparison between the two. One is legal in character, and humane in execution; the other is illegal and murderous.'[1]

This British attitude was not shared by the Vatican. The French representative, M. Gonse, explained in his despatch to the Quai d'Orsay, 'Rumours that the Pope condemns the German submarine warfare are unfounded. He regards it as the legitimate consequence of the British naval blockade of the Continent, which he considers an abominable crime.'[2] There was clearly little prospect of progress here, and the Pope decided to wait for a more auspicious occasion. It came earlier than he had expected.

During the summer of 1917, the Austrians displayed a greater desire for peace than did any of the other belligerents. The war was then going particularly badly for the Habsburg Empire, whose non-German and non-Magyar elements were on the point of capitulation. In the words of its Foreign Minister, Count Czernin, on 2 April 1917, 'I am convinced that another winter campaign is out of the question. By the autumn of this year, an end must be put to the war, at all costs.'[3] Accordingly, the Austrian Emperor Charles initiated secret negotiations through his brother-in-law, Prince Sixte of Bourbon-Parma, with the Entente Powers. They made little headway, as is explained by Count Czernin, who was in charge of them. 'The statesman of France and England,' he writes, 'are just like Ludendorff. None of them wishes to compromise. They look only for victory.' It was as a result of this failure that the Austrians turned to the Pope, and asked for his proposals.

During the summer of 1917 the Pope elaborated these, and at the beginning of August he published them to the world. They recommended an immediate armistice, to be followed by the evacuation of all occupied territory. Germany was to withdraw from Belgium and France, Britain was to return Germany's African colonies seized at the outbreak of war. Russia was to evacuate Poland and the Armenian territory taken from Turkey. Neither side was to receive reparations for the material damage which enemy occupation of their territory had caused (on the ground that these cancelled one another out). Other proposals dealt with territorial adjustments affecting Austria and Italy in the Alto Adige (or South Tyrol), and the return of Alsace to France. There was a clause about 'freedom of the seas', and a number of ethical recommendations such as, 'the moral force of law to take the place of the material force of arms'. The most desirable, if utopian, proposal was for the universal abolition of military service. 'For more than a century,' said the Pope, 'military conscription has been the bane and principal cause of the evils afflicting mankind.' He recommended the establishment of an arbitration tribunal which would, after the war, boycott any nation establishing compulsory military service.

These proposals were not well received by the Western Allies. Their view was that the Vatican had formulated them in collusion with the Central Powers, who stood to benefit most if they were accepted. The Central Powers, the Allies contended, were now aware that, as a result of the entry of the United States of America into the war, their defeat was certain. They therefore wanted to extricate themselves from a difficult situation while there was yet time; and they had enlisted the Pope to do it for them. In the British Foreign Office archives is a memorandum on this by Harold Nicolson:

The Vatican maintains, that their peace proposals were drafted without any previous consultation with Berlin and Vienna. But evidence from Mr Savery of our Embassy in Berne confutes this.[4] Mr Savery says that the Papal Legate in Berne, Mgr Marchetti, has been in constant contact since early 1917 with the German Catholic politicians, Erzberger and Lemnach, who came to Switzerland specially while the Papal proposals were being drawn up. It appears that Mr Savery himself was approached by the Papal Legate on the subject – whereupon Mr Savery told him, on our instructions, that Great Britain would enter into no peace negotiations so long as one single German soldier remained on Belgian soil. Whereupon Mgr Marchetti apparently became most agitated. 'The Vatican,' he said to Mr Savery, 'has had to fight tooth and nail with the German Government to get them to agree to the clause about withdrawing from Belgium.'

On this Mr Nicolson commented drily, 'This admission – that the German Government had cognizance beforehand of the Papal proposals – is significant. It completely confutes the Vatican contention that the proposals were drawn up without previous consultation with Berlin.'[5]

The Italian Government shared this view, as the report of its representative in Berne reveals. He too referred to the clause about the Germans evacuating Belgium. 'This,' he wrote, 'the Germans at first refused to agree to, and it required long and laborious negotiations with the Vatican to get them to accept. It seems that the Pope was reassured before issuing his peace proposals that they would be well received by the Central Powers and their allies, Bulgaria and Turkey.'

A further British objection to the proposals concerned the clause about 'freedom of the seas'. As the Royal Navy dominated the oceans of the world, this could be directed only against Great Britain. That at least was how the Central Powers saw it, in terms of the British blockade. What, asked the Germans, were the ports of Gibraltar, Malta, Suez, Aden, Cyprus, Singapore, or Colombo but so many bases for the British fleet? The Central Powers interpreted the Pope's suggestion about 'freedom of the seas' as indicating that these ports should be handed back by the British to their local native populations. The British of course would have none of this: these places were on the life-line to their Indian Empire. They also objected to the clause proposing the return of the German colonies. Britain regarded these not as pawns to be bargained over at the conference table, but as future additions to her Empire. Nor did the Pope receive support from the English Catholic hierarchy. Cardinal Bourne of Westminster stated, 'The Pope has proposed that all the belligerents should come to a compromise. No! We demand the total triumph of right over wrong. We do not want a peace which will be no more than a truce or armistice between two wars. There may be in our land some people who want peace at any price, but they have no following among us. We English Catholics are fully behind our war leaders.'

The French reaction to the Pope's proposals was even more obdurate. France had suffered most from enemy occupation, and that Germany should not pay reparations to her was unthinkable. The newspaper *Le Temps* summed this up: 'We French regard the war as a Crusade. To the Pope, it is evidently a lawsuit.' The French Ambassador in Washington wrote to the American President's representative in Europe, Colonel House, 'The Austro-Hungarian inspiration of the Pope's proposals is clearly revealed. . . . The fact that Serbia is not mentioned is surely significant of where Papal sympathies lie.' M. Gonse in Rome emphasized the French scepticism: 'Once again we see that the pacifist manoeuvres, apparently from the most diverse sources, are really unified – they all derive from Germany, which is ingeniously using the Pope. To reach their goal the Central Powers, having failed on the battlefield, are now mobilizing the Papacy.'[6]

It might be supposed that the American reaction would have been more sympathetic (President Wilson was later to make suggestions on similar lines in his 'Fourteen Points'). If anything, it was less conciliatory. Colonel House wrote to A. J. Balfour, the British Foreign Secretary, 'One of our main objections is that the Pope's proposals constitute no settlement, but only a return to the *status quo ante*, which would leave affairs in much the same position that furnished the pretext for the war. . . . It is hardly fair to ask the peoples of the Allied countries to discuss terms with a military autocracy – an autocracy which does not represent the German people . . . also, important issues such as the unrestricted submarine warfare are ignored.'[7]

The reaction of Russia was expressed by the Minister Tereschchenko to the Italian Ambassador in St Petersburg. He pointed out that no mention was made in the Pope's peace proposals about the evacuation of Russian territories invaded by Germany, only of Russian evacuation of Poland and Armenia; and that the Russians had occupied the latter only to 'terminate the unheard-of cruelties committed by the Turks there'. As for the omission of reparation payment, this, said Tereshchenko, 'eliminates all question of who was responsible for the war; it places Germany in an advantageous position, because her territory has not been touched by the war. So she has no reparations to claim anyway.'[8]

In connection with Russia, it is interesting to note that when, a year later, the Communists seized power in St Petersburg, they explained the Papal peace proposals in that special jargon to which we have in the last fifty years become accustomed. They said the Pope had wanted to submit his peace bid first, to forestall the 'peace-loving forces' of the International Socialist Congress in Stockholm which, under Communist guidance, was publishing its own peace plan. The Communists branded the Pope's proposals as 'a typical example of 'religio-capitalist hypocrisy'.'

The Italian reaction to the proposals was also predictable. The very fact that they emanated from the Vatican was enough to ensure condemnation by the powerful Socialist body in Monte Citorio. Moreover, it was unfortunate for the Pope that they coincided almost exactly with the Italian defeat at Caporetto in October 1917, for they were seized on by the Italian anti-clericals as having contributed to it. The British Ambassador in Rome, Sir Rennell Rodd, expressed the Italian view in his despatch of 2 November 1917: 'Caporetto is not regarded here as a defeat in the strict military sense, but rather a kind of general strike or refusal to fight by thousands of Italian soldiers. This was due, it is alleged, to the pacifist propaganda so long carried on by clerical circles and *encouraged by the Papal Peace Proposals* [italics author's].' The British Ambassador adds that Italian deserters fleeing before the Austrian advance were heard to cry *'Evviva il Papa!'* 'The Italian Foreign Ministry is convinced that the Vatican has been conniving with the Central Powers, by whom the peace proposals were inspired.'[9]

Some Italian newspapers went even further. The *Popolo d'Italia* attributed the responsibility for the Caporetto disaster quite simply to the Jesuits. But perhaps the most hysterical explanation of the Caporetto defeat was expressed in New York on 15 January 1918 – and by a presumably responsible politician. Here F. E. Walcott, later President Hoover's Minister of National Supply, stated before an audience comprising the flower of New York female society that 'Austria is in close agreement with the Pope, who was directly responsible for the disastrous retreat last October of the Italian Army at Caporetto.' He added that copies of the *Corriere della Sera*, containing defeatist propaganda and distributed among the troops, had been printed in the Vatican, and that the Pope ought to be brought to trial.[10] Some Catholic ladies in the audience were deeply offended by this, and they complained to the Vicar-General, Mgr Lavelle. He sent a letter of protest to the authorities, and Mr

Walcott was obliged to retract his words.

The result of all this diplomacy was that of the Western Allies, only the United States replied to the Papal proposals, and then negatively. France and Britain, being parties to the secret Treaty of London with its anti-Papal clause, could hardly reply. They were pleased to be able to extricate themselves from an embarrassing position by putting the onus of replying on their new ally.

On the other side, the Central Powers and their allies replied in most civil terms to the proposals, praising the Pope's initiative and deploring the negative attitude adopted by the Entente. The joint letter expressing this which the German Kaiser and his fellow sovereign, King Ludwig of Bavaria sent to the Pope, must also be one of the most hypocritical State documents ever penned. 'History has shown,' the two German Monarchs stated:

> that at the foundation of the German Empire, the German nation harboured no other or more earnest wish than to co-operate in peace and honour with other nations, in the task of *Kultur* for the benefit of mankind. Nothing was further in the minds of the peace-loving German nations and their governments than the prospect of attacking another nation, or striving by violence for territorial expansion – since neither conquest nor the acquisition of territory can, in their view, outweigh even in the remotest degree the fearful horrors of war, and its complement, the annihilation of cultural values. . . .

A copy of this letter is in the Italian Foreign Office files at the Farnesina;[11] but as the Vatican archives are not available for 1917, we do not know what the Vatican thought about this piece of disingenuousness.

Nevertheless, the German attitude towards the Pope's peace proposals hardened in the late autumn of 1917, because the fortunes of war took an unexpected turn in Germany's favour, with the collapse and capitulation of Czarist Russia. Germany could now concentrate her troops in the West for the decisive blow, and this required the continued occupation of Belgium (which Germany had earlier agreed to evacuate). In his memoirs Herr Erzberger writes, 'The Papal peace initiative of 1917 finally foundered on the refusal of Germany to make any concessions over Belgium.' He refers to 'a confidential seance of the German Supreme Command, in which the Chancellor Graf Hertling insisted that Belgian occupation was essential for the last phase of the war'.[12] However, after an initial success in that 'last phase', the great German offensive of 1918 in Flanders ground to a halt; the Central Powers had overreached themselves. Within another six months the war was over.

In the peace settlement of 1919 the Pope took no part; he had been specifically excluded from it by the victors under the secret Treaty of London. However, any regrets he may have felt at being unable to exercise the traditional good offices of the Papacy in reconciliation were soon offset, once the Peace Conference began, by his not being involved in the terms imposed on the defeated Central Powers, which the Vatican considered vindictive. In any case, the Vatican considered that the Conference was opening under most unfavourable auspices, by being held at Versailles instead of in a neutral country such as Holland, at the Peace Palace in The Hague. In the Vatican view, the choice of a belligerent capital was a psychological error; and the Conference was held too soon after the end of hostilities, when Allied hatred of Germany was unabated. Anyway, what could one expect of a Peace Conference dominated by Clemenceau, called 'The Tiger'? The Western Allied delegations should not have been totally led by men who had been wartime leaders and in office since 1914. Clemenceau's reference to the 'criminal deeds of the Germans' gave the first indication that revenge, not reconciliation, dominated the attitude of the Allied leaders, as did the absence of German and Austrian representatives at Versailles. These were only summoned at the very end, when they were presented with a *Diktat*. That, at least, was how the Vatican saw it.

The Vatican also deplored the dismantlement of the Austro-Hungarian Empire by the Trianon terms. The danger to Europe of such an event had been foreseen as early as 1916 by the Cardinal Secretary of State, Gasparri. The French representative in Rome, M. Gonse, reported the Cardinal's words at the time to the French newspaper *Le Journal*, which had referred to 'the likely dissolution of the Habsburg Empire'.

Destroy Austria? [exclaimed Cardinal Gasparri] My God! What madness! To what end? To hand it to whom? Let France and England reflect on the future they will prepare for Europe by such an act. The whirlpool of this terrible war will swallow up France too, even if she is victorious, if she does not recognize the perils which the triumph of this anti–Habsburg coalition will bring to Europe. Is it possible that France cannot recognize the Russian danger? If Austria goes, in a matter of years the Slavs will have swallowed up half Europe. France will lose all influence, and the Catholic religion will be under constant attack in all the countries of Eastern Europe.[13]

This remarkable prophecy was an unofficial warning, pronounced in 1916. After the Great War ended, it was repeated by the Vatican officially. 'Austria-Hungary,' it stated, 'is being unwisely dismantled, and replaced by an agglomeration of small independent states. These are bound sooner or later to come under the domination of Russia. They will form a Russian confederation stretching from the Carpathians to Constantinople, from Danzig to the Adriatic. Austria itself is being reduced to a rump, which will be incapable of holding its own against a hundred million Germans.'[14] The events of 1938 and 1945 were to confirm this abundantly.

What the Vatican did not appear to foresee during the conflict was that, since a new and more merciless form of warfare had been unleashed on the world, involving the risking of enormous material resources, from henceforth there could be no compromise; that the war could end only with the complete capitulation of one side or the other. Nevertheless, if the Pope had not made his plea for a compromise peace in 1917, he would have alienated public opinion, Catholic and Christian all over the world. For in the eyes of all religious denominations the Pope is, if nothing else, a 'man of peace'. Thus, he is expected at once to take part in international politics, and *not* to take part in international politics; to be at one point exclusively a spiritual leader, at another a temporal one. Thus, whatever he does is wrong. He knows this, so he simply does, as Benedict XV did in 1917, what he believes is right.

The result of his conduct was that the Papacy emerged from the war with its standing considerably enhanced, as certain anti-clericals were quick to note – and deplore. The French left-wing journal *La France Libre* complained on 15 May 1920, 'Fifteen years ago, the Vatican seemed on the point of collapse. . . . Now after the greatest war in history, in which all the belligerents suffered the most fearful destruction and loss of life, only one victor emerges –

the Vatican!' The Swiss *Semaine Littéraire de Genève* wrote, 'Since 1914, the Papacy has become again a power of the first order.' Even if these assertions were exaggerated, diplomatic confirmation exists. In 1914, only a handful of European diplomats represented their countries at the Vatican: there were two Ambassadors, of Austria and Spain; behind them four Ministers, of Prussia, Bavaria, Russia and Belgium. Apart from Latin America, that was all. By 1922, at the death of Benedict XV, some thirty-five countries had Ambassadors or Ministers at the Holy See – and it was not the Holy See which had solicited their presence.

To Benedict XV death came unexpectedly early, at the age of sixty-seven; and probably easily, a relief from the fearful burdens he had borne for four years of the greatest war in history. A fitting comment on his role during it came from an unexpected source – the only statue to him in the world, erected by the Turks in Istanbul. Engraved on it are the words: 'To the great Pope of the world tragedy, Benedict XV, the Benefactor of all Peoples, irrespective of Nationality or Religion – this Symbol of Gratitude from the East'.[15]

Conclusion

The Power of Rome? The question was asked at the outset. How great is it, as seen in terms of Stalin's celebrated, if apocryphal, question, 'How many divisions has the Pope?'. The question is well answered in Mr Peter Nichols' eloquent study of the Papacy today, entitled *The Pope's Divisions*. He shows that since the domination of European thought by the French anti-clerical intellectuals at the turn of the century, the increasing materialism of our age has turned mens' minds back to religion. 'At its height,' he writes of the Papacy, 'it was the greatest power in medieval Europe. It has now (1981) found a new vitality, at a time when fears are widespread for humanity's future, and the level of leadership in the purely political world is unusually low.' Mr Nichols quotes D.H. Lawrence:

> Give us gods. Oh give them us!
>   Give us gods.
> We are tired of men and motor-power.

In the period covered by this book we have seen a number of examples of this increasing Papal power. The first was Bismarck's *Kulturkampf* in 1871 against the Catholic Church in Germany (Chapter 6). After the Papacy's seven years of bitter struggle the French Ambassador in Rome, the Comte de Bourgoing, commented, 'Bismarck assumed the Papacy was weakened for ever [he is referring to the destruction of the Temporal power in 1870]. But this weakness is only apparent and superficial. Beneath the surface, the Pope still disposes of very great power . . . the Pope is now giving Bismarck sleepless nights. The victor of Sadowa and Sedan would not have attacked him so ruthlessly if he considered the Papacy infirm and powerless.' The Englishman, Henry Manning, commented, 'The German Empire, defended by a million bayonets and with legions of public and secret policemen at its disposal, celebrated, sung and idealized by an innumerable court of panegyrists as the first power in Europe, was forced to bow before 200 defenceless priests.'

An instance of Papal power of a more negative nature was the use of the *Veto* by the Emperor of Austria at the 1903 Conclave (Chapter 13). In that year, the Great Powers of Europe were already adopting positions for the military struggle ahead; the emerging adversaries, the Triple Alliance and the Triple Entente, were canvassing every potential support. At the Conclave of 1903, the favourite candidate for the Papacy was Cardinal Rampolla who, during his long period as Leo XIII's Secretary of State, had been consistently hostile to Austria and the Triple Alliance and friendly to its principal enemy, France. When it appeared certain that he would be elected, the Austrian Emperor invoked the age-old right of Catholic sovereigns, the *Veto*, which automatically disqualified Cardinal Rampolla. This was considered throughout Europe as extraordinary, for the *Veto* had long been regarded as lapsed. Nevertheless, the fact that it was invoked in 1903 was an indication that, although the Papacy had lost its temporal possessions, it still weighed heavily in the counsels of the Great Powers. For the war ahead, the Pope's sympathies must not lie with the enemy.

Perhaps the most significant example of Papal power was France where, in 1903, the socoalist-atheist government under Combes, confident that the Catholic religion was dead or dying, broke with Rome and suppressed all the religious Orders (Chapter 15). Yet within five years the French representatives abroad, the Ambassadors and Ministers in foreign countries of strategical or commercial importance to France, were writing to Paris, deploring the French loss of political and cultural influence through the closure of these missions. The Deputy, M. Gayrand, speaking in the Chambre on the subject of the Sisters of St Vincent de Paul in Jerusalem, said 'The best part of French influence here was due to these Sisters, their schools and institutions which cared for lepers. They did more for France than can a hundred-thousand bayonets.' Within two decades of its repudiation of the Papacy, the French government had to come deferentially to the Vatican and request that the French Missions be restored overseas. (After the rupture with France, the Pope had replaced them with missions from other

European nations.) The same thing was repeated in Portugal. They, too, experienced their Canossa, and had to return to the Vatican, penitent.

But the power of the Pope often operates in inverse proportion to the apparent felicity and prosperity of the Papacy; that is to say, when things are going badly, it is at its greatest. In the words of the French Senator Jenouvrier, when the Combes' persecution was at its height, 'Never has the Pope's presence in France been more deeply felt than today – when it has been banished. Never has his authority been more respected – since the day the government repudiated it. Never has the religious question been more alive and vital in France – since they stated that it did not exist!'

The secular rulers of the world, from Bismarck and Combes to Stalin and his heirs, still appear to ignore Machiavelli's famous maxim, *Perseguitatemi se volete farmi regnare*! Or, in the words of the valiant Pius IX, the most persecuted of all Popes in our time, 'Sometimes God sends a scourge deliberately to awaken men from their sloth. Just as many centuries ago, he sent Attila to reawaken the people to religion, so today he sends this modern Attila [Bismarck]. And this modern Attila who prides himself that he is destroying – he does not know that he is really creating.' Pius IX then called on believers to put their faith in 'a Church accustomed to triumph on Golgotha'.

The four Popes of the period described here were men of their time, of the Victorian bourgeois era, upright, hard-working, respectable, even dull. Certainly, compared with many of their 263 predecessors in the Chair of St Peter, they lacked colour. We are here far from the days when Julius III could raise his favourite, a fifteen-year old catamite, to the cardinalate, and cause his brother to adopt him. Or of the hedonist Popes like Paul II, whose reign was devoted almost entirely to the pleasures of the table, horse-racing, hunting-parties and the carnival. Nor did these four Popes possess any of the Maecenas quality of their Renaissance forebears, no open-handed patronage of artists and men of letters. Between 1870 and 1922, no Bramante, Michelangelo, Perugino, Raphael, or Sanseverino worked behind the Bronze Doors. One cannot name a single artist or architect of note whom the Popes of the 'liberal' period employed.

Of these four Popes the most successful – at least in re-establishing the power of Rome – was Leo XIII. His great achievement was to recreate some form of understanding between Church and State, after the events of 1870. To this end he was indifferent as to the *form* of government which the State assumed: monarchy or republic, democracy or autocracy. Such matters did not concern the Church, because the Church is above all nations and their governments. The latter he regarded as passing phenomena, imperfect but necessary instruments for the material ordinance of human life, ever in a state of flux, changing form sometimes violently, sometimes peacefully. In face of this, the Church can only adopt a waiting attitude, on the old Vatican principle of *cunctando regitur mundus*, mastery through delay. Then, and only then, when order has been re-established after the latest political cataclysm, and the new system appears to be functioning with public support and without undue friction, does the Church recognize it. Even then, it knows that it cannot last. Leo XIII did not live to see Mussolini; but he would have understood perfectly how a liberal monarchy could give way to an authoritarian rule which in turn gave way within a few decades to a liberal republic.

Novel as his political principles might appear, Leo XIII's religious principles were in no way different from those of his predecessors. Almost every word of his Encyclical *Immortale Dei*, on the relations between Church and State, might have been uttered by Innocent III, seven hundred years before. 'Human society' it announced, 'cannot dispense with morality, and the basis of morality is religion. God has divided the government of mankind between two powers, the ecclesiastical and the civil, the former placed over things Divine, the latter over human affairs. Since the Church's end is nobler, her power extends over all other powers, and can in no way be subject to civil authority.' The Pope finished with this superb claim: 'Wherever the Church of Rome has set her foot, she has straightway changed the face of things, and tempered the moral tone of the people with a new civilization, and with virtues before unknown. The Catholic Church remains the light of which civilization has been at all times the attendant shadow. All nations which have yielded to her sway have become eminent for their culture, their sense of justice, and the glory of their high deeds.'

Appendix

The Guarantee Laws of 13 May 1871

The main provision:

1 The Pope's person is sacred and inviolable, and crimes against him will be punished in the same way as crimes against the Majesty of the King of Italy. The Italian Government will show to the Pope the same tokens of honour as to other sovereigns.

2 The Pope shall have the right to retain the usual number of Papal guards for the defence of his person and palaces. He shall have full liberty to exercise all the functions of his office, and to post notices concerning that office on all the church doors of Rome.

3 The Pope will be paid by the State the annual sum of 3,225,000 lire, free from communal or provincial taxes.

4 The Vatican, the Lateran, certain basilicas in Rome, and the Papal palace at Castel Gandolfo are to be at the Pope's disposal; these properties can be neither taxed nor alienated.

5 When the Papal See is vacant, the Cardinals may freely assemble; the Government will ensure that Conclaves and Councils are not in any way disturbed.

6 No Italian officials may enter the Papal palaces, unless the Pope has given permission; it shall be forbidden to make domiciliary visits, or to confiscate papers, books or registers in the Papal offices and congregations engaged in spiritual work.

7 The Church's officials shall be protected by the civil authorities.

8 The Ambassadors of foreign powers to the Pope shall possess the rights and immunities due in international law to diplomatic agents; the same for Papal envoys to foreign governments. The Pope can without hindrance enter into communication with his episcopate abroad, and with the entire Catholic world.

9 The Pope may have his own post-office and telegraph facilities.

253

10   In Rome all seminaries, academies and colleges for the education of the clergy shall be subject solely to the Holy See.

11   The Government disclaims the right to appoint, or make suggestions as to the appointment to high ecclesiastical offices in Italy; and the Italian bishops shall not be required to take the oath of loyalty to the King of Italy.

12   *Exequatur, Placet regium*, and all other forms of governmental permission for the publication and execution of the decisions of the ecclesiastical authority shall be abolished.

Finally, new laws were promised for the preservation and administration of Church property throughout the Kingdom.

For further information see F. Nielsen, *The Papacy in the 19th Century*, pp. 408-10.

254

Notes

Preface

1 In 1860, the Papal States comprised ten provinces on the Adriatic, and ten on the Tyrrhenian coasts. By early 1870, all those on the Adriatic had been seized by Italy, and only five on the Mediterranean remained to the Papacy.
2 The *Divine Comedy, Paradiso* XXVII, 40–60; St Peter's philippic against the Church under Boniface VIII.
3 Cardinal H. E. Manning, *The True Story of the Vatican Council*, London, 1877.
4 Vat. Sec. Arch., Rubrica 255, No. 938, 23 September 1871.
5 Cardinal H. E. Manning, *op. cit.*

Chapter 1 *The Italian Seizure of Rome*

1 In his treatise *The Truth about the Papal Claims*.
2 Purcell, *Life of Cardinal Manning*.
3 F.O. 43/108 and 109, 8 April 1870, Report from Mr Jervoise on dissenting prelates.
4 F.O. 7/764, Report from Lord Bloomfield, British Ambassador in Vienna.
5 F.O. 43/108, 5 July 1870.
6 F.O. 45/165, 29 August 1870.
7 The Papal Zouaves (the word derives from French Algerian troops) were volunteers recruited from all parts of the Catholic world, chiefly from the Legitimist and Ultramontane families of France and Belgium. The officers came mostly from families with an illustrious history of fighting for the Catholic royal houses.
8 Vat. Sec. Arch. Rubrica 165, Despatch 2637.
9 F.O. 45/165, Memo dated 29 August 1870.
10 F.O. 43/1049.
11 Vat. Sec. Arch., Despatch 2579.
12 Vat. Sec. Arch. Rubrica 165, Fasc. 5, 14 August 1870.
13 Vat. Sec. Arch. 1870, Rubrica 165, Despatches 2580 *et seq*.
14 F.O. 43/109, Despatch 51, 15 September 1870, Mr Jervoise to Lord Granville.

15 Later, the French sent a frigate, *L'Orénoque*, for the same purpose.
16 The Italian force numbered 70,000 – against 6,000 Papal Zouaves. The Papal artillery was drawn by oxen.
17 'The Taking of Rome', from W. Kirkham's diary, reproduced in the English College magazine, *Venerabile*, April 1928.
18 Quoted by H. Johnson in *The Papacy and the Kingdom of Italy*.
19 F.O. 43/110, Despatch 80, 26 October 1870, Mr Jervoise to Lord Granville.
20 Vat. Sec. Arch. 1870, Rubrica 165, Fasc. 7, from *Documenti diplomatici relativi alle questioni communicati del Ministero degli Affari stranieri* ('Diplomatic documents concerning questions put by the Ministry of Foreign Affairs').

Chapter 2 *The Fulminations of Pius IX*

1 Vat. Sec. Arch. 1870, Despatch 2600, 10 December. It is significant that Pius IX never referred to 'the Italian Government', but only to 'the Piedmontese Government'.
2 Published in the official Legitimist organ, *L'Union*.
3 See Appendix, p. 253, for a summary of these Laws.
4 See Nielsen, *The Papacy in the 19th Century*, Vol. II, pp. 408-10.
5 The following details of the sequestration of the Collegio Romano given in F.O. 43/110, Despatch 92, 21 November 1870, Mr Jervoise to Lord Granville.
6 The 'White' aristocracy of Rome supported the Savoyard monarchy, as distinct from the 'Black', which was Papal.
7 F.O. 45/184, Despatch 223, 5 July 1871, Sir Augustus Paget to Lord Granville.
8 By this time, the term 'Ultramontana' had already lost its original Roman-centred connotation of 'beyond the Alps to the north', and had come, through use by the French, to mean 'south of the Alps', that is Italian. These prelates became a byword for their extreme views. The name was extended to any extreme traditionalist, Italian or not. (See Chapter 3.)
9 F.O. 45/311, Despatch 95, reported 25 March 1877 by Sir Augustus Paget.
10 F.O. 43/107, Despatch 76, 29 March 1870, from Mr Russell relating the 'Miss Dawkins affair'.
11 Some monks in Belgium even distributed to the faithful, wisps of mouldy straw on which the Pope was supposed to have been lying in the Vatican dungeons.
12 French Minister of the Interior of the short-lived Government of National Defence which was set up after Napoleon III's defeat at Sedan. He was obliged to escape from besieged Paris in this manner.
13 F.O. 43/114, Despatch 2, 2 January 1871, Mr Jervoise to Lord Granville.
14 F.O. 43/122, Despatch 37, 20 April 1873, Mr Jervoise to Lord Granville.
15 Quai d'Orsay, C.P., Tome 1055, 17 July 1872, Baron de Michelis to M. Remusat.
16 As a young man, Pius IX had intended to follow a military career. Only poor health, a tendency to epilepsy, had prevented him from becoming an officer in the Papal forces.

17   Vat. Sec. Arch., Ss. for 1870, Rubrica 165, Fasc. 8.
18   F.O. 43/110, Despatch 70, 7 October 1870. Mr Jervoise to Lord Granville.

Chapter 3 *The Turbolenti and the Zelanti*

1   Quai d'Orsay, C.P. Tome 1055, 2 November 1872, Bourgoing to the *Ministère des Affaires Etrangères* (Ministry of Foreign Affairs).
2   F.O. 45/236, Report of speech in Despatch 19, from Mr Jervoise, 21 June 1874.
3   F.O. 43/109, Despatch 64, from Mr Jervoise, 28 September 1870.
4   F.O. 45/336, Despatch 112, 7 February 1878, Sir Augustus Paget to Lord Derby.
5   Quai d'Orsay, C.P. Saint-Siège 1877, Tome 1062. This meeting was reported by the French Ambassador to the Holy See, Baron de Baude, on 1 June 1877.
6   Reported by Gregorovius in *The Roman Journals*, p. 396.
7   Vat. Sec. Arch. Ss. for 1889, Rubrica 241, Fasc. 3.
8   Reported in *L'Italie*, 1 June 1877.
9   Quai d'Orsay, C.P. Tome 1055, his despatch of 21 November 1872.
10   F.O. 45/241, Despatch 150, to Lord Derby, 15 October 1874.
11   Related in Gallenga, *The Pope and the King*.
12   F.O. 45/240, Despatch 29, 3 July 1874, Mr Herries from Rome.
13   F.O. 45/430, Despatches 297 and 307, 13 and 20 July 1881, Sir Augustus Paget to Lord Granville.
14   F.O. 45/430, Despatch 300, 15 July 1881, Sir Augustus Paget to Lord Granville.
15   F.O. 45/217, Despatch 71, 12 March 1873, Sir Augustus Paget to Foreign Office.
16   The Battle of Mentana near Rome (1867) was the last Papal victory, when the Pope's troops, aided by the French, routed Garibaldi's irregulars.
17   F.O. 43/115, Despatch 62, 13 April 1871, Mr Jervoise to Lord Granville.
18   Emile Zola in *Rome*.
19   Garibaldi, *Autobiography*, Letter dated 13 September 1870.
20   F.O. 45/259, Despatch 25, 1 February 1875, Sir Augustus Paget to Lord Derby.
21   *Ibid.*, this last according to Sir Augustus Paget, who had it from 'an authority which I cannot question'.
22   Quai d'Orsay, C.P. Rome 1875, Tome 1059, de Crouy's despatch dated 12 February 1875; and de Corcelle's despatch dated 19 April 1875.
23   Vat. Sec. Arch. 1882, Rubrica 241, Fasc. 3, 10 August 1882.

Chapter 4 *Democracy in Rome*

1   F.O. 45/259, Despatch 24, 30 January 1875, Sir Augustus Paget to Lord Derby.
2   Maurice Pernot, *Le Saint-Siège, l'Église Catholique et la Politique mondiale*.

3 Quai d'Orsay, C.P. Tome 1055, 20 August 1872, Baron de Michelis to Paris.

4 Three months after the occupation, Rome had suffered the worst flooding for three hundred years. F.O. 43/115, Despatch 54, 3 April 1871, reported by Mr Jervoise to Lord Granville.

5 From Emile Zola, *Rome*.

6 Quay d'Orsay, C.P. Tome 1052, Comte d'Harcourt's Despatch, 3 July 1871.

7 F.O. 45/180, Despatch 19, 12 January 1871, Sir Augustus Paget to Lord Granville.

8 F.O. 45/183, Despatch 201, 21 June 1871, Sir Augustus Paget's report to the Foreign Office.

9 Quai d'Orsay, C.P., Rome, Saint-Siège, 1877, Tome 1061. His allocution reported by the French Ambassador, the Baron de Baude, 18 March 1877.

10 Quoted from Noel Blakiston, *The Roman Question*.

11 Gregorovius, *The Roman Journals*.

12 F.O. 45/184, Despatch 223, 5 July 1871, Sir Augustus Paget to the Foreign Office.

13 Quai d'Orsay, C.P. Tome 1055, 18 June 1872. A full list of these conversions was reported by the French Ambassador, Comte de Bourgoing.

14 Gregorovius, *The Roman Journals*, pp. 400 *et seq*.

15 F.O. 45/199, Despatch 230, 1 August 1872, Sir Augustus Paget to the Foreign Office.

16 Quai d'Orsay, C.P. Tome 1053, reported by Baron de Michelis, 8 October 1871.

17 Quai d'Orsay, C.P. Tome 1056, 2 October 1872.

18 *Ibid.*, Tome 1052, Comte d'Harcourt's Despatches, 1 and 8 September 1871.

19 *Ibid.*, Tome 1058 for 1874, M. de Corcelle and the Vicomte de Crouy.

Chapter 5 *The Advent of Leo XIII*

1 Some doubt seems cast on this ceremony. The Papal Chamberlain at the time, F. A. MacNutt, describes it as 'a pious fiction', contending that the last occasion when it took place was in 1676 at the death of Clement X.

2 Cardinal (from *cardo* – a hinge). Until the sixteenth century the title applied to all priests. Only in this century was it confined to members of the Sacred College. Sixtus V limited its numbers to seventy (in keeping with the biblical seventy counsellors sent by God to Moses).

3 Quai d'Orsay, C.P. Saint-Siège, 1877, Tome 1062, the Baron de Baude's despatch 23 December 1877.

4 F.O. 45/337, Despatch 166, 22 February 1878, Sir Augustus Paget to Lord Derby.

5 Marcellus II was Pope for twenty-one days, from 9 to 30 April 1555. This conversation is quoted from Sodernini's biography of Leo XIII. The Pope gave him special access to his documents.

6 Related in Gallenga, *The Pope and King*.

7   F.O. 45/377, Despatch 12, 13 January 1879, Sir Augustus Paget to Lord Salisbury.
8   Milman, *Latin Christianity*, Book XIV.

Chapter 6 *The Fallacy of Prince Bismarck – the* Kulturkampf

1   Gregorovius, *The Roman Journals*, entry for 11 April 1869, p. 325.
2   Farnesina, Pacco 34, Despatch 59725, from Ambassador Orsini, 21 August 1908.
3   Vat. Sec. Arch. 1877, Rubrica 255, Fasc. 5-22, reported by Nuncio from Munich, Despatch 938, 23 September 1871. (This despatch has somehow found its way into the 1877 *Inventario* [inventory].)
4   *Ibid.*, Despatch 991, 24 September 1871.
5   *Ibid.*, Despatch 868, 13 June 1871. (Also in 1877 *Inventario*.)
6   *Ibid.*, Despatch 879, 4 July 1871.
7   *Ibid.*, Despatch 908, 11 August 1871.
8   *Ibid.*, Despatch 939, 25 September 1871.
9   *Ibid.*, Despatch 1025, April 1872.
10   Quai d'Orsay, C.P. Tome 1052, Despatch 28 from Comte d'Harcourt to Paris, 17 July 1871.
11   This was what Gladstone had feared, as expressed in his *The Vatican Decrees and their Bearing on Civil Allegiance* (see p. 16).
12   Vat. Sec. Arch. 1877, Rubrica 255, Fasc. 5-22, Despatch 988, 12 December 1871, from the Nuncio in Munich.
13   He was subsequently canonized.
14   The implication here is that the German Catholics would have preferred it on the head of a Wittelsbach in Munich or, more traditionally, on that of a Habsburg in Vienna.
15   Vat. Sec. Arch. 1878, Rubrica 255, Fasc. 1, Memo. from German bishops gathered at the tomb of St Boniface, Fulda.
16   Quai d'Orsay, C.P. Tome 1054, 27 February 1872, the Comte d'Harcourt to M. Remusat.
17   F.O. 45/199, Despatch 178.
18   Vat. Sec. Arch. 1877, Rubrica 255, Fasc. 5-22, *Carte relative alla Questione Germanica* ('Papers concerning the German Question'), Despatch 975, 22 November 1871, from Mgr Agilico, Papal Nuncio in Munich. See also (2.155) Ss., Rubrica 165 for 1890.
19   Quoted by E. Vercesi in *Tre Papi*.
20   See Schmidlin, *Papstgeschichte der neusten Zeit*, Vol. 2, p. 189.
21   Quai d'Orsay, C.P. Tome 1055, Comte de Bourgoing to M. Remusat, enclosure: Pope's allocution.
22   F.O. 45/312. These comments by Pius IX on Bismarck reported in Despatch 213, Sir Augustus Paget to Lord Derby, 22 May 1877.
23   F.O. 43/122, Despatch 62, Mr Jervoise to Lord Granville.
24   Goyau, *Bismarck et l'Église*.
25   Its progress in the 1870s is revealed by the figures: 1871, 57 seats; 1874, 94 seats; 1878, 103 seats.

26   Quoted from *Un Combat pour Dieu*, by M. Daniel-Rops, Papal historian.
27   See Josef Schmidlin, *Papstgeschichte der neusten Zeit*, Vol. 2('Pius IX and Leo XIII, 1846-1903'), p. 456.
28   Henry IV, King of the Germans in the eleventh century, was in constant conflict with Pope Gregory VII. At one point, after he was excommunicated, he was obliged to perform an act of penance at Canossa, a castle near Reggio nell'Emilia.
29   Quai d'Orsay, C.P. Tome 1055, Comte de Bourgoing's Despatch, 4 April 1872.
30   Goyau, *Bismarck et l'Église*.
31   Vat. Sec. Arch. 1886, Rubrica 1, Fasc. 20. This account of the Caroline Islands dispute is taken largely from this volume; also from a monograph on the subject, Louis Selosse, *L'Affaire des Carolines*.
32   This cannot be regarded as authentic, as there is no mention of it in the Vatican Secret Archives.
33   Vat. Sec. Arch., 1886, Rubrica 1.
34   *Ibid*.
35   *Ibid*.
36   In 1899 Germany bought the Caroline Islands from Spain and held them until the German defeat in 1918, when they passed under Japanese mandate. Following the Second World War control passed to the United States, of which they are a Trust Territory.

Chapter 7 *The Need for Reform*

1   Vat. Sec. Arch. for 1902, Ss., Rubrica 165, Fasc. 13-14, Commentary on *Roma, l'Italia e la realtà delle Cose*.
2   Vat. Sec. Arch. for 1902, Ss., Rubrica 165, Fasc. 14, Letter dated 2 November 1889.
3   Fénelon, François de Salignac, Archbishop of Cambrai (1651-1715), author of *Maxims of the Saints*, whose Christian Neo-platonism was condemned by Innocent XII. He recanted and withdrew it.
4   Vat. Sec. Arch. 1884, Rubrica 9, Fasc. 2, no date – description of Father Curci and his book taken from this – and also Vat. Sec. Arch. for 1902, Rubrica 165, Fasc. 14, no date.
5   Farnesina, Serie Politici P., Pacco 30, Stamped letter 050580, 14 September 1891.
6   *Ibid*.

Chapter 8 *Leo XIII and the French Republic*

1   The vessel remained there for four years, until 1874, causing great offence to the Italian authorities.
2   F.O. 45/219, Despatch 291, from Sir Augustus Paget, 8 August 1873. In it he quotes this from an article on French policy in *L'Italie*.

3   F.O. 45/220, Despatch 319, 23 October 1873, Sir Augustus Paget's explanation of Cardinal Bounechore's visit to Rome.

4   F.O. 45/241, Despatch 105, 26 August 1874, Mr Herries to Lord Derby.

5   Quai d'Orsay, C.P. Rome 1876, Tome 1060, Despatch from Baron de Baude, 27 December 1876.

6   From Adrien Dansette, *Histoire religieuse de la France contemporaine*, p. 435.

7   *Ibid*, p. 433.

8   Reported in Eduardo Soderini, *Leo XIII*, Vol. 2, pp. 123–274.

9   In 1301 Jean Nogaret, the representative of the King of France, physically assaulted Boniface VIII in his palace at Anagni, which led to that Pope's death a few weeks later.

10   Cardinal Consalvi restored the prestige and power of the Papacy in the 1820s after the Napoleonic ravages.

11   Farnesina, Serie Politici P.01778, Pacco 30, no date. (Berthier was Napoleon's Chief of Staff from 1795 until 1815.)

12   *Ibid*., Pacco 32, Despatch from Berne, 16 May 1900.

13   *Ibid*.

14   *Ibid*.

15   *Ihid*.

16   Farnesina, Serie Politici P.01778, Pacco 30, Report on the French pilgrims, (?) November 1891.

17   F.O. 45/666, Despatch 155, 2 October 1891, Mr Dering to Lord Salisbury.

18   Farnesina, Serie Politici P.056798, Pacco 30, Report on the French pilgrims incident by Ministry of Interior, 1 November 1891.

19   See descriptions of the Pantheon incident in Adrien Dansette, *Histoire religieuse de la France contemporaine*, and Eduardo Soderini, *Leo XIII*, Vol. 2.

20   A number of prelates were in favour of the Pope leaving Rome, and not only on grounds of safety. The Ultramontane French prelate Mgr Darboy stated: 'If the Pope, possessing the triple Majesty of his age, his misfortunes and his merits, were to leave Rome, if he were to travel all over the world as a pilgrim, a fugitive, he would shake the world under his feet. He would rouse the nations by the power of his tears alone. He would be a mortal curse to the enemies of the Church.'

21   His noisy rodomontades on this theme nearly led to another war with Germany. It was due to Boulanger's aggressive language that Bismarck demanded in the Reichstag a prolongation of military conscription in Germany, from three to seven years – with all that this later entailed for Europe.

Chapter 9 *The American Crucible*

1   Farnesina, Pacco 34, Italian Ambassador's Despatch, 28 August 1910.

2   Vat. Sec. Arch. Ss., Rubrica 280, Fasc. 10, *Rapporto sulle condizioni della Chiesa Cattolica negli Stati Uniti d'America* ('Report on the conditions of the Catholic Church in the United States of America'), November 1886.

3   Quoted from Robert D. Cross, *The Emergence of Liberal Catholicism in America*.

4   Farnesina, Pacco 31, Report of his visit by the Italian Consul in New Orleans, 19 March 1887.

5   The statistics of New York City between 1846 and 1876 reveal the arrival of some two million of these Irish emigrants.

6   Vat. Sec. Arch. for 1888, Rubrica 278p, Fasc. 1-3, Mgr Persico's Despatches and Report on the Irish situation.

7   Quai d'Orsay, C.P. Politique Etrangère, Saint-Siège, Relations avec les Etats d'Amérique 1897-1900, Vol. 1, M. Cambon's Despatch, 8 March 1898.

8   Reported in Robert D. Cross, *The Emergence of Liberal Catholicism in America*.

9   *Ibid*.

10   Farnesina, Pacco 33 1903-07, Report of the Italian Ambassador to the United States, 17 April 1903. An ironical explanation of the same phenomenon was given by the Jesuit journal *Civilità Cattolica*. 'Naturally,' it said, 'the Americans see it like this. The Cardinal will be with us for years, perhaps decades; an Italian Prime Minister probably for a matter of months.'

11   *Ibid*.

12   *Ibid*.

13   Quai d'Orsay, C.P. Politique Etrangère, Saint-Siège, Relations avec les Etats d'Amérique 1897-1900.

14   Quoted from Robert D. Cross, *The Emergence of Liberal Catholicism in America*.

15   Louis Bourdaloue (1632-1704), a prominent French Jesuit writer and orator, who attempted to convert the Protestants after the Revocation of the Edict of Nantes.

16   Quoted from Robert D. Cross, *The Emergence of Liberal Catholicism in America*.

17   Quai d'Orsay, C.P. Politique Etrangère, Saint-Siège, Relations avec les Etats d'Amérique 1897-1900, Vol. 1, M. Cambon's Despatch, 8 March 1899.

18   'A Protestant Tribute to Leo XIII', *Literary Digest*, 22 January 1898.

19   Quai d'Orsay, C.P. Politique Etrangère. Saint-Siège, Relations avec les Etats d'Amérique 1897-1900, Vol. 1, M. Cambon's Despatch, 8 March 1898.

20   Quai d'Orsay, C.P. Politique Etrangère, Saint-Siège, Relations avec les Etats d'Amérique 1897-1900, Vol. 1, M. Cambon's despatch, 1 May 1900.

21   Letter printed in *New York Herald*, 1 May 1899.

22   Described in J. Ellis, *Life of Cardinal Gibbons*, Vol. 1, Chapter XI.

23   Belief in God, but refusing to accept Revelation.

24   The Ku-Klux-Klan was founded after the Civil War to repress the Blacks. Officially banned in 1877, it was revived by the Methodist parson, Simmonds, when it took a violently anti-Catholic turn.

25   The Ku-Klux-Klan, which was avowedly anti-Catholic and in this sense less dangerous, numbered 200,000.

26   Vat. Sec. Arch. Ss. Rubrica 280, Fasc. 10.
27   Material taken from J. Ellis, *Life of Cardinal Gibbons*, Vol. 1, Chapter XII.
28   See *North American Review*, CXLV, August 1887, pp. 192–205.

Chapter 10 *The Irish Bane*

1   James Anthony Froude (1818–94), British historian and sometime follower of Newman (before the latter's conversion to Catholicism). His works include *The English in Ireland in the Eighteenth Century*, 1871–4.
2   The Fenian Brotherhood, also known as Clan-na-Gael, was founded in the United States and Ireland simultaneously in 1857. Its aim was to overthrow British rule in Ireland by any means, however violent. The name Sinn Fein ('Ourselves') was first used, as a slogan, in 1902.
3   Gregorovius, *The Roman Journals*, 29 November 1860.
4   F.O. 45/216, Despatch 7, 8 January 1873, from Sir Augustus Paget.
5   F.O. 45/217, Despatch 87, 25 March 1873, from Sir Augustus Paget.
6   F.O. 45/216, Despatch 7, 8 January 1873, from Sir Augustus Paget.
7   F.O. 45/220, Despatch 318, 23 October 1873, from Sir Augustus Paget.
8   F.O. 43/106, Despatch 13, 13 January 1870, Mr Russell to Lord Clarendon.
9   F.O. 45/426 Despatch 5, Sir Augustus Paget to Lord Granville.
10   Vat. Sec. Arch. for 1888, Rubrica 278, Fasc. 3, note on attitude of Rome to England.
11   F.O. 43/119, Despatch 65, 6 November 1872, Mr Jervoise to Lord Granville.
12   Vat. Sec. Arch. for 1888, Rubrica 278, Fasc. 1.
13   Vat. Sec. Arch. for 1888, Rubrica 278, Fasc. 1–3, Mgr Persico's Despatches and Report from Ireland.
14   In this way, several Irish M.P.s found themselves in gaol; as did the Major of Dublin, for having published an account of a proscribed Agrarian League meeting.
15   At the beginning of the war, a British Mission was accredited to the Vatican, first under Sir Henry Howard, then under Count de Salis.
16   F.O. 371/4890, 18 June 1920, Count de Salis's Despatch.

Chapter 11 *The English Anomaly*

1   King John had been placed under a Papal Interdict in 1212.
2   F.O. 371/7671, 22 October 1922, included in Report on Missions to the Holy See by Count de Salis to Lord Curzon.
3   Quai d'Orsay, C.P. Politique Etrangère, Saint-Siège, Relations avec la Grande-Bretagne, 1877–1907, reported in Despatch by M. de Courcel, French chargé d'affaires to the Holy See, 18 June 1904.
4   F.O. 45/210, Despatch 71, 12 March 1873, Sir Augustus Paget to the Foreign Office.
5   For account of the Noel incident: F.O. 45/183, Despatch 199, from Sir Augustus Paget; also F.O. 43/115, Despatch 93, 10 and 18 June 1871, from Mr Jervoise.

6 F.O. 45/242, Despatch 146, 21 December 1874, Sir Augustus Paget to Lord Derby.

7 Quai d'Orsay, C.P. 1876, Rome. Tome 1062, from M. de Corcelle, 28 April 1876; also Tome 1059, M. de Corcelle to the Duc Decazes, French Foreign Minister, 29 May 1875, various comments on Henry Manning.

8 F.O. 45/242, Despatch 146, 21 December 1874, Sir Augustus Paget to Lord Derby.

9 Gregorovius, *The Roman Journals*.

10 Vat. Sec. Arch. for 1883, Rubrica 278, Fasc. 3, Mgr Persico's Report.

11 Quai d'Orsay, C.P. Politique Etrangère, Saint-Siège, Relations avec la Grande-Bretagne 1897-1907, Amisard's Despatch, 28 January 1900 and 8 February 1900; see also M. Cambon's Despatch from London, 1 March 1900, on English Catholic dissatisfaction.

12 France had broken off relations with the Holy See in 1905 (see Chapter 15).

13 Auswärtiges Amt (Foreign Office), Bonn, Politische Beziehungen des Papstlicher Stuhl zu Deutschland ('Political Relations between the Holy See and Germany'), Politik 2, Band (Vol.) 1, March 1920–March 1924.

14 F.O. 371/2009, Despatch 438, Sir Rennell Rodd to Sir Edward Grey, 9 November 1914.

15 Farnesina, Pacco 34. Reported by Ambassador Cerruti to Rome from Vienna, 26 November 1914.

16 F.O. 371/3086, Comments on Mr Gregory's Memo.

17 F.O. 371/6189, Presbyterian Church of Scotland's complaint, 1921.

18 These Foreign Office comments are expressed in the file F.O. 371/9947, 28 October 1924.

19 F.O. 370/558, Memorandum on British Diplomatic Relations with the Holy See, drawn up by Stephen Gaselee, Michaelmas 1938.

20 In 1929, an Apostolic Delegate was appointed to the Court of St James, but without official status. In 1982 the British Ministry at the Vatican was upgraded to an Embassy.

Chapter 12 *The Achievement of Leo XIII*

1 F.O. 45/337, Despatch 178, 5 March 1878, Sir Augustus Paget to Lord Derby.

2 St Malachy, Irish Archbishop of Armagh (*c*. 1094–1148). A set of prophecies attributed to him is held to be a sixteenth-century forgery, but in any case is celebrated. They foretold in the form of individual Latin tags for each future Pope, from 1146 to 1996, what would characterize his reign. Some of them (not all) were remarkably prescient. Thus the heroic and persecuted Pius IX was *Crux in crucem* ('cross on cross'). Pius VI, whom Napoleon transported across Italy and France, was *Peregrinus apostolicus* ('the Apostolic Pilgrim'). The final date, 1996, is ominous.

3 F.O. 45/873, Despatch 158, 26 July 1903, Sir Rennell Rodd to Lord Lansdowne.

4 Farnesina, Pacco 32, for 1898, undated.

5   Farnesina, Pacco 32 for 1898, comment from *Gazette de Lausanne*, 5 May 1898.

6   Farnesina, Pacco 32, Rapporto della politica ecclesiastica della Santa Sede ('Report on the Ecclesiastical Policy of the Holy See'), 1898–99, 7 August 1899.

7   Vat. Sec. Arch. for 1895, Rubrica 165, Fasc. 3. Here it is reported how the finances of Rome had declined since the unification. In 1870, there were 300,000 gold scudi in the municipal coffers; by 1895, the City of Rome was 700 million lire in debt.

8   Vat. Sec. Arch. for 1880, Rubrica 1, Fasc. 71, 22 June 1880, Cardinal Rampolla's circular to the Nuncios in the Catholic countries.

9   Dante places the Simoniacal (office-selling) Popes, Nicholas III and Clement V, upside down in holes in a rock, with fire playing on the soles of their feet (Inferno, XIX.22 *et seq*.).

10   *Le Monde*, 31 May 1887.

Chapter 13 *Piux X – Signs of Conciliation*

1   Manning, *Sermons on Ecclesiastical Subjects*, Vol. 2, p. 83.

2   During his time in Madrid as Nuncio, Cardinal Giustiani had attached himself so closely to Charles IV's second son Don Carlos that the Queen, Maria Christina, had reason to fear that, if he became Pope, he would place difficulties in the way of her daughter Isabella's accession to the throne. As monarch of Spain, she therefore invoked the *Veto* against his candidature.

3   F.O. 45/874, Despatch 166, 7 August 1903, Sir Rennell Rodd to Lord Lansdowne.

4   J. Schmidlin, *Papstgeschichte der neusten Zeit* ('Papal History of Recent Times'), Vol. 3.

5   John xviii. 14.

6   (French:) 'No doubt Your Eminence is an Italian Archbishop. In which diocese?'
     (Italian:) 'I don't speak French.'
     (Latin:) 'In which diocese are you the Archbishop?'
     (Latin:) 'I'm the Patriarch of Venice.'
     (Latin:) 'Don't you speak French?'
     (Italian:) 'No.'
     (Latin:) 'Then you're not *papabile*, seeing that the Pope has to speak French.'
     (Latin:) 'By the most great Lord, that's true. I'm not *papabile*. Thank God!'

7   F.O. 45/874, Despatch 169, 19 August 1903, Sir Rennell Rodd to Lord Lansdowne.

8   Merry del Val's father Don Raphael was a Spanish diplomat descended from the O'Hollicans of Hy-main in Connaught, who had immigrated to Spain in the seventeenth century, where they changed their name to Merry, later marrying into the Trinidad del Val family. His mother was also Spanish, with descent from a Scottish grandfather and a Dutch grandmother. The new Secretary of State was born in England (where his father was *en poste*),

educated in Belgium, became a Spanish diplomat, and spent most of his life after taking Orders in Italy.

9   Farnesina, Pacco 34, Despatches relating to the Nathan incident by the Duke of Averna, Italian Ambassador in Vienna, for October and November 1910.

10   Quai d'Orsay, C.P. Politique Etrangère, Tome 13, Relations avec l'Italie, 1903–1907, M. Nissard's Despatch, 1 May 1903.

11   Quai d'Orsay, *ibid.*, M. Nissard's Despatch, 8 April 1904.

12   In F.A. MacNutt, *A Papal Chamberlain*.

13   Quai d'Orsay, *ibid.*, same Despatch of M. Nissard, 8 April 1904.

14   F.P. 45/889, Despatch 67, 16 May 1904, Sir Francis Bertie to Lord Lansdowne.

15   This year is, coincidentally, almost exactly halfway between 1870 and the full reconciliation of 1929.

16   Quai d'Orsay, *ibid.* M. de Courcel's Despatch, 27 May 1904.

17   *Ibid.*

18   F.O. 371/1659, Sir Rennell Rodd to Sir Edward Grey, 11 February 1913. Later, in F.O. 371/3810, 13 September 1919, he said, 'This was the first war Italy had waged as a united country, and it created a new spirit.'

19   In J. Hergenrother and A. Hoch, *Pius X, ein Bild Kirchlicher Reformfahigkeit* ('Pius X, a Portrait of Ecclesiastical Reforming Ability').

20   Farnesina, Pacco 33, Report by the Italian Minister in Nicaragua, 18 November 1906, on the Matzenauer incident.

Chapter 14 *The Power of the Pope*

1   In C. Falconi, *I Papi del Ventesimo Secolo* ('The Twentieth-Century Popes').

2   *Ibid.*

3   F.O. 371/262, Mr Cartwright to Sir Edward Grey from Munich, 1 September 1907.

4   From J. Schmidlin, *Papstgeschichte der neusten Zeit*, Vol. 3, p. 167 *et seq*.

5   Don Sturzo described this Papal audience in a letter he wrote many years later to Conte Sforza: see Piva and Malgeri, *Vita di Luigi Sturzo*, p. 149, footnote 36.

6   F.O. 371/469, Sir Edward Egerton's annual report from Rome to Sir Edward Grey, 1 January 1908.

7   Vat. Sec. Arch. Ss. for 1897, Rubrica 256, Fasc. 2; the Apostolic Delegate reported from The Hague, 16 December 1896, that the Catholic group in Parliament had saved the Conservative Government and coalitions on many occasions.

8   Quai d'Orsay, C.P. 1897–1918; M. Gonse's reports are in the single file, No. 598 *bis*, under the heading 'Italie', and dealing with the Holy See during the First World War.

Chapter 15 *French Atheism and the Rupture with France*

1   For their fallacy here, see the account of Leo XIII's attitude to capitalism, in Chapter 7.

2   Vat. Sec. Arch., Ss., 1902, Rubrica 248, Fasc. 1-12, 7 March 1901; these contain full reports of the attack on the Church in the Chambre.

3   Quai d'Orsay, C.P. Politique Etrangère, Saint-Siège, Tome 22, Relations avec la France, January-July 1904, Papal interview reportedly by French Embassy in Rome – M. Camille Parrieu (signature illegible), 10 January 1904.

4   The Austrian Emperor, Franz Josef, had respected these Papal wishes, and did not return the visit the King of Italy made to him in Vienna. The King of Portugal behaved in the same manner.

5   Farnesina, Pacco 34, Despatch 23 June 1910.

6   Quai d'Orsay, C.P. Politique Etrangère, Saint-Siège, Tome 22, Relations avec la France, January-June 1904, M. Barrère's Despatch, 13 May 1904.

7   The Protestants in France were a small but mixed collection, including (principally) the French Methodists, the French Lutherans, the French Calvinists, the Reformed Church of Alsace-Lorraine, and the Church of the confession of Augsburg (this last fundamentally Lutheran), as well as many smaller sects.

8   In F.A. MacNutt, *A Papal Chamberlain*.

9   See Chapter 6.

10   The Socialists in the Hautes-Pyrenées were more concerned with the effect on local trade in Lourdes; and they persuaded the Government to make an exception here, and not close its many conventual establishments.

11   Quai d'Orsay, C.P. Saint-Siège, Relations avec la France, Tome 24, Mgr Guthlin's Report, 19 January 1907.

12   F.O. 370/11050, reported by Sir Eric Phipps from Paris.

13   Quai d'Orsay, C.P. Saint-Siège, Tome 23, Relations avec la France, July-December 1904, unsigned Despatch (presumably from Ambassador), 13 July 1904.

14   Article in *Le Gaullois*, 18 July 1912.

15   Vat. Sec. Arch. Ss. 1902, Rubrica 248, Fasc. 1-12, 7 March 1901, quoted from debate in French Chamber.

16   *Ibid.*, quoted from British Parliament.

17   F.O. 371/13248, Sir John Tulley to Sir Austen Chamberlain, 4 January 1928.

18   Quai d'Orsay, C.P. Politique Etrangère, Tome 22, Relations avec la France, January-June 1904, Memo by M. Delcassé to the President of the Council of Ministers, 10 February 1904.

19   *Ibid.*, Tome 25, M. Bompard from Pera, 17 March 1913.

20   Quai d'Orsay, C.P. Politique Etrangère, Tome 25, Saint-Siège, Relations avec la France, 1910-1913, Memo dated 17 March 1913.

21   *Ibid.*, Memo dated 10 April 1913.

22   *Ibid.*

23   France attempted to offset this disadvantage during the war by sending the Deputy M. Denys Cochin to the Holy See; but, not having official status, he could achieve little.

24 A Memo in the German Auswartiges Amt (Foreign Office), Bonn, reports that the French diocese of Coutances alone, for example, lost 112 priests and seminarists killed in the war.
25 Only 800 of the 7,000 priests succumbed to this blandishment.
26 Farnesina, Pacco 34, Despatch M.071755, Lisbon, 23 October 1910.
27 F.O. 371/12705, Foreign Office Historical Memo on Portuguese colonization, 1927.

Chapter 16 *The Achievement of Pius X*

1 Farnesina, Pacco 34, Report M.18327, 9 March 1911.
2 F.O. 371/258, Despatch to Sir Edward Grey, 8 February 1907. This estimation of Merry del Val's personality is not generally shared.
3 F. Segmuller, *Pius X*.
4 From F. A. MacNutt, *A Papal Chamberlain*.

Chapter 17 *The 1914 Dilemma – Benedict XV*

1 Farnesina, Pacco for 1913, Report M.039118, Averna from Vienna, 20 May 1913.
2 *Ibid.*, Report M. 036881, Squitti from Belgrade, 9 May 1914.
3 *Ibid.*, 2 July 1914.
4 Benedict XV is reported to have said after his election, 'I remain the pupil of Leo XIII and Cardinal Rampolla.'
5 Quai d'Orsay, C.P. Saint-Siège, 1897–1918; the one file on the war, marked 598 *bis*, dealing with the Vatican in the war, is supposed to cover February 1915-June 1918, but is marked 'Incomplete file found in Warsaw after the Second World War'! This comment by M. Gonse is dated 20 November 1916.
6 F. A. MacNutt, *A Papal Chamberlain*.
7 F.O. 371/7671, Report from Count de Salis to Lord Curzon on Mission to Holy See, 22 October 1922.
8 Here the Vatican's fears were unfounded. Far from wanting the Russians on the Bosphorus, Britain had gone to war in 1854 in the Crimea to prevent it; and again to the brink of war with Russia at the Congress of Berlin in 1878.
9 F.O. 371/2377.
10 Quai d'Orsay, C.P. Saint-Siège 1897–1918, on the single file 598 *bis* (see earlier note), M. Gonse's Despatch, dated 8 November 1915. Pius V organized the campaign in which the Spanish and Venetian navies defeated the Turks at the Battle of Lepanto in 1571.
11 *Ibid.*, Despatch of 19 December 1915.
12 Farnesina, Santa Sede 1920, Pacco 1258, M.66895, the Italian Ambassador in Prague, Sig. Bordonaro, to Count Sforza, Italian Minister of Foreign Affairs; from series of letters, 22 August 1920.
13 F.O. 371/2946, for 1917; the Gerlach affair is described in this Despatch, 9 March 1917, from Sir Rennell Rodd in Rome to A. J. Balfour; also by Sir

Henry Howard in F.O. 371/2377, 27 May 1915; also by Count de Salis in his Report on the Mission to the Holy See, F.O. 371/7671, 22 October 1922.

14   Farnesina, Santa Sede 1915–1918, Report on Gerlach from Italian Legation in Berne, 29 June 1917.

15   F.O. 371/2684, Despatch 10181, 17 January 1917.

16   Quai d'Orsay, C.P. Saint-Siège 1897–1918, 598 *bis*, M. Gonse's Despatch dated 20 January 1916.

17   Farnesina, Santa Sede 1915–1918; this interview reported only on 24 January 1918.

18   Quai d'Orsay, C.P. Saint-Siège, 1897–1918, 598 *bis*; letter undated, but after 30 August 1917. 'The Greek Kalends' means a non-existent date, never; the Romans celebrated the Kalends on the first of each month which, to the Greeks, was just like any other day.

19   *Bayerischer Kurier*, 23 July 1925 and subsequently.

20   M. Loiseau, *Politique romaine et sentiment français* ('Roman policy and French feelings'), p. 30.

21   The Germans provided the Vatican with evidence that in occupying Poland, Russian troops had fired a Catholic church full of people who, as they attempted to escape from the flames, were shot down by the soldiers.

22   On the contrary, it was found after the war that many of the 'German atrocities' in Belgium, such as cutting off little girls' arms, had been invented by Lord Northcliffe and his ilk as propaganda.

23   Farnesina, Santa Sede 1915–1918, in a document in French, La Guerre allemande et le Catholicisme ('The German War and Catholicism').

24   German 'White Book' in Farnesina files, Santa Sede, 1915–1918.

25   *Ibid*.

26   Reported in H. Johnson, *Vatican Diplomacy in the First World War*.

Chapter 18 *The Failure of Benedict XV's 1917 Peace Proposals*

1   F.O. 371/3081, Count de Salis's Despatch.

2   Quai d'Orsay, C.P. Saint-Siège, 1897–1918, 598 *bis*.

3   From Col. House, *The Intimate Papers of Colonel House*, Vol. 3, Chapter 6.

4   As a neutral island in a sea of warring Europeans, Switzerland and its capital Berne had taken on considerable importance. The letter-heading 'Berne' crops up continually in the diplomatic archives of all the belligerents.

5   F.O. 371/.3083–4, Memo from Harold Nicolson, dated 5 September 1917.

6   Quai d'Orsay, C.P. Saint-Siège, 1897–1918, 598 *bis*, M. Gonse's Despatch dated 2 February 1917.

7   From *The Intimate Papers of Colonel House*.

8   Farnesina, Santa Sede 1915–1918, Pacco 177, Despatch from Italian Ambassador in St Petersburg, 31 August 1917.

9   F.O. 371/2948, Despatch from Sir Rennell Rodd to A. J. Balfour on defection of Italian 2nd Army and Vatican influence on it, 2 November 1917.

10 The *Corriere della Sera* was then a Milanese paper of mildly anti-clerical hue. Mr Walcott was confusing it with the *Osservatore Romano*, which is printed in the Vatican.

11 Farnesina, Santa Sede 1915–1918, Pacco 177 includes the joint letter.

12 M. Erzberger, *Erlebnisse* ('Experiences').

13 Quai d'Orsay, C.P. Saint-Siège 1897–1918, 598 *bis*, M. Gonse's Despatch, 24 January 1917.

14 F.O. 371/7671, Count de Salis to Lord Curzon, 22 October 1922; in his Report on Mission to the Holy See.

15 See J. Schmidlin, *Papstgeschichte der neusten Zeit*, Vol. 3.

Bibliography

de Barral, E., *Histoire des Zouaves pontificaux,* Paris, 1932.

Barrès, M., *La grande Pitié des Églises de France,* Paris, 1914.

Blakiston, N., *The Roman Question,* London, 1962.

Bonomelli, Mgr, Bishop of Cremona, *Roma, l'Italia e la realtà delle Cose,* Milan, 1902.

Cheetham, N., *Keepers of the Keys,* London, 1982.

Cross, R.D., *The Emergence of Liberal Catholicism in America,* Chicago, 1958.

de Cesare, R., *The Last Days of Papal Rome* (translation), London, 1909.

Curci, C.M., *L'Italia nuova ed i vecchi Zelanti,* Florence, 1881.

Dalpiez, V., *Cardinal Merry del Val,* London, 1937.

Daniel-Rops, M., *A Fight for God 1870-1939* (translation), London, 1966.

Dansette, A.M., *Histoire religieuse de la France contemporaine,* Paris, 1951.

Ellis, J., *Life of Cardinal Gibbons,* Milwaukee, 1952.

Erzberger, M., *Erlebnisse im Weltkrieg,* Stuttgart, 1920.

Falconi, C., *I Papi del Ventesimo Secolo* Milan, 1967.

Fogazzaro, A., *Il Santo,* Milan, 1906.

Gallenga, A., *The Pope and the King* (translation), London, 1879.

Garibaldi, G., *Memorie Autobiografiche,* Florence, 1888.

Gioberti, V., *Il Primato civile e morale degli Italiani,* Turin, 1845.

Gladstone, W.E., *The Vatican Decrees and their Bearing on Civil Allegiance,* London, 1874.

Gorman, J., *Converts to Rome,* London, 1910.

Goyau, G., *Bismarck et l'Église (4 vols),* Paris, 1911-13.

Goyau, G., *Papauté et Chrétienté sous Benôit XV,* Paris, 1922.

Gregorovius, F., *The Roman Journals 1852-1874* (translation), London, 1907.

Hare, A., *Walks in Rome,* London, 1897.

Hergenrother, J., and Hoth, A., *Pius X. Ein Bild kirchlicher Reformfähigkeit,* Leipzig, 1901.

House, E.M., *The Intimate Papers of Colonel House,* London, 1926.

Jemolo, C., *Chiesa e Stato in Italia negli ultimi cento anni,* Turin, 1948.

Johnson, H., *Vatican Diplomacy in the First World War,* Oxford, 1933.

Johnson, H., *The Papacy and the Kingdom of Italy,* London, 1926.

Leo XIII, *Encyclical – Immortale Dei,* Vatican, 1885.

Leo XIII, *Encyclical – Rerum Novarum,* Vatican, 1891.

Loisy, A.F., *L'Évangile et l'Église,* Paris, 1902.

271

MacNutt, F.A., *A Papal Chamberlain*, London, 1936.

Manning, H.E., (Cardinal), *Sermons on Ecclesiastical Subjects*, London, 1844–50.

Manning, H.E., *The Vatican Decrees in the Bearing on Civil Allegiance*, London, 1875.

Manning, H.E., *The True Story of the Vatican Council*, London, 1877.

Merry del Val, R., (Cardinal), *The Truth about the Papal Claims*, Vatican, 1901.

Marshall, C.C., *The Roman Catholic Church in the Modern State*, London, 1931.

Milman, H.H., *Latin Christianity*, London, 1854–5.

Niboyet, J-P., *L'Embassade de France au Vatican 1870-1901* (thesis), Paris, 1912.

Nichols, P., *The Pope's Divisions*, London, 1981.

Nielsen, F., *The Papacy in the 19th Century*, London, 1906.

Pernot, M., *La Politique de Pie X, 1906-10*, Paris, 1910.

Pernot, M., *Le Saint-Sîee, Église Catholique et la Politique mondiale*, Paris, 1974.

Piva and Malgeri, *Vita di Luigi Sturzo*, Cinque Lune, 1972.

Purcell, E.S., *Life of Cardinal Manning*, London, 1895.

Schmidlin, J., *Papstgeschichte der neusten Zeit* (Vols 2 and 3), Munich, 1935–6.

Schwaiger, G., *Geschichte der Päpste im 20. Jahrhundert* (paperback), Munich, 1968.

Segmuller, G., *Pius X*, Einsiedeln, 1926.

Selosse, L., *L'Affaire des Carolines*, Paris, 1886.

Soderini, E., *The Pontificate of Leo XIII* (translation), London, 1934.

Strachey, L., *Eminent Victorians* (Cardinal Manning), London, 1920.

Tyrell, L., *Christianity at the Crossroads*, London, 1909.

Vercesi, E., *Tre Papi*, Milan, 1929.

Zola, E., *Rome*, Paris, 1896.

Index